"First Among Equals"

"First Among Equals"

Abraham Lincoln's Reputation During His Administration

Hans L. Trefousse

Fordham University Press

New York   2005

Library of Congress Cataloging-in-Publication Data

Trefousse, Hans Louis.
    First among equals : Abraham Lincoln's reputation during his administration / Hans L. Trefousse.—1st ed.
        p. cm.
    Includes bibliographical references and index.
    ISBN 0-8232-2468-6
    1. Lincoln, Abraham, 1809–1865—Public opinion. 2. United States—Politics and government—1861–1865. 3. Public opinion—United States—History—19th century. I. Title.
E457.2.T74 2005
973.7'092—dc22   2004028482

Printed in the United States of America
07 06 05   5 4 3 2 1
First edition

*In memory of my dear wife
Rashelle F. Trefousse*

Contents

Introduction

In 1994, Merrill D. Peterson published his revealing book, *Lincoln in American Memory*. Most appropriately, he entitled his first chapter, "Apotheosis," and followed by tracing the deification of the Great Emancipator after his martyr's death.[1] Whether Lincoln's reputation was in any way comparable while he was still alive is a question that remans to be answered.

Some fifty years earlier, J. G. Randall, the famous Lincoln biographer, in an article entitled, "The Unpopular Mr. Lincoln," concluded that his hero was largely unappreciated during his lifetime. He wrote:

> For in the eyes of contemporaries Lincoln was a President who offended conservatives without satisfying radicals, who issued a tardy and incomplete emancipation proclamation after showing his willingness to conserve slavery, who had little if any success with Congress, who suppressed civil rights, headed a government marred by corruption, bungled the war, and then lost the peace, his post-war policy being blocked by congressional regional leaders in his lifetime before being wrecked in the reconstruction period.

He concluded that if Lincoln, like Woodrow Wilson, were to be remembered by what his enemies said, his reputation would be very different.[2]

It is of course true that Lincoln had many enemies who denigrated him throughout his career. In the South, this feeling was widespread, as was to be expected; in the North, Democrats

attacked him incessantly for being too radical and too antislavery, while radical Republicans faulted him for being too slow
in freeing the slaves. He was viewed as hesitant, wavering, and
indecisive. The hostile press marked him as a baboon and a
gorilla, and no terms seemed too demeaning to downgrade the
Civil War president.[3]

Yet, there is another side to the picture. Surprisingly enough,
any number of observers became aware of Lincoln's greatness at
an early time. Nor was he totally unknown—another mistaken
assertion. Ever since his election to the Illinois legislature as a
Whig in 1836, Lincoln's reputation had steadily grown. Even
during the election campaign, an observer wrote to the *Sanga-
mon Journal* "A girl might be born and become a mother before
the Van Buren men [the Democrats] forget Mr. Lincoln."[4]
Toasting Lincoln at Athens on August 3, 1837, E. D. Baker, one
of the volunteers present, called him "The people's choice,"
adding, "They will glory in sustaining him while he serves them
faithfully." Others, mentioning his faithful carrying out of his
friends' expectations, called him one of "nature's nobility."[5] Of
course, his opponents charged him with dictatorial ambitions
and clownishness, accusations that Democrats continuously repeated whenever the occasion seemed ripe.[6] Yet his friends,
stressing his "great talents, services, and high standing," referred
to him as a most suitable candidate for governor.[7] In 1846, Lincoln was nominated for a seat in Congress. At a meeting in
Petersburg, the Whigs of Menard County, endorsing Lincoln
for the nomination, resolved that in integrity and character they
considered him equal to any, while in respect to services ren-
dered, they thought his claims "superior to all."[7] After his election, the *Chicago Daily Journal*, welcoming his presence at the
Harbor and River Convention at the Windy City, aired its faith
in the congressman-elect. It had no doubt that its expectations
would be realized, "for never was reliance placed in a nobler
heart, and a sounder judgment." Once he had taken his seat, the

New York Tribune characterized his remarks favoring internal improvements as "a very sensible speech," while favorably comparing his intellectual endowments with his great physical height. During the War with Mexico, Lincoln's Spot Resolutions, which called on President James K. Polk to indicate the exact spot on American soil where Mexican attacks had allegedly taken place, received wide publicity, with the *New York Herald* highlighting his remarks and the St. Louis *Missouri Republican* labeling his speech one "of great power and replete with strongest and most conclusive arguments." When, after campaigning for the election of Zachary Taylor, Lincoln was not rewarded with a desirable position, Illinois friends angrily characterized the administration's course toward "our able & faithful representative" as highly reprehensible, while Bloomington Judge David Davis emphasized his belief in Lincoln's great legal ability.[8]

He was not forgotten after his term had ended. In 1854, the *Quincy Whig,* cited in the Springfield *Illinois State Journal,* expressed its regret that Lincoln did not fill Douglas's seat in the Senate, which it argued would have been better for the West and the peace of the Union. Correspondents praised him for his firmness and integrity, and even Joshua Giddings, the antislavery leader, said he would walk to Illinois to elect Lincoln to the Senate.[9] As Elihu Washburne, the influential Illinois congressman, wrote to Lincoln from Washington in January 1855, "You would feel flattered at the great interest that is felt for you here by all who know you, either by reputation or personally." In 1856, mentioned for vice president on the Republican ticket, he was called a "soldier tried and true." Then, at the Republican convention in Springfield in June of 1858, he was nominated for the Senate against the longtime Democratic Senator Stephen A. Douglas. It was on this occasion that he delivered his famous "House Divided Against Itself" speech, declaring that "this government cannot endure, permanently half *slave* and half *free,* a speech that the *Chicago Tribune* referred to as "a powerful summing up of the issues for the people—clear, concise, argumentative, unimpassioned and courteous."[10] Speaking at Joliet on June 30, 1858, the radical antislavery leader Owen Lovejoy said, "I am for Lincoln . . . because he is a true hearted man, and that, come what will, unterrified by power, unseduced by ambition, he will remain true to the great principles upon which the Republican Party is organized." More conservative observers were equally impressed, the *New York Times* reporting that "all the old Whig feeling is aroused in favor of Mr. Lincoln."[11]

The senatorial campaign involved a series of debates with Douglas in all parts of the state. During these, his fame spread throughout the country, the contest being called the "campaign of the year." As he heard from Pennsylvania five days before the first debate at Ottawa, "The eyes of freemen here are on you." In its account of that meeting, the New York *Evening Post* published a summary of Lincoln's life. Stressing his rise from poverty and deprivation, its reporter exulted, "At first a laborer, splitting rails for a living—deficient in education, and applying himself even to the rudiments of knowledge—he, too, felt the expanding power of his American manhood, and began to achieve the greatness to which he has succeeded. . . . I was convinced he has no superior as a stump speaker." The *New York Tribune*, edited by the radical Horace Greeley, agreed that he had the advantage over Douglas. It found his doctrines better and more correct than those of his antagonist and believed he stated them with more propriety and cogency and an infinitely better temper. He was urged to accept an invitation to speak in Danville, Illinois because his popularity with the masses would give him more influence in the right direction than the oratory of any other man. Following the Freeport debate, in which he challenged Douglas to reconcile his views on "popular sovereignty"—the idea of letting territorial settlers decide the slavery question—with the Dred Scott decision denying congressional power to outlaw slavery in the territories, the New York *Evening Post* commented upon his ability to appeal to both left and right, while Samuel Galloway, the Ohio educator and legislator, commenting on the debates at Ottawa and Freeport, wrote to him, "You have sustained yourself at both places, but especially at Freeport."[12] Highlighting the fact that his popularity was not confined to the West, a Rochester, New York correspondent wrote that the New York Republicans who were in love with Douglas were now rather more inclined to take a different view. They had found much to admire and praise in Lincoln's conduct of the campaign so that he had made many warm friends in the East,[13] and Judge David Davis considered his final, somewhat conservative, speech at Charleston "most admirable." At the conclusion of the contest, when he lost the senatorship but gained a popular majority, a number of correspondents predicted that his way was now clear for the 1860 presidency.

The prediction was not far from the mark. As Lincoln heard from Pennsyvania, the defeat was not a defeat, and people would not forget him until they put him into the White House. By March of 1859, the *New York Times* reported that the Rockford, Illinois *Republican* was proposing Lincoln for the vice presidency, and it was said that some of Old Abe's friends were looking still higher for him. In April, T. J. Pickett of Rock Island offered to start his drive for the office, and Ethelbert Oliphant of Uniontown, Pennsylvania insisted that Lincoln must be president.[14]

His popularity as an orator had become so pronounced that in 1859 he delivered speeches all over the Midwest. After his address in Dayton, Ohio, in September, the local newspaper characterized him as "remarkable for vigor of intellect, clearness of perception, and power of argumentation, and for fairness and honesty in the presentation of facts," while the editor Horace Rublee reported from Madison, "You have many friends in Wisconsin who want to see you and hear you." Members of

the Ohio Republican State Central Committee ordered several
thousand extra copies of his speeches at Columbus and Cincinnati and assured him that they had attracted general attention
from the thinking minds of the state. "I believe you are the man
for the times," a fellow townsman wrote him, while a Kansan
informed him that his name was a household word in that
state.[15]

Of course, opponents had made charges against him from
the moment he entered public life, accusations that were very
similar to those that pursued him throughout his career. He was
alleged to be dictatorial and in 1839 was accused of dictating
who should be elected from Menard County. When he was a
candidate for elector for Harrison in November that year, the
Springfield Democratic *Illinois State Register* wrote that he could
not meet the arguments of his opponent, Stephen A. Douglas,
and had responded with stale anecdotes—a favorite theme of
critics ever after, and in 1848, after he had introduced the Spot
resolutions, he was called a Benedict Arnold.[16] In the course of
his campaign, Douglas brought up all the points that were to
be made incessantly during the presidency—the accusation of
defying the Supreme Court because of the Dred Scott Decision,
of endangering the Union in the "House Divided Against Itself"
speech, his opposition to the Mexican War, his alleged love for
the Negroes, and a a purported plot to destroy the Democratic
and Whig parties with the new Republican organization.[17]
While the conservatives thought Lincoln was an abolitionist, the
radicals considered him too mild on slavery. The Columbus,
Ohio *Statesman* opined that he was so bad a speaker that it
would be good for the Democrats if he spoke every day until
the election, as he was allegedly not an orator and could hardly
be classed as a third-rate debater, an opinion shared by the *Cincinnati Enquirer,* which repeated it in 1859.[18] Although it has
been said that he was less known than any previous candidate,
by 1860, despite Democratic assertions to the contrary,[19] Lincoln
was hardly an obscure figure.

"First Among Equals"

1 Nomination and Election: 1860–1861

Thus, while Lincoln's comparative lack of recognition in the East has often been asserted, he had long been a source of interest for those who watched political developments. When Springfield Republicans in January 1860 organized a Lincoln Club in order to further his quest for the presidential nomination and passed a resolution asserting that they regarded Abraham Lincoln as the "expounder and defender of sound National Republican principles," they were not merely promoting a local celebrity.[1] Two weeks later, Lincoln heard from a Washington friend that his candidacy for either president or vice president was very much alive in that city, while a Juneau, Wisconsin correspondent wrote that Lincoln's name was a "tower of strength" in the state. He was asked to come to various cities in different parts of the country and traveled extensively. Then, in December 1859, he consented to write a brief account of his life, which was widely reprinted as a campaign biography.[2] How his reputation was enhanced by the Cooper Union speech, which skillfully set forth his antislavery views to New Yorkers, has often been mentioned. "Mr. Lincoln is one of Nature's orators, using his rare powers solely and effectively to elucidate and to convince, though their inevitable effect is to delight and electrify as well," stated the radical *New York Tribune* on February 28, the following day. The famous poet and editor William Cullen Bryant thought Lincoln "made quite a stir" in New York, and James A. Briggs, who had been on a committee inviting him there, sent him a check for $200 and wrote that he wished it were $200,000, "for you are worth it."

He added, "You hit the nail on the head fine & long, very long will your speech be remembered in this City." The Ohio legislator Samuel Galloway stated to John Covode, the Pennsylvania congressman, that Lincoln was the best man for the Republicans in the West because all the elements of the opposition could be united upon him. "The heart of the masses of our people is ardent for Lincoln," he asserted.

After his visit to New York, Lincoln embarked on a visit to New England to visit his son Bob, then at school at the Philips Exeter Academy. The fact that "our noble Lincoln" was "making a fine impression in his tour East" encouraged his fellow Illinoisans, who expressed the hope that he would be their standard bearer.[3] His trip to New England also convinced Republicans that he would be a better candidate than New York Senator—and former governor—William H. Seward, the party's front runner. An Indiana correspondent wrote to the prospective nominee that he had walked twenty miles to hear him speak, and when he heard his name mentioned for the presidency, it aroused feelings that he could not put down on paper. He wanted to see Lincoln nominated, "not only on personal grounds, but because there are few men who stand exactly in the right position to combine the whole vote of the opposition in the North."[4] In presenting Abraham Lincoln to the Chicago Republican National Convention as a candidate for the presidency, the *Chicago Tribune* explained that it was actuated "by a profound and well matured conviction that his unexceptional record, his position between the extremes of opposition in the party, his spotless character as a citizen, and his acknowledged ability as a statesman" would give him an advantage before the people that no other candidate could claim.[5]

His nomination brought forth many new encomiums. The *New York Tribune* commented, "Mr. Lincoln's romantic personal history, his eloquence as an orator, and his firm personal integrity, give augury of a successful campaign. . . ." The people of the Northwest were wont to designate him," HONEST OLD ABE!" the article continued, pointing out that this rude designation expressed the entire and confident affection which the heart of the masses felt for Lincoln wherever he was known. It declared the popular certainty that his was "a nature of sterling stuff, which may always be relied upon for perfect integrity, and constant fidelity to duty. . . ." The New York *Evening Post* called him "a man of high-toned character, noted for his probity and benevolence," who would, if elected, administer the government with frugality, independence, and honor. In the House of Representatives, Illinois Republican Elihu Washburne not only enthusiastically praised Lincoln's rise from common laborer to "his present exalted position," but also declared, "He stands today, as a private citizen and public man, unassailed, and unassailable—An HONEST MAN, the noblest work of God." Washburne's Ohio colleague, Harrison Gray Otis Blake, joined him by asserting that the Republican party had nominated "one of the noblest scions" of the West, a fit representative of the battle between slavery and freedom.[6] Other commentators expressed their satisfaction at his alleged conservatism, his former activities as a Whig, and his bold and determined oratory, while radicals like Benjamin F. Wade and Joshua Giddings were also satisfied. The radical antislavery journal, The *Independent,* though unhappy about Lincoln's endorsement of the Fugitive Slave law, predicted he would run well because he had spoken boldly against slavery. As Giddings put it in a letter to Lincoln, his selection was made on two grounds: "1. That you are an honest man, 2nd That you are not in the hands of corrupt or dishonest men."[7] Rutherford B. Hayes, later president, noted that the nominee was taking well in Ohio. Hannibal Hamlin, the vice-presidential nominee, was informed that a stronger ticket could not have been nominated, while the leading antislavery senator, Charles Sumner, though worried that the nominee had very little acquaintance with government and was called him "a man of agreeable manners, a ready and forcible speaker, self-made and self-taught, and personally popular among the burly sons of the West."[13]

Foreign opinion varied. The British envoy, Lord Richard B. Lyons, thought of Lincoln as "a man unknown, a rough Westerner of the lowest origin and little education." When he heard more about the candidate, he learned that "he was a rough farmer who began life as a farm laborer and got on by talent for stump speaking," whose election, because of Republican high tariff policies, would affect Great Britain adversely.[14] The *Edinburgh Review* was more complimentary. As it wrote in October, "Mr. Lincoln, of fair fame in his own State, and not unknown in Congress, as a shrewd and sensible politician of a homely sort, prudently keeps quiet. . . ." But the French traveling scion of the noted banking family, Salomon de Rothschild, considered him an extremist who would improve Stephen Douglas's chances.[15]

It was natural that favorable characterizations continued during the following presidential campaign. Confessing that he was worried that somebody with bad associates might be nominated, William Cullen Bryant expressed his relief in a letter to the candidate. As he put it, "It is fortunate that you have never gathered about you a kind of political confidants who have their own interests to look after."[16] New York was a crucial state, with its large electoral vote, and Lincoln's increasing popularity in the Empire State—in spite of disappointment with the defeat of William H. Seward—was a good omen. Expressing his regret at the favorite son's failure, the local politician George W. Pratt nevertheless exhorted fellow Republicans at a Rochester ratification meeting to "give to 'honest Abraham Lincoln' the same enthusiastic support which we gave to the gallant Fremont in 1856." In the House, Ohio Congressman Harrison G. Blake called the nominee "a fit representative of this great battle between *freedom* and *slavery* . . . a truly representative man . . . ;"

and the Indiana representative and later vice president Schuyler Colfax in Washington, quoting fellow congressmen from Buffalo and Chautauqua, had heard that in New York Lincoln would obtain one thousand more votes than Seward.[17] There were similar reports about Vermont, Missouri, and Minnesota, as well as other states. Lincoln was praised for being a true follower of Henry Clay, for being steadfast and incorruptible.[18]

Because the Democratic party, unable to coalesce in June, had nominated two tickets—one favoring Douglas and popular sovereignty, and the other favoring Vice President John C. Breckinridge and a federal slave code for the territories— Lincoln's probable success became more and more likely. Cartoons appeared showing the party breakup as "The Last Rail Split by Honest Old Abe," and a Republican triumph was now generally expected. "You will be elected President, my friend," wrote the Boston antislavery advocate Edward L. Pierce, "and I trust you will be found equal to the responsibility."[19] Other antislavery agitators were equally satisfied. "You have the advantage of being without entanglements and go into the White House as free I trust as you are now," wrote Owen Lovejoy. "It would be a treat such as the nation has not enjoyed for a long time to have the office seek the man rather than have the man seek the office." Charles Sumner assured the candidate that he was looking forward with joy "to the opportunity of mingling with your fellow citizens in welcome to you here at the national capital next 4th March." Frederick Douglass, the famous black abolitionist, praising Lincoln's great firmness of will, industriousness and honesty, and considering him a radical and not a compromiser, called him "a man of unblemished private character, a lawyer standing near the front rank of the bar of his own State."[20]At the same time, conservatives continued to picture him as "not dangerously ultra," and as "a sound, safe, national man, who could not be sectional if he tried."[21] Lengthy accounts of his life appeared, and he was shown to be a true

American, having risen from rags to riches. His moderation and kindliness were frequently mentioned, as were his oratorical skills. On October 19, Alexander K. McClure, the Pennsylvania politician, congratulated Lincoln on the confidence with which the country hailed his certain election.[22] Even some Southerners still had good things to say about him. The Georgian Alexander H. Stephens, the later vice president of the Confederacy, who knew Lincoln well, wrote that his election would not cause him to favor disunion. "In point of merit," he wrote, "I have no doubt Lincoln is just as good, safe, and sound a man as Buchanan, and would administer the Government as far as he is individually concerned just as safely for the South and as honestly and faithfully in every particular." Various North Carolina newspapers expressed the hope that the presidency would make Lincoln careful, and pointed out his lack of power should the Senate remain Democratic, while even the hostile *Richmond Enquirer* admitted that he was honest and resolute. Thus, it was left to members of the Northern opposition and the Southern majority to attempt to denigrate him.[23]

They tried hard. Alleging that no conservative could vote for Lincoln, the *Providence Daily Post* insisted that he was "the true representative of the Radicalism which Rhode Island repudiated last April" and that his record was that of "an abolitionist from beginning to end." The Albany *Atlas and Argus* continued its attacks, asserting that Seward had never been defeated while Lincoln had never succeeded.[24] Southern observers naturally opposed him from the beginning. The *Louisville Daily Journal*, conceding that it had a favorable opinion of Lincoln's personal and even political integrity, but, stressing his "House Divided Against Itself" speech, asserted that he was "a sectional candidate and only a sectional candidate."[25] The *Richmond Enquirer*, though admitting that he was no disunionist, maintained that he wanted gradually to build up the Republican party in the South, which would lead to the eventual end of slavery and the loss of property in Negroes. It criticized him for openly asserting eternal hatred of slavery and for allegedly preaching Negro equality.[26] The Montgomery, Alabama *Weekly Mail*, decrying what it considered the horrors of miscegenation, maintained that Lincoln's nomination showed that the North believed in it. *The Charleston Mercury* was more outspoken: "A horrid looking wretch he is, sooty and scoundrely in aspect, a cross between the nutmeg dealer, the horse swapper, and night man, a creature fit evidently for petty treason, small stratagems, and all sort of spoils. He is a lank sided Yankee of the uncomeliest visage, and of the dirtiest complexion. Faugh! After him, what decent white man would be President?"[27]

On November 7, 1860, Lincoln, with 39 percent of the popular ballots, won a majority of the electoral votes and thus the election. His triumph naturally brought out triumphant expressions of delight from his supporters. "THE GREAT VICTORY. . . . HONEST OLD ABE ELECTED," headlined the *Chicago Tribune*. The *New York Tribune* reprinted a letter from a Springfield professional gentleman to a friend in Boston, who wrote, "Mr. Lincoln is a man whom all will respect and love who know him. There is goodness of soul, generous nature, and, above all, great simplicity of character which deeply impresses everyone who hears his voice." Iowa Senator James M. Grimes thought the triumph was achieved more because of Lincoln's respected honesty than because of the Negro question. Papers all over the North praised his integrity, wisdom, and patriotism; private observers were delighted, and the New York Republican Preston King assured his Democratic friend Samuel Tilden that the benefits of the victory would be a gain for the whole country.[28]

Many radicals were also pleased. In a speech at Concord on November 7, Charles Sumner expressed his satisfaction that Lincoln had all the characteristics to weather the crisis because he was calm, prudent, wise, and also brave. The *Independent* exulted in "A Victory Gained for Freedom," and Ben Wade was told that Lincoln's honesty and good common sense would enable him "to manage the ship of state." In Congress, in December, the Senator defended the president against Southern attacks by calling attention to his conduct and character from his youth on to prove that he would not trespass on the rights of any man.[29] William S. Thayer, the later consul in Alexandria, was reassured by Senator Lyman Trumbull of Illinois that Lincoln was against compromise and as much opposed to Thurlow Weed's program of yielding as Trumbull himself. Even Wendell Phillips, the extreme Boston abolitionist, valued the moral effect of the victory, because Lincoln, hardly thought of as an antislavery man, consented to represent an anti-slavery idea. And even though William Lloyd Garrison's *Liberator* refused to back Lincoln because of his alleged support of the Fugitive Slave Law, it admitted that, given the choice between him and his opponents, his election was "a great and encouraging triumph."[30]

Democrats and Southerners judged the result from vastly different points of view. The Albany *Atlas and Argus* conceded that Lincoln's position was not an enviable one. But the newspaper predicted that he could do little and would carry on much like his predecessor. William Medill, the former Democratic governor of Ohio, thought that abolitionism had at length done its work, while Senator George E. Pugh of Ohio, asserting that Lincoln was totally unknown to most people, questioned why the government could not exist half slave and half free; and John Logan of Illinois, the later radical but then still a Democrat, questioned whether it was possible that Lincoln, opposed as he was to the Mexican War, could possibly attempt a policy that would bring on civil war.[31]

Southerners were much more vehement. Extremists, like the leading elements in South Carolina, considered Lincoln's election grounds for secession, and the Palmetto State took immediate steps toward that end. The New Orleans *Daily Crescent*, quoting various of his antislavery speeches, insisted that they proved him to be a "radical Abolitionist, without exception or qualification." Howell Cobb, the outgoing secretary of the treasury, in a letter to the people of Georgia, while admitting that without a majority in Congress, Lincoln could not do any harm to the South "at present," nevertheless warned that he was a representative of the Republican party, organized on antislavery principles and allegedly favoring Negro equality.[32] Senator Thomas L. Clingman of North Carolina asserted that the Illinoisan had been elected because he was known to be a dangerous man who would make war upon the South until its social system was destroyed; and Jefferson Davis, soon to be president of the Confederacy, thought that by following the policies of his predecessor, Lincoln would bring about a civil war while leaving a Democratic administration responsible for it. The Georgia fire-eater Robert Toombs, convinced that the president-elect's object was to abolish slavery, declared that he would inaugurate emancipation in the territories and then turn to the states; and Senator Alfred Iverson of the same state opined that while Lincoln would not commit any overt acts, the power of the government would be so extended against slavery that the institution would not last ten years. The Democratic Tennessee politician A. O. P. Nicholson called the election of Lincoln on the Republican platform a declaration of war against the South, and the Texas extremist Louis T. Wigfall accused Northern Republicans of nominating "two of the most fanatical of your sect as candidates for President and Vice President."[33]

Moderates, however, both Southerners and Northern Democrats, stressed Lincoln's conservatism and his inability to accomplish anything in view of the continued Democratic control of the Senate. "In a minority in both Houses of Congress, with the Supreme Court to expound the laws and restrain all illegal and unconstitutional acts, the President will be utterly powerless for evil, if he should have the disposition to do wrong," said Douglas on November 13. The following day, Alexander H. Stephens told the Georgia legislature, "I do not anticipate that Mr. Lincoln will do anything to jeopardize our safety and security, whatever may be his spirit to do it; for he is bound by the constitutional checks which are thrown around him; which at this time render him powerless to do any great mischief. . . ." Supreme Court Justice John Campbell, entertaining the same opinion, went further. Writing that Lincoln was chosen because he was more conservative than his opponent, he said he had been assured by reliable gentlemen who knew the president-elect that "he is not the object of fear."[34]

As the secession crisis worsened, these views did not change much. Representative John Sherman, the general's brother, believed that the new administration would do much to dissipate Southern feeling against the North, and the former Know-Nothing leader Daniel Ullman heard from one of his correspondents in upstate New York that the rebellion needed a man of indomitable will who would act prudently and with decision. Such a man, he thought, was Mr. Lincoln. A New York female supporter was so impressed with him that she sent him two hats, "As a slight testimonial of my admiration for you as a man, a patriot, and a statesman." [35] On December 11, Washburne informed Lincoln that Seward was expressing the greatest confidence in his "wisdom and ability" in office, and a week later assured him that General Winfield Scott wished that he were already in office. He was not alone; the New York banker George Worthington Dow, wrote the same thing a week later. Carl Schurz, the famous German-American leader, assured his wife on December 17 that he had complete confidence in Lincoln's honesty as well as in his courage, and Charles Sumner lost none of his regard for the president-elect: "All that we hear of the new President—who lives 800 miles from Washington—is favorable," he stated. "He is calm & decided."[36] On the day after the secession of South Carolina, the Springfield, Illinois *State Journal* pointed out that the Founding Fathers would be found on Lincoln's side because they believed as he did in freedom preferable to slavery-free territories and the ultimate extinction of the institution. Trumbull was repeatedly informed that Lincoln was the best man for the times, that he was another Jackson, and that Illinois was proud of its "old Abe."[37]

As the inauguration drew nearer, this praise continued. Andrew Johnson, the most famous Southern Unionist, heard from a fellow townsman on January 2, 1861, that the administration of Lincoln would be all that could be asked for by all good citizens because he was no abolitionist but a patriot who would anxiously care for the perpetuity of the Union. C. H. Ray of the *Chicago Tribune* wrote to Washburne that he could trust Old Abe. "He is rising every day in the estimation of all who know him," he wrote. "He is wiser and more sagacious than I thought he could ever be. Our Const. Is dearer to him than anything else!"[38] He was praised as firm, steadfast, and a man of principle, and, as the New York *Commercial Advertiser* pointed out, he would administer the government with vigor and discretion. At any rate, Charles Case of Indiana reminded his fellow legislators, his ideas were originally Jefferson's, and J. F. Farnsworth of Illinois added that Lincoln would rather die than make concessions as the price of his inauguration.[39]

Lincoln's cabinet choices received mixed reviews. The *Cincinnati Gazette* found that it showed his conservatism, and labeled stories of his indecisiveness ridiculous, and the *Cincinnati Commercial* believed that his choosing a cabinet without going to Washington would please the people because it indicated "a timely disposition to accept responsibilities." On the contrary, however, Senator Lyman Trumbull, unhappy about the inclusion of Simon Cameron among the president's advisers, thought Lincoln ought to come to the capital to assert public sentiment. Illinois attorney Leonard Swett, usually a firm supporter, criticized the idea of uniting all the elements of the party in the cabinet.[40]

Southerners, of course, continued their attacks. The St. Louis *Missouri Republican* challenged Lincoln to accept the Crittenden Compromise, an arrangement that would have permitted slavery south of 36°30', both in the existing territory of the United States and areas that might thereafter be acquired. George W. Hughes of Maryland declared that it was not the election of the individual, Abraham Lincoln, that had created the excitement in the South, but "the election of the representative man, Mr. Lincoln, representing principles hostile to the rights, the honor, and the interest of the slave-holding states." Albert Rust of Arkansas pointed out that obviously the Illinoisan thought personal rights more important than property rights, and William T. Avery of Tennessee again accused the president-elect of favoring racial equality. The Virginian John S. Millson avowed that Virginia would never submit to Lincoln, and James M. Leach of North Carolina again warned that what Lincoln had in mind was the ultimate extinction of slavery.[41]

In view of complaints about Lincoln's silence since the election, when he finally spoke on his trip to Washington, his remarks and activities were widely reported. His Farewell Address in Springfield appeared most impressive to the Springfield *Illinois State Journal*. "We have heard him speak on a hundred different occasions" the article said, "but never saw him so profoundly affected, nor did he ever utter an address, which seemed to us so full of simple and touching eloquence, so exactly adapted to the occasion, so worthy of the man and the hour." Francis Springer, the Springfield superintendent of schools, wrote him, "When the train bearing you passed my residence this morning, my heart said, God bless Lincoln, & make him second to none but Washington!" James Garfield, the later president, saw Lincoln for the first time in Columbus and, while he was disappointed in some aspects, he felt that in general Lincoln surpassed expectations. Ovations greeted him wherever he traveled and, according to the *Cincinnati Gazette*, the people be-

lieved that he was the second savior of his country—one of the
first public comparisons of Lincoln to George Washington. The
New York *Sun* praised the "the frank and hearty manner" in
which he expressed himself and believed that his assurances of
noninterference with the domestic institutions of the South
ought to be satisfactory to Southerners who trusted their fellow
men.[42] He was widely criticized, however, when, because of
threats against his life in Baltimore, he went to the capital in
secret. *Harper's Weekly* published a hostile cartoon, "The Flight
of Abraham," although his safe arrival in Washington greatly
reassured many. According to the *New York Times,* the country
had avoided the lasting disgrace of a presidential assassination,
an assessment shared by the *Chicago Tribune*. In the House of
Representatives, Ohio Republican Congressman Benjamin Stanton called attention to the fact that the president-elect was a
prudent and sensible man who would not resort to the use of
force if it could possibly be avoided.[43]

Southerners, however, still charged him with advocating racial equality and the eventual eradication of slavery. Reporting
that his speeches showed that he would use force to uphold the
government, they insisted that the talks revealed him as a stump
orator.[44] The Kentuckian, Henry C. Burnett, maintaining that,
in his Cincinnati speech, Lincoln had told Kentuckians to prepare for war, shouted, "What fatuity! What madness!" The Virginian Muscoe R. H. Garnett accused the president-elect of
having made warlike statements, while his colleague, Thomas S.
Bocock, charged that the Illinoisan refused to see the problems
facing the country, that he was refusing to yield, and that there
was not anyone who took a more repulsive position than he.
The *Charleston Mercury,* radical as ever, thought the secret trip
to Washington was the last straw. "Everybody here is disgusted
at this cowardly undignified entry" (into Washington), it wrote.
The fire-eater Louis T. Wigfall, during the last days of the 36th
Congress, still taunted the Republicans with having taken up a

man because he was "an ex-rail-splitter, an ex-grocery keeper, and ex-flatboat captain, and an ex-Abolitionist" from whom he could not expect any great information as to the government which he was to administer.[45] It is therefore evident that at the eve of his inauguration, Lincoln was neither totally unknown nor unpopular, and was the object of praise as well as of denigration.

2   The First Year

I f Lincoln was neither totally unknown nor generally dis-
liked prior to his inauguration, his assumption of office certainly made the country familiar with his views afterward,
and while his popularity, like that of all presidents, experienced
its ups and downs, a number of people were impressed with
him from the very beginning.

His inaugural address, in which he disavowed any aggressive
intentions and reaffirmed his support of the Constitution, was
generally well received. The *Philadelphia Inquirer* considered it
"in admirable tone and temper" and added that "no man can
read it without being convinced that the new President is a patriot in the sincere desire to dispel groundless apprehension
growing out of his election." The New York *Commercial Advertiser* felt that "those familiar with M. Lincoln's past career, ac-
quainted with his general conservatism and character, and
aware of his firmness, honesty, and directness, expected nothing
else from him than the manly, frank, and conciliatory words
that he employed." The Springfield *Republican* thought the
speech would "give general satisfaction to the people of the free
states" which could "hardly fail to have the best effect on all
sections of the country." The *Cincinnati Commercial* agreed,
calling the address "at once firm, conciliatory, and persuasive."[1]
Governor Edwin D. Morgan of New York, expressing his total
satisfaction with it, asserted that it could not fail to win the
confidence of the North and the respect of the South, while
Congressman Justin Morrill of Vermont believed it was "just
what it should be. . . . A paper of extraordinary ability, and . . .

extraordinary tact." A fellow citizen from Havana, Illinois, wrote to Trumbull, "The inaugural suits us here exactly. We cannot find telling terms to express our admiration of it. Its moderation, its wisdom, its conciliation, its firmness are above all praise." From Michigan, the senator heard that Lincoln stood erect and lofty mentally and as well as physically. "We have a President at last!" his correspondent wrote, and similar reports came from California. *Frank Leslie's Illustrated Newspaper* now printed a full-page portrait of the new executive.[2]

Benjamin B. French, the commissioner of public buildings, believed that "words could not have been selected & framed into sentences that could better express the ideas of those who have elected Abraham Lincoln to the Presidency." He characterized the inaugural as conciliatory but firm and thought it would have "more tendency to bring back the seceding States than anything else." The Philadelphia editor Sidney George Fisher thought the speech established Lincoln's character as a "man of talents and honest purposes," while the temperance advocate Neal Dow, thanking the president "for the noble words" of the inaugural, assured him that "they inspire the country with confidence and fill the hearts of your friends with joy."[3]

Radical observers were also impressed with the document. The *New York Tribune* praised its brevity and added, "The Address can not fail to exercise a happy influence upon the country. The tone of almost tenderness with which the South is called upon to return to her allegiance, can not fail to convince even those who differ from Mr. Lincoln that he earnestly and seriously desires to avoid all difficulty and disturbances while the firmness with which he avows his determination to obey the simple letter of his duty must command the respect of the whole country, while it carries conviction his earnestness of purpose, and of his courage to enforce it."[4] Governor John Albion Andrew of Massachusetts, who heard that the address had stopped further secession, sent his private secretary to the president to

assure him of his state's "cordial concurrence" with the views expressed in the address. Even Garrison's *Liberator*, though critical of the defense of the Fugitive Slave Law, expressed relief that there was going to be no bloodshed and praised Lincoln's "manly courage."[5] And Charles Sumner, though worried about Lincoln's inexperience, expressed his trust that the administration would show itself able to deal with events as they occurred.[6]

Some conservatives and the Democrats differed, of course. The *New York Herald* criticized the inaugural for its alleged vague generalities and its failure to spell out concrete policies for the future. The Albany *Atlas and Argus* concluded that it was a stump speech that would initiate civil war, an interpretation with which Senator Stephen A. Douglas disagreed, stating that the inaugural was characterized by ability, but he had reservations that required further elaboration.[7] And while Senator Thomas L. Clingman of North Carolina insisted that it was a declaration of war, Douglas pointed to the passages safeguarding slavery as a refutation of this interpretation.[8] The Weekly *New-Yorker Staats-Zeitung*, bitterly hostile, declared that the inaugural lacked all strength and impetus, while the equally hostile Columbus *Crisis* stated that Lincoln had left himself plenty of elbow room, an opinion that it still maintained a week later with the hope that he wanted to be the president of the whole nation, though cautioning that he would face opposition from his own party.[9]

Southerners could hardly be expected to be pleased In general, they continued with their aspersions, mostly agreeing with the Richmond *Semi-Weekly Enquirer*, which labeled the inaugural a "Declaration of War." Charlestonian Emma Holmes wrote, "Old Abe was inaugurated today amidst bayonets bristling from the housetops as well as on the streets. . . . His speech was just what was expected from him, stupid, ambiguous, vulgar and insolent, and is everywhere considered a virtual declaration of war."[10] Senator Clingman voiced a similar opinion in the Sen-

ate. Vigorously denying Lincoln's assertion that the Union was unbroken, he tried to show that the remaining Union forts in the South could not be held without a conflict, and Wigfall of Texas, as well as the Virginian James M. Mason, fully agreed.[11]

Others, however, even in the South, were not so sure. The Virginia Unionist James D. Davidson thought that the inaugural showed Lincoln would be careful, that he had no intention of coercion, and if war came, the South would have to start it. His North Carolina counterpart, Jonathan Worth, was sure that the inaugural breathed peace to any candid mind.[12] The Raleigh *North Carolina Standard* wrote that the inaugural was not a war message and that it was not unfriendly to the South, an idea which the *Knoxville Whig* substantially shared by endorsing Lincoln's "temperance and conservatism."[13] Some were simply perplexed. The mayor of Savannah was told the inaugural was a queer production, meaning this and that, or that it might mean neither. Mary Chesnut, the literary wife of the senator from South Carolina, though thinking Lincoln an "insidious villain," was equally puzzled. "Means he war or peace?" she queried. The New Orleans *Picayune* also found the inaugural indecisive, a matter of great concern to Southern observers.[14]

Foreign opinion was as divided as its domestic counterpart. The London *Morning Chronicle* was impressed with Lincoln's honesty and fairness and the fact that his ideas about the South were the same as they had been when he was still a comparatively unknown Republican orator, though it predicted that his effort to collect tariffs would lead to war. The Paris *Moniteur* reported that the English press generally applauded his message, "which clarifies the facts with frankness and lucidity, although it does not indicate any elements of solution."[15] In Germany the *Frankfurter Journal* stressed the fact that every mention of the Union was greeted with enthusiasm, but it feared that the speech did not please the border states. The tiny Republic of San Marino conferred honorary citizenship upon him. The London

Times, however, hostile from the beginning, and regretting that Lincoln did not give any clue to his future policy, characterized him as "still the local politician, the honest man of a farming Western State, with all the simplicity which belongs to the pioneers of civilization." According to the editors, he could not emancipate himself from the hackles of a legal mind and left no room for negotiations, only for war.[16]

Foreign diplomats in Washington tended to be dubious about the inaugural. Henri Mercier, the French minister, thought that it expressed no fixed idea, but in "an excellent way" analyzed and discussed the outstanding difficulties of the situation. He believed Lincoln did not favor war, not only because it was repugnant to his patriotism, but also because he recognized that at the moment the South was better prepared.[17] His Russian colleague, Baron Edouard de Stoeckl, agreed. Though he admitted that the president had an agreeable and honest facial expression, he averred that Lincoln, influenced now by the radicals and now by the conservatives, had no fixed program and did not realize the seriousness of the situation. Rudolph Schleiden, the representative of Bremen, disagreed. He characterized Lincoln as a simple *Naturmensch* of healthy intelligence and of best will, who seemed to be aware of his great responsibilities and could not be unduly swayed. Lord Lyons, on the other hand, was sure that radical influences predominated.[18]

Lincoln's choice of cabinet met with a mixed reception. Justin S. Morrill thought it did not foreshadow an honest administration or a very Republican one, largely due to Seward's influence. Radical Governor Andrew of Massachusetts, on the other hand, heard that everyone admitted that the president had selected good and able men for "engineers," but that they did not all look the same way.[19] According to the *Philadelphia Inquirer*, however, this was no reason why the cabinet could not last. Charles W. Dennison of the *United States Naval Gazette*,

expressing his gratitude that the president's life had been preserved, shared his satisfaction at his choice of a cabinet.[20] Criticism of the cabinet, however, tended to become a steady means
of attacking the administration.[21]

The first month of Lincoln's tenure of office was generally
viewed with favor. Praising the continuance of peaceful conditions, the *Cincinnati Gazette* emphasized its satisfaction that the
president recognized all of the South's constitutional rights, that
Southern property was safe, and that new territories had been
organized without mention of slavery. The *Philadelphia Inquirer*
gave the president credit for his steadfastness, calling him "Jacksonian in his positive adherence to a line of policy from which
he could not be moved" According to the New York *Commercial Advertiser,* Lincoln had found the country in shambles, but
his vigor had gone far to restore public confidence The South
Bend *Register* was certain of his "unshaken faith in his coolness,
his judgment and his determination."[22] John Greenleaf Whittier
also expressed his confidence in him, as did William T. Sherman
and others in various parts of the country. "The country has
got rid of a wicked & imbecile Chief Magistrate and a new one
by the blessing of God has been inaugurated which already gives
evidence of wisdom, honesty, & patriotism, three qualities
which have long been wanted at the head of our Nation as well
as in all the subordinate branches of the government," George
W. Dow wrote to his cousin.[23] John W. Forney, the Philadelphia
journalist, clerk of the House and soon to be secretary of the
Senate, wrote to Lincoln, "It gives me great pleasure to assure
you that the policy of your administration, as far as the public
can understand it, meets with almost universal approbation."
Even the Californian James A. McDougall, upon his election to
the Senate as a Free Soil Democrat, assured Lincoln that he had
faith in him.[24]

Others criticized the "uncertainty of the policy of the administration," a situation which, according to one of Andrew John-

son's correspondents, weakened the Union. The irascible Count Adam Gurowski, a Polish radical, although asking Lincoln for a position, regretted that the month of March had passed with the administration seemingly enjoying the "most beatific security." Charles Sumner, radical as ever, and thinking the president ignorant, was nevertheless in hopes that the administration would be able to deal with events as they occurred.[25]

Most Democrats and Southerners, however, had not changed their minds. Delaware Senator James A. Bayard not only criticized Lincoln for allegedly being unable to understand the difference between the relations of a country to a state and those of a state to the federal government, but also castigated him again for extending the Declaration of Independence to all men, including blacks. While Stephen Douglas still maintained that the president, a lawyer, and a conservative, would not perjure himself by either blockading the South or collecting revenues from forts without authority from Congress, John C. Breckinridge, though asserting his personal respect for the executive, criticized him for his belief that freedom was the normal condition of the territories. The *Charleston Mercury* questioned whether Lincoln's indecision was feigned to deceive the South of his true purposes. However, the paper also considered it possible that this shortcoming merely mirrored the enemy's incapacity. The Virginia convention appointed a committee to induce the executive to clarify his policy, the uncertainty of which it considered most injurious to the adjustment of difficulties.[26]

The federal government had retained control of only four forts in the South, of which Fort Sumter in Charleston Harbor was the most important. Though urged to evacuate it, Lincoln refused and, on April 12, the Confederates attacked it, thus starting the Civil War. His firm stand on the fort, however, had widespread support. As James Watson Webb, the journalist and future envoy to Brazil, wrote to the president on the day before the Confederate attack, "The recent action of the Govt. has most favorably developed the real state of public feeling and its patriotic impulses. Nineteen twentieth of the people of the Free States rejoice in what has been done. . . ." After the assault, the Washington *Evening Star* pointed out that the government had done nothing wrong. Had not the "oligarchy," as the *Star* called the Confederates, attacked although the administration had sent no arms or supplies to Major Robert Anderson, the fort's commander, till he was cut off? In the same vein, after war had begun, the *New York Tribune* editorialized, "None should forget the earnest, anxious forbearance with which the President and his supporters have sought by every conceivable means to avoid a bloody collision." And the *New York Herald*, long hostile, now came to Lincoln's support.[27] Lincoln's call for troops on April 15 met with general approval, as did his blockade of Southern ports, which the *Chicago Tribune* called a blow upon the insurgents. As one former opponent confessed, "Every honest, wise, good and true American . . . will with heart and hand unite . . . to stand as one body to our beloved, just, and wise President. . . ." The New York *Belletristisches Journal*, pointing out that the president had written the document himself, stressed that it displayed the simple, strong wording that marked the author's character. Charles Sumner, who had had his doubts, now felt that the President spoke simply and plainly of the state of country and understood it. He wrote to a friend, "As I see more of him, I like him better." Orville Browning, Lincoln's confidant in Quincy, convinced that his friend was adequate to the emergency and that he would meet it as it should be met, wrote to him, "Everybody is delighted with the measures you have adopted, and the vigor with which you are pushing them." Henry P. Tappan, the president of the University of Michigan, declared, "The heart of the great West—the heart of the entire North—is with you in the defense of our beloved country. You cannot ask of us too much." And *Harper's*

Weekly contributed a cartoon, entitled, "Consulting the Oracle," which showed the president asking Columbia, "What Next?" and Columbia, holding the Constitution, answering, "First be sure you're right, then go ahead." Two weeks later, the *Weekly* published its first Brady photograph of him. Southerners, on the other hand, thought the call for troops dissolved the Union.[28]

At the end of the first two months of the administration, the *New York Times* praised it for having achieved what it had promised. Senator Henry Wilson of Massachusetts, who had at first encountered the belief that the administration would go down before it had begun, now found "almost everyone hopeful, confident, satisfied." He wrote to Lincoln, "Today our friends are full of confidence in you and your Cabinet. They now feel that you are doing the right thing and that all will be done in your power to put down treason." The *Philadelphia Inquirer*, calling attention to the administration's tremendous achievements within three weeks, reminded its readers that Washington and Fort Pickens were now safe, and that New York, New England, and the West were alive with regiments. At the end of June, John Esterbrook of Bunker Hill, Illinois, let Trumbull know how much he continued to admire the executive. "We still have the utmost confidence in Mr. Lincoln," he wrote. "The only wonder among us is, that he survived so long, that the Leeches, hangers on and Blood Suckers at Washington haven't utterly ruined and prostrated him long before now."[29]

The suspension of the writ of habeas corpus between Philadelphia and Washington, though highly controversial, also met with approval. Pointing out that the Constitution authorized this when the public safety required it, the *Cincinnati Gazette* defended Lincoln's action .The *Springfield Republican* severely criticized Chief Justice Roger B. Taney's ruling against it. The Washington *National Intelligencer* agreed, pointing out that the president had the right to suspend the writ when Congress was not in session. And the *Philadelphia Inquirer*, referring to this justification, asserted that the existing state of affairs was infinitely stronger than the various precedents to which others had referred.[30]

The Democrats, always eager to find fault, though supporting the Union despite their opposition to the administration, berated Lincoln for waging an unconstitutional war. His suspension of the writ of habeas corpus, which was authorized only in Article One of the Constitution, dealing with the powers of Congress, aroused their special ire. Calling the conflict a disgrace, they tended to accuse Lincoln of incompetence and sought to picture themselves as defenders of American liberty. "Like Jack Cade's, Mr. Lincoln's mouth has become, not merely Congress, Constitution and Law, but also the judiciary," asserted the Columbus *Crisis*. Again and again, they attacked his establishment of a blockade, the suspension of the writ of habeas corpus, and the expenditure of funds. But they could not prevail against popular opinion to the contrary.[31]

Foreign assessments varied. The *Manchester Guardian* blamed Lincoln for the war, while the *Frankfurter Journal* stressed the loyalty of the North to the president. Quoting one of Cassius Clay's letters, the *Moniteur* showed that Lincoln, fighting to maintain American nationality, considered secession to be treason that must be opposed and punished, and that the blockade would end the war within a year. And a spokesman for the merchants of Liverpool assured the president that the businessmen of that city warmly sympathized with him and felt that he was acting with energy to put down an unjustifiable rebellion. These differing opinions would change little during the following years.[32]

On July 4, 1861, Lincoln sent a message to the special session of Congress expounding his views about the causes of the war and explaining his actions—a missive that was widely sanctioned. The *Cincinnati Gazette*, crediting the president with writing the message himself, believed that it gave universal satisfaction; the New York *Commercial Advertiser*, pleased with its chaste style, its modesty, and its patriotism, labeled it "in every way a document worthy of the Chief Magistrate of a great republic." The New York *Sun* was sure that it deserved and received general approbation for its "direct, manly, and forcible statement of the facts and principles involved in the present crisis of our national affairs." The Washington *National Intelligencer*, likewise praising its "clearness of style," commented that the president shown that he had "rightly estimated the nature of the task," while *Harper's Weekly* called it, "truly American" and "thoroughly democratic." The Vermont delegate to the Washington peace conference, Lucius Eugene Chittenden, wrote in his journal, "The Message and Reports meet with universal favor all over the country"; and one of Seward's correspondents, delighted with the message, considered it "just right."[33] The Philadelphian Sidney George Fisher, reading it with great satisfaction, thought it showed remarkable power of thought and argument. "In this hour of its trial," he wrote, "the country seems to have found in Mr. Lincoln a great man." From Mount Morris, Illinois, Elihu Washburne heard that, as a whole, the message was well received, and although some faulted it for falling a little below what the times demanded, yet on the whole, it was popular, "being unmistakenly and most decidedly Lincolnish." Vice President Hamlin was also impressed with the message, and Congress quickly acted to legitimize the measures the president had taken during the recess. To be sure, the radical *New York Tribune* conceded that the president exceeded his authority in calling out the militia and making other provisions for suppressing the rebellion. But, it added, "He would have been a fool and a traitor had he done otherwise." The same point was made by his defenders in Congress during the debates concerning the actions.[34]

As usual, the opposition found fault.. The president's most

stringent critic was the Copperhead Congressman Clement L. Vallandigham, who was totally opposed to any tampering with the constitutional guarantees of states rights. Denouncing the congressional effort to legitimize the president's acts, he declared that the inaugural had been uttered with forked tongue. "I assert here . . . ," he said, "that every principal act of the Administration since has been a glaring usurpation of power, and a palpable and dangerous violation of that very Constitution which this civil war is professed waged to support." As the most unequivocal representative of the opposition, he spoke for his colleagues when he accused the executive of instituting an illegal blockade, suspending the writ of habeas corpus, and illegally raising armies. Vallandigham would remain a roadblock in the administration's procedures ever after.

The attacks of Vallandigham and others in Congress must, however, be viewed against widespread defenses of the president by Republican representatives and senators. "It is my belief that the administration has already done all that could be expected or desired in the vast preparations for war which have in so short a period of time been made—bringing the country in a few weeks, from the long quietude of a peace establishment . . . to our present condition of security and power," said Senator James Dixon of Connecticut on July 15. This was an idea reinforced by Indiana Senator Henry S. Lane the next day, and Lincoln's friend Orville H. Browning naturally also defended him in the Senate.[35]

On July 21, the Union forces suffered a severe defeat at Bull Run. It might be expected that after this setback, Lincoln's popularity would decline. But confidence in the executive did not materially diminish. "The President may rest assured of the cordial and hearty support of the country in whatever measures he may deem necessary for the vindication of the national honor, and the maintenance of the Constitution and the laws," wrote the *New York Times* on August 1. While the cabinet was widely criticized—as Congressman John Covode was told, people had confidence in Lincoln, but none in his advisers. Granville Moody, the president of the Union of Protestant Clergymen, declaring that Bull Run had not shaken people's conviction of the righteousness of the cause, asked the Kentucky antislavery advocate Cassius M. Clay to assure Lincoln of "our sympathy with him with the responsibilities providentially devolved upon him" and Senator Trumbull was advised: "Say to the President, who must be sorely grieved at our recent defeat, that we will stand by him and the government no matter what the cost." On August 16, the Philadelphia *Press* alluded to the ever more common comparison of Lincoln to George Washington. The first president, the *Press* pointed out, had also been attacked, just as Lincoln was attacked at present. But, it remarked, the attacks were ceasing, and even the president's opponents always conceded that he was honest. As his friend Browning reminded him, he ought to be hopeful of his future. He had it in his power to make his name "one of the most justly revered and illustrious in the annals of the human race."[36]

At the end of August, Lincoln asked General Frémont to modify the order to his department calling for the emancipation of the slaves so that it conformed to the recently passed Confiscation Act, which applied only to bondsmen used militarily against the Union. Even this seemingly conservative action was viewed favorably by many in the North. "The President, whose kindness of heart is only equaled by his firmness in what he believes to be right, has performed the duty in a manner that General Frémont will appreciate as full of consideration towards himself," wrote the New York *Commercial Advertiser*. Of course he did not change the order, but two days later the paper, conceding that the West depreciated Lincoln's interference, nevertheless wrote that the more the measure was looked into, the more it showed "the wisdom of the President." The Washington *National Intelligencer* praised the president for seeking to keep

faith with his promise merely to restore the Union and asked
that he be sustained in the "just and loyal attitude he has taken;"
and the Springfield *Republican* reasserted its confidence in the
integrity and patriotism of the president, though it also expressed equal confidence in Frémont.[37] Seward was told that
had the president not acted as he did, a protest meeting would
have been held in every regiment in General Banks's division,
so it was "the best stroke of administrative policy thus far during the war." Even Frémont's removal in October was accepted
by some of the public. "So far, Mr. Lincoln has proved himself
to be actuated only by great and generous considerations,"
wrote the *Philadelphia Intelligencer*, while the New York *Commercial Advertiser* was certain that the subject was looked at
carefully by the cabinet and president, and they deemed the
removal necessary for the Union cause in Missouri.[38]

Many radicals, however, long dubious about the administration because of their lack of faith in the president's commitment
to antislavery, were most critical. As early as April 7, Charles
Sumner, sure that Lincoln was undertaking "what no mortal
can do," feared he lacked executive ability. Count Gurowski,
growing ever more bitter, not only criticized the blockade, but
compared the president to Pope Pius IX, who in 1847–48 also
had many bad advisers. Ben Wade, who thought the South had
to be punished and traitors hanged, possibly by constitutional
means, warned, "The stern demand for justice of a united people must not be babbled by the imbecility and perverseness of
one man though he be the President of the United States." Governor Andrew of Massachusetts received similar complaints
about Lincoln's alleged indecisiveness. Wendell Phillips thought
the executive was not bold enough, while one of Ben Butler's
correspondents considered Lincoln "the greatest of our woes."[39]
The revocation of Frémont's emancipation order seemed to
confirm the doubts these radicals had about the president. "The
President's letter to Gen. Fremont has cast a funeral gloom over

our patriotic city," Joseph Medill of the *Chicago Tribune* wrote to Secretary Chase. "We are stricken with a heavier calamity than the battle of Bull Run." As Charles Sumner complained, "This weakens all our armies. . . . Our Presdt is now dictator, imperator-what you will but how vain to have the power of God and not to use it God-like." Garrison's *Liberator,* condemning "this timid, depressing, suicidal letter of President Lincoln," cited the *Boston Transcript* for containing a scathing attack upon a "weak, hesitating mistaken policy," while the *Cincinnati Commercial* feared the failure to sustain Frémont would increase the rebels' confidence.[40]

In order to retain some popular support, the Democrats now had to shift gears somewhat, after having abused Lincoln day in and day out, with General McClellan going so far as to call him "an idiot." The Albany *Atlas and Argus,* which on September 18 had cited the appointment of Frémont as an example of his incapability, on the next day had to concede that the Democratic press of the North was rallying to the support of the president whenever he placed himself upon the platform of the Constitution, and they defended him against assailants of his own party. The *New-Yorker Staats-Zeitung,* which in August had severely criticized the president's indecisiveness as well as his cabinet, on September 19 referred to his "calming letter," which had allegedly strengthened Unionists, while the Columbus *Crisis,* a usual critic, commented that "we must cheerfully give Mr. Lincoln credit for this very prompt and decided act."[41]

The South, on the other hand, did not change. It had kept up its constant attacks on the man it considered its arch foe. Holding him responsible for the start of the war and accusing him of tyranny, it called his blockade ineffective and continually underestimated him.[42]

Foreign observers' opinions varied. The *Moniteur* explained that Lincoln, considering the loyalty of Kentucky especially important, could not afford to be taken for an abolitionist. The

London *Quarterly Review* believed that the vigor with which he had swept away "every vestige of constitutional liberty" deserved grateful recognition at the hands of all admirers of strong government. The London *Times,* generally pro-South, called him ignorant of diplomatic etiquette, and the *Frankfurter Journal* thought Frémont was absolutely right. The British diplomat Sir Henry Bulwer-Lytton mused that when the president was "so bewildered by his own armies," America had more to learn from England than England from America.[43]

The final recall of Frémont resulted in more controversy. Frederick Law Olmsted, the famous builder of parks in New York and Brooklyn, believed that the recall caused the administration and the country to stand stronger, while the New York *Commercial Advertiser* commented that the subject had been carefully considered by the cabinet as well as by the president himself, and was deemed necessary for the sake of the Union cause in Missouri. Even Secretary of the Treasury Salmon P. Chase, radical as he was, was thoroughly persuaded that, in all Lincoln had done concerning Frémont, he had been guided by a true sense of public duty. The *Philadelphia Inquirer* was also critical of the general. Concerning the dismissal, it wrote, "So far, Mr. Lincoln has proved himself to be actuated only by just and generous considerations."[44]

More radical Republicans were outraged. The general's soldiers were furious, reported the New York *Tribune*; in his journal Frank Leslie called it "a great blunder," a characterization that the *Cincinnati Commercial* shared. Wade was convinced that not since Admiral Byng [who was executed] "was sacrificed by a weak and wicked Administration to appease the wrath of an indignant people" had any public man suffered so unjustly as General Frémont. Nevertheless, *Harper's Weekly,* though it considered the moment ill chosen, felt that things were indeed better in Missouri, and that the nation, which believed implicitly in the president's honesty and singleness of purpose, would acquiesce.[45]

It did. Lincoln's popularity in October and November of 1861 was as high as ever. On October 19, Rutherford B. Hayes, the future president, trying to convince his hostile wife that she was in error, insisted that he did not know any other man that was to be preferred to the president. The pastor of the Presbyterian church in Warrington, Pennsylvania, expressed his great confidence in Lincoln to the secretary of state, and George Gordon Bennett, the changeable editor of the *New York Herald,* assured Lincoln of his deep sympathy. From the border state of Kentucky, Thomas Batman of Louisville assured Lincoln that he was winning the confidence of the plain people throughout the loyal states. As Benjamin B. French put it on November 27, "Everybody that knows him loves him." No wonder his private secretary, William O. Stoddard, could say, "Our worthy Chief Magistrate is in excellent spirits."[46]

In November, Captain Charles Wilkes of the U.S. Navy captured James M. Mason and John Slidell, Confederate emissaries to Britain and France aboard the British steamer *Trent* and took them to Boston for detention. This violation of international law caused the British government to demand their release and threaten war. It was generally believed that the matter was largely resolved by Seward rather than by the president. Yet, the executive had been advised that, according to international law, the United States was in the wrong and that if Great Britain demanded it, the prisoners must immediately be given up, especially since war with the United Kingdom would be a calamity, and Lincoln had used his influence with Seward to maintain the peace. In the army, Major Henry Livermore Abbot mused that some were saying we could hang pirates because we had Mason and Slidell. "The idea of the good natured Old Abe pursuing such a fiendish policy as that is laughable," he added.[47] Charles Sumner, in hopes that peace might be preserved, was reassured by the president's statement to him that there would be no war unless Britain was bent on having one. Knowing that Lincoln was astonished by Britain's outrage, he wrote to the English liberal, John Bright, "He is essentially honest, & pacific in his disposition, with a natural slowness." Because Lincoln had told the senator that there would be no war unless Britain was bent on having one, Sumner was reassured. Democrats like August Belmont regretted that the president did not immediately give up the two captives, but when the administration finally did surrender them, the executive heard from Maine that this resolution was received with great satisfaction there. "I have never known so important a decision by an administration which is so universally acceptable," wrote his correspondent. And in Germany, the *Münchner Neuste Nachrichten,* reporting that Lincoln sanctioned the return of the commissioners, quoted him to the effect that one could not wage two wars at one time.[48]

The president's 1861 message to Congress provided his followers with the usual opportunity for approbation. The New York *Commercial Advertiser* praised it highly, labeling it an "admirable document . . . the work of a clear-headed man, sensible of the gravity of the time, and responsive to the vast burden of care devolved upon him." The *Philadelphia Inquirer* agreed, particularly focusing on the excision of Simon Cameron's call for the arming of the slaves as evidence that the president was not ultra.[49] According to the Washington *Evening Star,* the effect of the document would as surely be to secure from him the hearty and active support of the loyal people as to unite against him the noisy band of fanatics, and it cited its neighbors the *Intelligencer* and the *Republican* as sympathetic with its opinion. To the radical *New York Tribune,* Jefferson Davis was the better grammarian, though preaching in a sanguinary spirit; but Lincoln, not moved by this unseemly display of rage and indignity, was a speaker of admirable spirit and laudable brevity. The Springfield *Republican,* though partially critical, agreed that the message was a model of compactness, while the *New York Times* liked its "plain clear common sense."[50] The New York *World*, not yet bitterly hostile, headlined its report, "The Right Man In The Right Place," and compared Lincoln to George Washington. Lincoln's correspondent T. S. Bell, the president of the Kentucky division of the U. S. Sanitary Commission, wrote him that the message was all that could be desired. "You have my grateful thanks for it," he insisted. "You have constantly gained upon my confidence until I feel it is to be no kind of a stigma to be called a Lincolnite." The Massachusetts statesman Edward Everett liked its "temperate and conservative tone," a sentiment James A. Hamilton, the son of the first secretary of the treasury, shared. And while there was criticism of Lincoln's style, the general praise was evident, even the Democratic Albany *Atlas and Argus* admitting that the message was of a character that admitted of no condemnation.[51]

Naturally, there were many critics. Charles Harry Brewster, a Massachusetts soldier, thought that the message did not amount to anything because "he don't tell nigger enough," an idea seconded in better language by the abolitionist Gerrit Smith as well as the *Independent.* The *Belletristisches Journal,* certain that the document would not satisfy anyone, opined that it would have been better had it shown more of the spirit of a statesman than of a rail-splitter. That the rift between Lincoln and the radicals was not unbridgeable, however, was confirmed by Charles Sumner, who confided to Wendell Phillips that the president had assured him that in a month or six weeks "we should all be together." Southerners thought the document was unique in style and sentiment, but its doctrines were infamous and unconstitutional, with the *Richmond Enquirer,* boasting that the message mentioned no defeats, declaring that its recounting of the progress of the war thus far would be disreputable to a child.[52]

Obviously, Southern opinion was not shared in the North.

On Christmas Eve, General Sherman was able to write, "I don't find fault with the administration—they have done their best—all that is possible—same of the President . . . ," and at the end of the year, the Maryland legislature passed a resolution asserting "that our confidence in the wisdom, firmness, and moderation of President Lincoln remains undiminished."[53]

Lincoln's popularity was evident again in the New Year. Conservative as he was, and not willing to cast doubt on his Unionism, Senator Garrett Davis of Kentucky assured the president that, "I am your true and unwavering supporter in waging this war, and in the reconstruction of the Union . . . upon the principles which you have proclaimed to the people of the United States and will vote to strengthen your hands with every constitutional power to bring the war to a speedy and successful close." Several other opponents, particularly the Democrats Hendrick Bradley Wright of Pennsylvania, John B. Steele and Fernando Wood of New York, and Samuel S. Cox of Ohio, also expressed their satisfaction with Lincoln's conservative course. The Springfield *Illinois State Journal,* citing the *Philadelphia Saturday Post,* reported that universal testimony was borne to the honesty and sincerity of the president and that even those who doubted the wisdom of his policy admitted the uprightness and honesty of the man. Encouraged by his reputation for "kind feelings and truest honor," Mrs. Sherman appealed to him to intervene in her husband's case (he had been accused of insanity), and the *Cincinnati Commercial* quoted a former supporter of Stephen A. Douglas, who predicted that if Lincoln succeeded in putting down the rebellion he would be second only to Washington.[54]

When Lincoln dismissed Cameron in January and appointed the former Democratic attorney general Edwin M. Stanton secretary of war, public opinion approved of the choice. John Covode heard that people approved, and the New York lawyer Edwards Pierrepoint wrote to Lincoln that the whole nation was thanking God that he had the wisdom and courage to make the change. *Frank Leslie's Illustrated Newspaper* expressed its agreement; the *Philadelphia Inquirer* spoke of almost universal expressions of satisfaction, particularly because the president had gone outside of his party to find a cabinet member, a fact that also impressed the New York *World.* The *New York Herald* also approved, calling Honest Abe Lincoln in this affair a "man of fixed principles, strong will . . . in some ways, like Old Hickory."[55]

In Congress, too, Lincoln was strenuously defended. In the House, Burt Van Horn of New York powerfully refuted attacks on the administration concerning a planned Confiscation Bill. "We stand by the President and his Administration with a firm trust in his patriotism and fidelity to the great cause of constitutional liberty and the right, and should expect that the President and his Administration will stand by us, and give faithful execution to the laws we shall pass to crush this rebellion . . . ," he said. Alexander Diven, soon to become a general, sought to defend the president against radical attacks, maintaining that the party must unite and that the president's doctrines were simply those acknowledging his constitutional powers. William D. Kelley, himself radical, regretted that Democrats were defending the president, who, he said was a conservative, "alike loyal to the love of liberty . . . and his duty to the Constitution." In the Senate, the archconservative Garrett Davis called him "as honest and as pure a man as lives," a sentiment shared by the much more radical senator from Maine, William Pitt Fessenden.[56]

Lincoln retained his popularity in the army as well. Soldiers had long admired him, as the Boston Brahmin and later colonel of the 54th Masssachusetts Colored Regiment, Robert G. Shaw, had already written in April 1861: "Lincoln knows what he is about." Others were also favorably impressed. As Elisha Hunt Rhodes of the 2nd Rhode Island Infantry observed when he first saw him, "He looks like a good honest man and I trust that with

God's help he can bring our country safely out of its peril."
Thus, it was not surprising that on January 25, 1862, Lincoln
heard from a soldier in Missouri, "You are very popular in the
army. All patriots admire you." Of course, there were those who
were critical, and his relations with General McClellan were very
touchy, but as a whole, the president's popularity in the army
remained constant.[57]

Various individuals also expressed their approval. Governor
Richard Yates of Illinois, not particularly fond of his fellow Illinoisan, confessed to Trumbull that what he was saying of Lincoln "cheers me indeed." One of Joseph Segar's Virginia
constituents had sent him two dozen terrapins for "Honest Abe
Lincoln," which the representative transmitted, fully sharing the
sentiments. Frederick Law Olmstead wrote to his sister, "Old
Abe . . . grows in our respect. A straight forward, shrewd,
quaint, ready and rough old codger." Using similar words, the
conservative New York diarist, George Templeton Strong, who
thought Lincoln a barbarian in respect to outside polish, nevertheless conceded that he was "a sensible, straight forward old
codger. The best President we have had since old Jackson's
time."[58] When the Lincolns' son Willie died, expressions of
sympathy were general, and Andrew Curtin, the Governor of
Pennsylvania, assured the president that he had never enjoyed
to a fuller extent the respect and confidence of the people of
the state. Thus, when the first anniversary of the administration
rolled around, the New York *Evening Post* was able to write,
"Surely, our excellent President, to whose judgment, courage
and decision the people owe so may of the triumphs of the past
year, will not allow the occasion to pass for securing the greatest
good to his country, the most beautiful fame for himself that
ever was offered to a mortal."[59]

3 Second Year: Sustaining Popularity

One of Lincoln's greatest gifts was his uncanny sense of timing. Knowing exactly when to launch a new measure so that it might be adopted, he habitually chose the proper moment to advance administration programs. As Karl Marx observed, "President Lincoln never ventures a step forward before the tide of circumstances and the call of general public opinion forbids further delay. But once 'Old Abe' has convinced himself that such a turning point has been reached, he then surprises friend and foe alike by a sudden operation executed as noiselessly as possible."[1] The choice of fewer than 40 percent of the electorate, he had to secure the Democrats' support for the war, to say nothing of maintaining the loyalty of the border slave states. Thus, he continually stressed that the purpose of the war was to restore the Union and not to extinguish slavery. Nevertheless, on March 6, 1862, he felt the time was ripe for a message calling on the border states to emancipate their bondmen in return for compensation.

The document was generally well received. "The promulgation of the President's mild Emancipation Message is a presage of the universal adoption of this great principle which alone" can win, one of Lyman Trumbull's Chicago correspondents stated to the senator. Henry Raymond, the editor of the *New York Times*, agreed. "I regard the message as a master-piece of practical wisdom and sound policy," he wrote to Lincoln. "It is marked by that plain, self-vindicating common sense which, you will permit me to say, has preeminently characterized every act of your Administration." Governor Thomas Hicks of Maryland—a slaveholder—congratulated the president on the patriotic, sensible, prudent message, as he called it, and thanked him for it. The document was also popular in some army units. "The President's Proclamation is liked very much by all officers I have seen," Massachusetts Lieutenant Stephen Minot Weld wrote to his father.[2]

Many newspapers were equally impressed. According to the *Cincinnati Daily Gazette,* "The views expressed by Mr. Lincoln will, or at least ought, to meet the approbation of earnest Union men everywhere," an idea shared by the *New York Tribune.* "For our part, we thank God that Abraham Lincoln is President of the United States, and the whole country, we cannot doubt, will be thankful that we have at such a time so wise a ruler," it exulted.[3] The *Philadelphia Inquirer* praised the "temperate and statesmanlike spirit" of the message; the Washington *National Intelligencer* hoped that it would be adopted, while the *Chicago Tribune* was glad that it showed the president was aware of slavery as the cause of the rebellion and knew that it must disappear. The *Belletristisches Journal* declared, "This message breathes more statesmanship than any other emanating from the executive during the last fifty years," and the *Springfield Republican* not only spoke of the universal satisfaction with it but, on March 27, asserted, "Nobody is making reputation faster and surer now than President Lincoln. When Congress assembled, he was at a discount in both branches. . . . Now all are hastening to do him reverence."[4]

Radical reaction varied. The ultra radical Wendell Phillips, rarely friendly to the administration, was positive. He called the message, "A voice from the sanctuary of God." Frederick Douglass, speaking for his race, was delighted. "A blind man can see where the President's heart is," he said, calling Lincoln "a brave man, trying against great odds, to do right. An honest patriot endeavoring to save his country in its day of peril." Other radicals, however, anxious for total emancipation, were less laudatory. Count Gurowski thought it a mere crumb; the *Liberator,* decrying its style and offer of a bounty to traitors, was unhappy with it; and some radicals thought that it amounted to nothing.[5]

Most Democrats, making use of the country's widespread opposition to a war for the liberation of the blacks, also criticized the message, declaring that it was ill-timed, impolitic, and beyond the power of Congress. Senator Willard Saulsbury of Delaware was sure it indicated abolitionist intentions, which he deplored, and the New York *Sun* regretted that Lincoln had allowed the abolitionists to beguile him into a false step.[6] The Albany *Atlas and Argus* chastised the president for impulsiveness in sending the message without preparation, a want of consideration on his part giving a sense of insecurity. But the equally Democratic weekly *New-Yorker Staats-Zeitung* admired the fact that the president had taken the wind out of the abolitionists' sails. The South was naturally hostile and called the message hypocritical and its author a "miserable wretch"[7]

Foreign opinion tended to be generally favorable. In spite of much disdain in England, where many considered it incomplete, John Bright was able to write to the historian and diplomat George Bancroft, "The late message of the President on the subject of 'compensated abolition' has given much pleasure here to all friends of the United States." The London *Spectator,* the Liverpool *Post,* the London *News and Star,* and the *Saturday Review* all printed laudatory comments, which were quoted in the New York *Commercial Advertiser,* while even the generally hostile London *Times* conceded that the president had ventured to tackle a question that had been on the minds of many. The *Moniteur* commented on the popularity of the message in England; other French papers commended the president's humanitarianism, although the procurator general of Nancy considered the proposition insufficient for bringing about a solution. And in Germany the *Münchner Neuste Nachrichten* thought the executive expected great results from his initiative.

The worldwide antislavery feeling was very helpful to the chief executive.[8]

On March 11, the president published an order establishing four *corps d'armée*, stripping McClellan of overall command, but leaving him in charge of the Department of the Potomac. He also gave Frémont a new department in the Shenandoah Valley. This new arrangement also met with approval. The *Chicago Tribune* was certain that the change would be the occasion of sincere satisfaction; the *Cincinnati Commercial*, though worried about the restoration of Frémont to command, regarded the division into corps as a good policy; the *New York Herald* believed it to be "well adapted to vigorous prosecution of the war"; and the *Cincinnati Gazette* expressed its satisfaction that the president was now in command.[9] "There can be but one opinion of the entire wisdom of this policy," wrote the *Philadelphia Inquirer,* while the New York Chamber of Commerce passed a resolution of praise and honor to the president "for the wisdom, patriotism and skill which have directed the recent movement of the National forces." *Harper's Weekly* was of the same opinion. "It is fortunate for the country and for the world that it is a wise and calm civilian and not a soldier who is our Chief Magistrate," it mused. Pointing out that Lincoln had remarked that not since George Washington had any president faced so difficult a situation, it predicted history would record Lincoln had been "wrought with a similar wisdom."[10]

The bill for the emancipation of the slaves in the District of Columbia, which Lincoln signed in April, was controversial. Although Lincoln had always insisted on a prior referendum of the inhabitants, he was induced to forego this demand, and while the *New York Herald* reminded its readers of his previous position, it nevertheless thought that, because the bill provided for compensation and possible colonization, the radicals had not gained much.[11]

The Washington *National Intelligencer* gave the president

credit for evidence of great good sense and of a practical sagacity inspired by a sound theory of political action, and both Trumbull and Washburne heard from different towns in Illinois that local people were much pleased with the emancipation act.[12] The *Boston Journal* was certain that "the great mass of the loyal people of this country" would "hail the President's approval of the bill abolishing slavery in the District of Columbia with profound delight." Though there had been some pressure on him to veto the measure, "we thought we knew him well enough to feel no doubt of his final action. . . . He has taken his time and the result is his name will go down to all future ages on the decree which extinguishes human bondage in and around the Capital of the United States." Even the radical Benjamin F. Wade, now happy to be able to praise a Republican chief executive, defended the president in the Senate. The Democrats were less enthusiastic.[13]

By this time, Lincoln's popularity had spread to such an extent that instead of the usual brief prayer of blessing for a president, Congregation Mikve Israel in Philadelphia added a blessing for the president "for his sterling honesty, . . . for his firmness and moderation," and asked God "to rekindle with joy his domestic hearth. . . ." And William O. Stoddard, the president's private secretary, wrote on April 21, "The fact is, that at present the country has entire confidence in no one else, and we might almost say, 'after him the deluge' in view of our present condition." Kentuckian John J. Crittenden, the famous author of the most popular compromise proposal, in a speech on the pending Confiscation Act, put it even more strongly:

> I voted against Mr. Lincoln, and opposed him honestly and sincerely. But Mr. Lincoln has won me to his side. There is a niche in the temple of fame, a niche near to Washington, which should be occupied by the statue of him who shall save his country. Mr. Lincoln has a mighty destiny! It is for him,

if he will step into that niche; it is for him to be but a President of the people of the United States, and there will be his statue. It is in his power to occupy a place next to Washington, the founder and the preserver side by side![14]

The European radicals Ledru Rollin, Joseph Mazzini, and Karl Blind were equally impressed. "Ever since the outbreak of the fierce contest in which you are so nobly battling against domestic rebellion . . . the hearts of the nations with whose aspirations for freedom we are identified, and in whose name we address you, have not for a moment ceased to be with you," they wrote to him. By May 23, the *New York Times* noted, "The most conspicuous feature of the war thus far is the strong hold which the Administration of President Lincoln has been steadily gaining upon the confidence of the great body of the people. There has been nothing like it in the recent political history of the country." Blacks naturally expressed their gratitude for his part in the emancipation of the District of Columbia, and the army esteemed him because of his personal attention to individual soldiers. As Colonel Robert McAllister of the 1st New Jersey Infantry put it to his wife, "Abraham Lincoln and Genl. McClellan . . . are destined to be among the world's grate [sic] men."[15]

When on May 9, General David Hunter issued an order freeing all slaves in his Department of the South, Georgia, Florida, and South Carolina, within ten days Lincoln declared it void. Reminding all of his emancipation offer to the border states, the president nevertheless reserved to himself decisions affecting slavery . The general reaction to this was similar to that toward his action concerning Frémont's edict. "The proclamation will please the sober mass of the people," opined the *Cincinnati Commercial.* "It is gratifying to observe, while the President is an anti-slavery man, he is not a heedless obstructionist, while he is in favor of using all indispensable means for crushing the rebellion, he is not enamored of the impossible schemes of the

impracticables."[16] Referring particularly to the executive's reference to the border states message, the New York *Commercial
Advertiser* thought it "impossible to read this portion of the
proclamation without feeling one's admiration for President
Lincoln vastly heightened." The *Philadelphia Inquirer* praised
the president's "wise policy," and the Washington *National Intelligencer* exulted in the "universal expressions of assent and
approbation" of the loyal press. Some radicals reluctantly approved. The New York *Evening Post* admitted that "Mr. Lincoln
has acted with so much sagacity, prudence, and moderation in
his general treatment of the subject [slavery], that whatever
course he may see fit to adopt will be readily acquiesced in by
the loyal men of the whole country." The *New York Tribune*,
though approving of Hunter's idea and not doubting that the
president held a different position, found it necessary to bow
to his decision. That Democrats like General McClellan wholly
approved was not surprising.[17]

Many radicals, however, were deeply troubled. Even Secretary of the Treasury Salmon P. Chase expressed his dismay to
the general. Garrison called it a wet blanket thrown by Lincoln;
the editor James Wien Forney severely condemned it; and Joseph Medill, the editor of the *Chicago Tribune,* was sure that a
more unjust edict had not been issued since the war began.[18]

Lincoln gained further acclaim when, in response to a congressional resolution demanding an explanation of the corruption in Simon Cameron's department, he assumed all
responsibility himself. "It is impossible not to admire the candor, the sense of justice, and the magnanimity which lead the
President to interpose his own character and authority between the House and the objects of its undeserved censure,"
commented the New York *World*. The Springfield *Republican*
praised "The forbearances and magnanimity of the president in
volunteering this statement," which "exhibits that strong sense
of justice which is so prominent a trait in the president, and

which has given him so strong a hold upon popular confidence." Other papers fully agreed, the *Chicago Tribune* commenting that the "inherent nobility of Abraham Lincoln" had never been more clearly shown." And a correspondent wrote to Washburne that the message was another proof of the president's honesty and patriotism—indeed that he was placed in the chair he occupied "by the Great God of Heaven."[19]

In Congress, a number of Republicans strongly defended Lincoln against Democratic attacks. The Pennsylvania representative Edward McPherson, later the clerk of the House, declared that the administration was justly entitled to the unreserved and generous confidence of people, particularly the president, who had overcome prejudices and won the respect and admiration "by unfaltering and singled minded devotion to duty." The Ohioan Luther Hanchett, defending the suspension of the writ of habeas corpus, thought the executive had been entirely right in the exercise of all powers which he had used, not only in this matter, but also in the arrests which had been ordered; and his colleague John W. Killinger, comparing Lincoln to his predecessor, who had left the legacy of a government verging on dissolution, could point to the people's "unbounded confidence in the integrity of the President and the stability of the Government."[20] Even radicals like Charles Sumner expressed their satisfaction with Lincoln's moves against slavery. The New York *Evening Post* strongly denied the charge that there was a deep rift between him and the radicals; and a habitual critic like General McClellan, who had called Lincoln a "baboon" and an "idiot," as well as "an original gorilla," now temporarily considered him his best friend. Moreover, the call for 300,000 additional troops, hailed by the papers, met with the approval of William T. Sherman, who was not always intrigued with Lincoln's actions.[21]

The Confiscation Act, which provided for the seizure of rebel property, including slaves, was passed by Congress in June, and signed by the president only after he insisted on amendments he considered constitutionally warranted. This pleased many of his supporters. Some radicals, however, were put off by his hesitation in signing it. But as Lyman Trumbull pointed out in the Senate, believing, as he did, that the executive, eminently patriotic in his purpose, "pure, upright, honest, and honorable in his intentions," deserved the support of Congress, which ought to conform to his wishes. Senator Morton S. Wilkinson rejoiced at "the warm republican heart of our worthy Chief Magistrate" who agreed with Congress in signing the measure.[22] And when Lincoln granted an interview to a number of abolitionists who urged him to proceed against slavery, the New York *World* stated that while his views were not theirs, his repudiation of their methods resulted from no want of sympathy with their objects. As the Springfield *Republican* pointed out, "Can a reasonable man doubt for a moment Mr. Lincoln's interest in the poor African?" He had done more for the blacks than any previous president, the paper noted, and with his "noble and generous nature, "ought to rank with the honored names of Clarkson and Wilberforce."[23]

In the meantime, General McClellan's failure to capture Richmond caused misgivings. Democrats blamed the president for failing to send reinforcements to the general, but even radicals like Senator Chandler defended him. Asking which one of two people was responsible for the setback, he said, "The one is the President of the United States, Abraham Lincoln, whom I believe to be a patriot, whom I believe to be honest, and honestly earnest to crush out and put down this rebellion; the other is George B. McClellan, general of the Army of the Potomac, of whom I will not express a belief."[24] *Frank Leslie's Illustrated Newspaper,* asserting that Lincoln was right in removing Frémont; now urged him to proceed likewise with McClellan. And when Lincoln went to visit the Army of the Potomac, the Washington *Evening Star* commented, "The country will thank him for the promptness with which he repaired to the Peninsula on this occasion, to examine for himself into the condition of the Army of the Potomac. . . . His presence in its midst have had the happiest conceivable effect of it; for, men and officers, high and low, all its components have implicit confidence in his patriotism and sagacity."[25]

On July 21, William D. Stoddard, musing about the president's popularity, wrote, "He is the most perfect *representative* of the purely American character now in public life—perhaps the most perfect that ever has existed. This is why the mutual understanding between him and the people is so perfect." The *New York Herald,* not always friendly, fully agreed. "President Lincoln has the confidence of the country," it asserted. "No man doubts his honestly or his patriotism." And as the radical William D. Kelley put it in a letter to Lincoln: "I would not write to you of politics if I did not believe that the success of your administration is the only possible means of saving my country."[26]

By this time, the question of emancipation was becoming ever more crucial. The president, who had written his emancipation proclamation in June, presented it to his cabinet on July 22, only to be told that he ought to wait until federal forces had secured a military success. Consequently, he held it in abeyance, but in order to make any such message more popular, he invited some blacks to the White House to urge them to start a colonization movement. According to the *Cincinnati Gazette,* this showed his good feelings toward the colored race. Did he not want them to have all the rights they did not or could not obtain in the United States? The *New York Semi-Weekly Spectator* characterized his address to the blacks as marked by good sense.[27] But when Horace Greeley expressed disappointment with the president's failure to act and published what he called "The Prayer of Twenty Millions," urging immediate emancipation, Lincoln answered with characteristic clarity that his aim was to restore the Union. If it could be done by freeing some slaves, he would do it, if it could be done only by freeing all slaves, he would do it, and if it could be done only by freeing none, he would do that also, although he reiterated his personal conviction that all men everywhere ought to be free.[28]

Although some radicals were disappointed, the reply was very popular. "In no act of his official life has Mr. Lincoln shown more tact and sagacity than in his reply to the officious letter of Mr. Greeley," commented the *Cincinnati Commercial.* The *Philadelphia Inquirer* called it "the most admirable controversial paper elicited by the Rebellion," while *Harper's Weekly* pointed out that in this position the president would undoubtedly find himself supported by the bulk of the people of the country. Orville H. Browning, who had already informed Lincoln that even the Irish, generally Democrats, were becoming "somewhat enthusiastic" for him, now wrote that the letter had been the occasion of general joy to the people. The chairman of the 1860 Republican convention, George Ashmun, also assured him that the people were with him and would sustain him, and William A. Stearns, the president of Amherst College, called the reply "the clearest and most straight forward policy document of the times." Even the Democrats praised the executive for placing stress on the preservation of the Union rather than on the abolition of slavery.[29]

After McClellan's failure to capture Richmond, his troops were ordered to aid John Pope near Washington, but Pope was defeated at the Battle of the Second Bull Run, and Lincoln was forced to recall McClellan. This action was well-liked in the army, but McClellan himself accepted only after, coming to Washington "mad as a March hare," he had a plain talk with General-in-Chief Henry W. Halleck and Lincoln.[30] The president's popularity was only marginally affected. Still, George Templeton Strong thought that disgust with the government had become universal: "Even Lincoln himself has gone down at last, and like all our popular idols of the last 18 months, this honest old codger was the last to fall, but he has fallen. Nobody believes in him anymore," he entered in his diary. But he himself still had some faith in him.[31]

He was not alone. "The hearts of the people were never more warm for you than they are today," Orville H. Browning wrote to Lincoln, while the Presbyterian Synod of Genesee resolved "that we renew our expression of confidence in the President of the Untied States, and our cordial approbation of the vigorous persecution the war in the use of all the means in his power for the speedy overthrow of the rebellion," sentiments shared by the Wesleyan Methodist Church of the Miami Conference in Ohio and by the citizens of Westchester County in New York. And when a horse ran away with the president, endangering his life, Stoddard remarked how "we were shocked into an appreciation . . . of how deep an interest we all had in the safety or our WISE Chief Magistrate."[32]

McClellan now won a victory at Antietam, finally giving Lincoln a chance to embark on the most controversial action he ever took, the Emancipation Proclamation. Carefully wording it to affect only slaves in territories still in rebellion on January 1, 1863, and restating his purpose as commander in chief of the armed forces to restore the Union, Lincoln succeeded in having it widely accepted by his supporters. As two Erie, Pennsylvania correspondents wrote to him, "God bless you for the word you have spoken! All good men upon the earth will glorify you, and all the angels in Heaven will hold jubilee!" Another assured him that his proclamation was "the choicest document issued this century," and a Philadelphian asserted that the virtuous, intelligent, and patriotic people "hail your edict with delight and bless and thank God that he put it in your heart to issue it." The Missouri radical B. Gratz Brown called it "the noblest act of the age on this continent"; and Vice President Hamlin predicted that future generations would say, as he did, "God bless you for the great and noble act."[33] The New Hampshire physician John

Milton Hawks thought that "the name of Lincoln in spite of all his follies, must stand forever emblazoned in letters of living light"; the radical Benjamin F. Wade stated to George W. Julian, "Hurrah for Old Abe, and the *proclamation*," and the equally radical editor of the *Independent,* Theodore Tilton, wrote to Lincoln, "God bless you for a good deed." Charles Sumner thanked God that he had lived to enjoy this day. "The Administration belongs to us now, and we belong to the Administration," he declared. And in 1864 the artist Francis Bicknell Carpenter painted the well-known picture of the event.[34]

Many newspapers agreed. "We have no doubt that the President's policy . . . will be approved by an immense majority of the people of the United States who are loyal to our republican form of government," stated the *Cincinnati Commercial;* the *Liberator,* though regretting the postponement of emancipation until the first of January, was certain that September 22, 1862, would henceforth be a memorable day in the nation's history. The *New York Times* thought the wisdom of the step taken was unquestionable and its necessity indisputable; the New York *Evening Post* called it the most glorious day of Lincoln's life; and the Springfield *Republican* believed that Lincoln's "integrity, his prudence, his courage, his supreme fidelity to the constitution, and his purpose to do nothing which did not evidently tend to the salvation of the Union" were "fully, nobly, triumphantly vindicated." The *Portland Transcript* called it an important step forward; the *Chicago Tribune* exulted, "President Lincoln has set his hand and affixed the great seal of the nation to the grandest proclamation ever issued by man," while the *New York Tribune* wrote, "It is the beginning of the end of the rebellion; the beginning of the new life for the nation. GOD BLESS ABRAHAM LINCOLN!"[35]

The army was less favorably impressed. Allen Morgan Geer of the 20th Illinois Volunteer Regiment thought it a "fearful experiment." Colonel David Hunter Strother of West Virginia, commenting that Lincoln had neither sense nor principle, was afraid the proclamation would make a speedy peace impossible, a fear shared by others. George Whitman, stationed near Antietam, thought Lincoln would have to lick the rebels before he could free the Negroes.

Even among the soldiers, however, there were those who admired the president for his act. As Joseph Jones of the 45th Illinois wrote to his wife, "The proclamation is a death blow to Slavery. . . . The name of Abraham Lincoln will be handed down to posterity as one of the greatest benefactors of his country, not surpassed by the immortal Washington himself."[36]

The Democrats, again relying on the country's racism, thought to make the most of Lincoln's alleged departure from the Chicago platform adopted in 1860 and his own inaugural address. "President Lincoln has swung loose from the constitutional moorings of his inaugural address and his messages at the opening of two successive sessions of Congress under his administration," charged the New York *World*. Asserting that the president was striking at the idea of "the Constitution as it is" and "the Union as it was," the Columbus *Crisis* concluded, "We have at last hit upon the lower round of national existence." The Albany *Atlas and Argus* complained that the abolitionist pressure had been too strong for Lincoln to resist, while the *Louisville Journal* vowed that Kentucky would never acquiesce in this unconstitutional act.[37] The army surgeon Thomas Ellis thought that every patriotic lover of his country must deplore this act which would merely inflame the South. The *Chicago Times*, though conceding that the president had been all right so far, believed he had now cut loose from the Constitution. The *Brooklyn Eagle*, asserting that he could not even write good English, also castigated Lincoln for having allegedly violated the Constitution. And, according to the *New York Evening Express*, he had done his best to divide the Northern states as well as to prolong the war indefinitely.[38]

Southerners, who considered the proclamation "a diabolical move," published cartoons of "King Abraham Before and After Issuing the Emancipation Proclamation," showing Lincoln taking off a mask and revealing the face of the devil. Nevertheless, they generally thought it would not change much. This was the opinion of the fire-eater Edmund Ruffin, who held that it was good for the Confederacy because it showed what the North allegedly wanted all along, an opinion also voiced by the Richmond *Dispatch,* which asserted, "The Yankee Government has at last laid aside all disguise. Lincoln openly preaches the abolition of slavery throughout the South." Frank M. Gailor, the Confederate quartermaster thought Lincoln had played his last card; and the war clerk J. B. Jones believed that it would only intensify the war and add to Southern armies in the field. In Louisiana, Kate Stone, a determined secessionist, was sure that there was little chance of a happy hereafter for Lincoln and that a thousand years of repentance would be but brief time to wipe out his sins against the South.[39]

Although the proclamation was in part intended to strengthen the Union's position abroad, leading foreign journals failed to be impressed. In Britain, *Punch* called it "Abe Lincoln's Last Card." The London *Times* not only agreed, but accused him of starting a servile war; and Benjamin Moran, at the American legation in London, commented that "this great measure of liberty has been received with laughter and jeers by England." The *Edinburgh Review* considered the action "one of vengeance," with no indication of the fate of the blacks once they were freed, while the London *Spectator,* while conceding the limitations of Lincoln's powers, called it merely a hopeful promise, disregarding the principle at stake. In France, the *Moniteur* was dubious about it, and in Germany, the *Frankfurter Journal* considered it unimportant. The Russian envoy Edouard de Stoeckl regretted Lincoln's having yielded to the abolitionists.[40]

Contrary reactions, however, were also in evidence. The German-American activist Gustave Koerner wrote from Europe that Germany was very sympathetic to the Union, and noted that, had the Emancipation Proclamation reached him there or in Switzerland, he would have found people even more sympathetic. And when Chancellor of the Exchequer William E. Gladstone, in a speech at Newcastle, said that Jefferson Davis and his collaborators had made an army, were making a navy, and what was more, a nation, the Birmingham writer Samuel A. Goddard, in a letter to the *London American*, chastised him for having delivered the talk when he already had in his possession the president's Emancipation Proclamation, which the writer called, "probably the most important to humanity of any document published during the present century.[41]

Two days after issuing the Emancipation Proclamation, Lincoln issued a second document, widely suspending the writ of habeas corpus. This too, though extensively criticized by the opposition, was approved by important journals. The *New York Times* expressed its satisfaction that both proclamations showed that the administration now had a determined policy, and the *New York Tribune* called it "an evidence of the earnestness with which he means the war shall now be prosecuted. . . ." The *Philadelphia Inquirer* was certain that the president adopted this second proclamation only after the fullest deliberation "with far greater knowledge of its necessity than . . . by any . . . mere lookers-on. . . ." And when Congress met in December, Republican senators and representatives defended both proclamations against Democratic attacks, Maine Senator Lot M. Morrill declaring that he was exercising precisely the functions the Constitution conferred upon him, the Ohioan Wells A. Hutchins calling the proclamation necessary to end the cause of the rebellion, and William Pitt Fessenden characterizing the executive as generous and magnanimous. Hostile papers and politicians, however, had a new issue on which to aim their criticism of the president.[42]

In spite of these favorable comments, the Republicans suffered severe losses in the 1862 midterm elections. Nevertheless, Lincoln's popularity endured. The *New York Herald,* while blaming the setbacks in Ohio and Indiana on the proclamation, nevertheless asserted that the results strengthened the president against the radicals. Others thought that the result was due, not to the document, but to want of vigor in the conduct of the war. When further losses followed in November, even Lincoln's supporters admitted that the elections were worrisome. But as the Springfield *Republican* surmised, it was the Republican party, not the administration of Mr. Lincoln, that had been condemned by the people, who had pronounced for a more vigorous prosecution of the war. Other papers were less charitable, but they generally agreed that a determined war policy was required.[43] Still, Lincoln's popularity persisted. Schuyler Colfax, the later vice president, rejoicing at his reelection to Congress, contrary to the *Herald,* thought the Emancipation Proclamation had come just in time to secure victory for successful Republicans. "God bless you," he wrote to the president." Though admitting that the elections were a call to the administration to do better in the future, the New York *Evening Post*—which some weeks earlier had already asserted that because of Lincoln's great successes, if he pushed forward, his fame would be as great as that of Washington—now stated, "The Administration has at its head a most pure, patriotic, and upright man, a man of clear understanding, who can read the lessons of events as they arise, and who sincerely desires to govern his public course by the wisdom they teach. What we expect from such a man is, that he will discard the sluggish policy role the people have as decidedly condemned and that he will insist on precipitating our whole military force upon the enemy." Private commentators agreed that more vigor was needed, and one of John Sherman's correspondents already saw some "indications of a more determined and vigorous purpose in the president, since the late elections."

The New York attorney David Dudley Field, calling himself a most sincere well-wisher of the president, advised him that people were dissatisfied because of failure of the conduct of the war, the arrest of citizens, and the unconstitutionality of the proclamation. "It is no merely personal regard which prompts me to write it but the conviction that the continued confidence of the people in you is important to the safety of the country."[44]

The Democrats took a different approach. The Albany *Atlas and Argus* expressed its satisfaction that the Democrats were now coming to the rescue of the president and were relieving him of radical pressure. The New York party activist S. L. M. Barlow urged Governor-elect Horatio Seymour to go to see Lincoln in order to invigorate the administration, something that he said the cabinet could not do. As usual, the response to the elections showed that the president's personal popularity was such as to withstand political as well as military setbacks.[45]

This fact became evident again immediately after the elections, when Lincoln dismissed McClellan and appointed Rhode Island General Ambrose Burnside in his stead. The New York politician Daniel S. Dickinson, emphasizing that the rural districts did very well in the recent elections, sent his approval, as did Schuyler Colfax, who added, "Our people send grateful thanks for Burnside's appointment changing despair into confidence & hope." Governor William Sprague of Rhode Island agreed, as did the Indiana banker and farmer Calvin Fletcher, who called the change "a deserved censure of McClellan, who showed himself totally unfit for his position. . . ." Pittsburgh Congressman James K. Moorhead wrote, "Permit me to thank you, as I do, from the bottom of my heart. Whatever the result may be you have done your duty and the country will congratulate you upon it, and rally around you."[46] The *Cincinnati Daily Commercial,* contending that the motives of the president in the discharge of his public duties were above suspicion, pointed out that he knew the facts and had long been friendly toward the discharged general. As the *Philadelphia Inquirer* put it, "We should all remember that the President has been, through good report and through bad evil report, the steadfast friend of General McClellan, and we must therefore accept his order transferring General McClellan's command as an act done in good faith, because of controlling reasons of public policy." In Rye, New York, Cornelia Jay believed that "many think the Administration, disappointed in the recent elections, has wreaked revenge of the favorite general of the Democratic party, but I think too well of Mr. Lincoln to believe he would be influenced in so important a matter by such motives." In Oswego, New York, Caroline L. Frey wrote to Ludlow Frey, "Aren't you rejoiced at the removal of McClellan? It gives great satisfaction here." And the radical *New York Tribune,* which, like other radicals, had long been critical, expressed its satisfaction that the president, at the last hour, but not too late to save the country, had relieved McClellan.[47]

The army, however, had grave misgivings about the change. There was even talk of resignations because of it. But even among the officers, there was some understanding of the president's action. As Oliver Wilcox Norton of the 83d Pennsylvania Volunteers informed his sister, the army thought as much of McClellan as ever, and he believed the president too, had full confidence in McClellan when he removed him, but the pressure of public opinion made him do it. Some enlisted men were equally understanding, Charles H. Moulton of the 34th Massachusetts Volunteer Infantry, calling it "a very wise idea."[48]

The Democrats made the most of the move. The Columbus *Crisis,* while admitting that the president had always manifested the strongest desire to act for the best of the country, said that he had gone too far. The *New York Evening Express* called it a "fatuity," and felt that "never was the adage 'Whom the Gods wish to destroy they first make mad' more fully verified." Others spoke of the "criminality of McClellan's removal," and continued to urge the restoration of the "Little Napoleon."[49]

Lincoln's December 1862 message was again received with much praise. "It is a document marked by unmistakable ability and by an earnest and sincere patriotism," commented the *Philadelphia Inquirer,* while the *New York Times* labeled it "concise, clear and perspicuous." The *Cincinnati Gazette,* emphasizing his treating the Emancipation Proclamation as "a thing accomplished," reported that the message was widely spoken of as the best written and best considered of any he had ever submitted. According to the Washington *National Intelligencer,* it could not be read without "feeling respect for his candor and patriotic inspiration," and even the *New York Herald,* often critical, felt constrained to say, " It is marked throughout by the characteristic simplicity of style and honest and earnest patriotism which distinguish all the official production of its author." As Private Oliver Wilcox Norton of the 83d Pennsylvania Volunteers wrote to his sister, "I have been much interested in the President's message. . . . It meets my views exactly. . . . Nothing he has ever said or done pleased me so much as his reasons for his policy, and his earnest appeal to Congress and the people to support it." The Indiana banker Calvin Fletcher called it fair, and the Pennsylvania observer Samuel Conway thought it "a great paper indeed."[50]

Because of the president's suggestion about colonization, as well as an amendment for general emancipation with compensation by 1900, a number of radicals, still eager for a total war against slavery, were critical. "I could hardly credit my ears when I listened to the whole message, and heard not a word or sentence that indicated that the administration intended to push the war to a triumphant conclusion," wrote Gerrit Smith to the educator Burke Hinsdale, calling the proposed amendment "a most weak, absurd scheme." While conceding to the president the "honesty of purpose," the *Liberator* decried "the

folly and infatuation" of his plan "for buying up 'Southern treason' in lots to suit purchasers." Charles Sumner, however,
thought that the last paragraph vindicating emancipation was
everything. The New York *Evening Post*—though complaining
that the president was not a rhetorician nor a formal logician
whose reasoning was not always rigid—nevertheless wrote, "He
is thoroughly conscientious in what he does, devoted to the best
interests of his country, with more than an average share of
sagacity, and a good deal of that homely wisdom which springs
from honest purposes." And the radical *New York Tribune*, emphasizing the lack of difference between the Emancipation Proclamation and the proposed amendment, which did not affect
conquered areas, expressed its satisfaction that in the stormy era
in which the country found itself, it was well that it should have
one among its leaders whose integrity, patriotism, and uncalcu-
lating devotion to the noblest ends, all may and do confide, . . .
Abraham Lincoln."[51]

Southerners continued their vilification. In Georgia, the Rev-
erend C. C. Jones thought the message breathed "the same
heartless, cold-blooded, and murderous fanaticism that first
began and has marked the war." The Richmond *Dispatch* labeled it "beneath contempt," and the Virginia secessionist Lucy
Rebecca Buck was certain that it was a most sublimely ridiculous composition showing the difference between Jefferson
Davis and Lincoln.[52]

The month of December 1862 was one of great difficulty for
Lincoln. General Burnside lost the battle of Fredericksburg, and
a congressional committee representing a Republican caucus
demanded that the president change his cabinet and appoint
reliable generals. As the critics were chiefly interested in removing Secretary of State Seward, he resigned, but Lincoln then met
with the protesters in the presence of the entire cabinet, which
denied many of the charges against it, principally initiated by

Chase, who now also resigned, making it possible for Lincoln to keep both controversial secretaries.[53]

That these problems caused widespread criticism of the president was natural—the Albany *Atlas and Argus* complained that the president merely continued cracking his jokes—but even then, Lincoln's popularity persisted. "Assure the President that all earnest men & women are praying for him daily, that God will give him the wisdom he needs in this hour of the Nation's agony & hope," the Illinois Republican Wait Talcott wrote to Lyman Trumbull on December 19. The Connecticut Assembly passed a resolution expressing its confidence in the patriotism and integrity of the president, and the Union nurse Hannah Ropes expressed her conviction that his honesty was a gain over anything the country had had for some time. James Wien Forney urged the reporter John Russell Young to endorse the president's action during the cabinet crisis; the Washington *Evening Star* also hailed it. And, referring to the cabinet crisis, *Harper's Weekly* chastised the Senate for attempting to dictate changes in the cabinet. "The Constitution confers upon them no more right to demand the resignation of an obnoxious secretary than to appoint a mayor of New York city," it wrote. "For the Senate to attempt to dictate to the executive, is at least as intolerable as it would be for the President to assume legislative powers."[54]

In Congress, Republican members reaffirmed their trust in the administration. Indiana Senator Henry S. Lane, condemning the attacks on Lincoln, said, "The country will withstand these assaults, the President will withstand them. He stands erect in the conscious honesty of his purpose, the purity of his intention, the loftiness of his patriotism, and he will stand as the granite cliff repels and beat back the wild waves of the ocean. So far, the President, if he has erred at all, has erred upon the side of mercy." On December 15, Samuel C. Fessenden of Maine introduced a resolution declaring the Emancipation Proclamation constitutional, and two days later, the Missouri representative John W. Noell strongly defended the suspension of the writ of habeas corpus.[55]

Most of Lincoln's radical critics obviously denigrated him at the time. Robert Gould Shaw believed him to be on the verge of lunacy, and Count Gurowski repeated his loss of confidence; Charles Sumner, however, pitied him. "He wants to do right and save the country," he wrote to Longfellow. Admiral Samuel F. DuPont also was sorry for him. And Zachariah Chandler, although privately considering him weak and an imbecile, nevertheless wrote to Governor Austin Blair of Michigan that Old Abe promised to stand firm, and he believed him. The New York Tribune commented on Lincoln's known kindness but said he had not yielded and had retained his cabinet. And Benjamin F. Wade, most critical as usual, was urged to speak to Lincoln, who would certainly do his duty.[56]

As the New Year neared, some opponents were still in hopes that Lincoln would not carry out his emancipation policy. But they were wrong. As Sumner reported to John Murray Forbes, the president said he could not stop the proclamation if he would, and he would not if he could. And when he did issue it on January 1, 1863, although the reaction was most varied, the high estimation of the executive became more pronounced than ever. "I improved yesterday to my satisfaction in reading the President's Proclamation!" wrote the New Yorker Abby Howland Woolsey. "The Lord reigneth, let the earth rejoice!" Lincoln heard that the blacks were delirious with joy and hailed him as liberator of a people. General Julius Stahel, somewhat too optimistic, sent him his best wishes and added, "May you be spared to enjoy the anniversary of this day when your wisdom & patriotism shall have restored peace & plenty to our united country." From Brooklyn, he was told, "Language has no words to express how much we thank you for your glorious Proclamation. . . . Only see the Proclamation carried out and how brightly the name Abraham Lincoln will shine through all times and ages. How richly laden with blessings will your Proclamation be handed down to future generations, as great a document as the Declaration of Independence, and your memory as much honored and beloved as that of Washington." A delegation of German-American citizens also likened the executive to Washington; poems sang his praise; and Lyman Trumbull heard from his home state that while the Democrats were furious, most Republicans approved of the proclamation.[57]

Republican newspapers were equally enthusiastic. "The President's proclamation . . . marks an era in the history, not only of this war, but of this country and the world," wrote the *New York Times,* while the *Chicago Tribune* called it "A New Year's Gift to Humanity," The *Cincinnati Gazette* called it "the foremost document of the century." The Springfield *Republican* fully approved of the proclamation "as a fit and necessary war measure for suppressing the rebellion" and praised the president for having issued it in his capacity as commander in chief of the army, in spite of his personal antislavery feelings, an assessment with which the New York *Commercial Advertiser* fully agreed.[58]

The radical faction, now regaining some faith in the president, though unhappy about the omission of the border states, was also generally satisfied. As the *New York Tribune,* though regretting the proclamation's limitations, put it, "Let it not be said that we cavil at the Proclamation and seek to undermine it. It is worth very much, even though it might have been made worth far more"; and its editor, Horace Greeley, informed Lincoln that his message fully satisfied the expectations of his friends, and was received with great enthusiasm. The *Independent* was more positive. "The news of the President's great act was received with a thrill thought the loyal North," it commented. The New York *Evening Post,* criticizing the president for not having acted earlier, hailed "his acceptance of the true policy nonetheless." The *Liberator,* generally critical, carried a headline, "Glory, Hallelujah"; George Livermore, the Cambridge businessman and bibliophile, wrote to Sumner, who had let him know that the "act" would be firm throughout time, "God bless Abraham Lincoln, & God bless Charles Sumner!," and the Massachusetts Anti-Slavery Society passed a resolution expressing its joy that "at last the President was constrained . . . to proclaim the emancipation of more than three millions of slaves."[59]

One of the reasons for the proclamation was Lincoln's hope that it would create sympathy for the Union in Europe. On December 31, the workingmen and citizens of Manchester, in a letter printed in the *Manchester Guardian*, praised him for his antislavery measures and congratulated him on the impending issue of the proclamation. Henry Adams wrote to his brother from London, "The Emancipation Proclamation has done more for us here than all our former victories and all our diplomacy. It is creating an almost convulsive reaction in our favor all over this country." His father, the American envoy to Great Britain, said the same: "Since the issue of the President's proclamation there are signs of extensive reaction in the popular feeling toward the United States," he wrote to Edward Everett. Baptist Wriothesley Noel, in his book, *The Rebellion in America,* stressed the same thing, as did Edward Dicey, who tried to explain that the president could go only as far as he did, so that any dissatisfaction with the limitations of the document was not justified. Samuel Goddard, in answer to Sir Robert Peel's criticism, asserted, "The act, instead of 'odious,' will be declared by posterity to be the greatest movement of this century, and will immortalize the President." The *Caledonian Mercury* in Edinburgh agreed: "The more the text of the president's Message is considered, the higher must be our appreciation of its calm thoughtfulness, so different from the rowdyism we were wont to receive from Washington when Pro-Slavery Cabinets were in the ascendance." And Frederick Douglass heard from an observer in Liverpool that the 1st of January 1863 would be a day ever to be remembered in the history of America.[60]

The London *Times,* however, hostile as usual, categorized the proclamation as a complete lack of success of federal politicians to bring English sympathy to their side, and continued to insist that the policy was a failure. The *Times* was not alone. "Notwithstanding the manifest importance of Mr. Lincoln's Emancipation Proclamation, the British press almost universally carp at and condemn it," Benjamin Moran observed. French opinion was equally critical. According to the *Moniteur,* there was great opposition to the document, with Lincoln being blamed, and the Procurator General of Colmar called the proclamation "truly monstrous." Did it not, in line with Lincoln's orders, keep slaves in Union territory while freeing them in that of their neighbors?" The poet Alphonse de Lamartine considered slavery but a pretext for a war of jealousy against the South, because, as Lincoln himself had stated, nobody in the North considered the Negro a brother. The *Courier du Havre* accused the president of a type of tyranny in which the tsar of Russia would not have indulged.[61]

The Democrats made the most of the final proclamation. "The Deed Is Done! The Dictator Presumes to Speak! The Negro in the Ascendant!" headlined the Columbus *Crisis,* complaining "that one should not be surprised at this last act of the half-witted usurper who, in an evil hour, was elected under the forms of the Constitution by a minority of the American people. . . ." The Albany *Atlas and Argus* was certain that no one believed in the proclamation, not even the president himself, and that it was a step in the progress of separation. Colonel Charles S. Wainwright, arguing that Lincoln virtually admitted he issued it to please the radicals, mused, "What is to become of us with such a weak man at the head of our government, be he ever so honest?" In the Senate, Willard Saulsbury said that the call on the freedmen to abstain from violence would "light their author down in dishonor to the remotest generation," while his Kentucky's colleague Lazarus W. Powell also charged the president with instigating rebellion among the slaves.[62]

The South expressed similar opinions. The Confederate States "could not consent to an armistice of a single day or hour, so long as the incendiary proclamation of the atrocious monster now bearing rule in Washington city shall remain un-revoked," was the wording of a resolution introduced into the Southern Congress by Tennessee Representative Henry S. Foote; Catherine Edmundston complained about the "infamous" proclamation which caused its author henceforth to stand forth a perjured man; the *Richmond Enquirer* called it "the indecent expression of Lincoln's rage," and the *Southern Illustrated News* republished a *Punch* cartoon ridiculing the call-up of black troops.[63]

While Democrats attacked the president because of the Emancipation Proclamation, they could agree with their opponents in praising him for revoking General Grant's order expelling Jews from his department. "The conduct of the President and the General-in-Chief in thus promptly countermanding such an outrageous, unconstitutional, and inhuman order, meets with my hearty approval. I commend them for it," said Lazarus W. Powell in the Senate, thus echoing Republican newspaper opinion. The reaction to the removal of General Benjamin F. Butler from his command in New Orleans, where he had been accused of being too radical and of a tendency to corruption, was a different matter. Although Lincoln received letters of thanks from local supporters, radical critics thought he had made a bad mistake. Butler's quartermaster thought Lincoln acted like a child, and sought to enlist Cameron and Republican members of Congress to see Lincoln in order to protest against the removal.[64] But on the whole, the president had maintained his popularity throughout the year.

4   Defeat and Victory

I n the year 1863, the nation—as well as the chief executive—was confronted first with defeat, and then with victory, interrupted once again by a setback, but finally ending in the victory at Chattanooga. Notwithstanding the reverses, however, Lincoln's reputation remained favorable and rose with each new military success.

As early as January 11, the Philadelphia Union League called for the president's renomination. In the House of Representatives, Ohio Representative John A. Bingham defended him against Vallandigham's incessant attacks, and Wisconsin's James Doolittle did the same in the Senate by answering Lazarus W. Powell's complaints about military arrests: "The President of the United States (and a more honest and patriotic man does not live)," he said, "believing that, under the Constitution of the United States, he is acting by virtue of that authority which that instrument gives him, has made these military arrests. . . ."[1] From Iowa, William Leighton wrote to New York Collector Hiram Barney that he supported "our noble President" in all of his acts, and according to Representative Hendrick B. Wright of Pennsylvania, it was the duty of all Democrats to support Lincoln because of his appointments of men from different political parties. At the same time, the president's financial message calling for a uniform currency was widely praised. "We have read the message carefully, and for our lives cannot see any cause for dissatisfaction with what the President has done," commented the New York *Evening Post;* the New York *Tribune* endorsed every word of the message, while the Washington *Daily Morning Chronicle* considered Lincoln's pleas an "irresistible argument."[2]

In the meantime, the usual attacks on the administration continued. The *New York Leader* was certain that the "shameful malpractices of the Administration have disgusted the country and crippled the national credit." *The New York Evening Express* thought "the best thing that can be done is for Mr. Lincoln to resign, and go home to Springfield, with Mr. Hamlin to follow him. These resignations would be worth twenty victories, and would reestablish public confidence. . . ." The weekly *New-Yorker Staats-Zeitung* wondered whether the president was to be pitied or despised, and after publication of the McDowell Court of Inquiry report justifying the general's actions during McClellan's campaigns, Lincoln was blamed for the 1862 defeats. Kansas Representative Martin Conway announced that Lincoln was evidently not the man for the job, though even he admitted that the president was "amiable."[3] As before, however, Lincoln's popularity survived these put-downs.

If his opponents utilized the McDowell report to denigrate the president, the latter's supporters used it for the opposite purpose. After McClellan had moved to the peninsula, Lincoln wrote a letter setting forth his reasons for holding back troops for the defense of Washington; the letter was published in the McDowell report and the *New York Times* stated that it showed Lincoln's "most earnest anxiety to do always the best in his power . . . for ceaseless action in the field against the rebels. Whoever may be responsible for the inaction and delay which enabled the rebellion to grow from an easily repressed revolt . . . it is not the President." Even Count Gurowski thought it showed sound common sense, and the *Chicago Tribune* labeled it "a complete and unanswerable vindication of the Administration." It also took the Copperheads to task for calling him a tyrant and an enemy of popular liberty. "You lie, you scoundrels," it wrote; "you know you lie. You know that his thoughts, hopes, wishes, expectation and toilsome labor among difficulties of Alpine magnitude, are all for the dear land and the institutions that our fathers framed."[4]

The praise continued. In the Senate, on January 19, Joseph A. Wright of Indiana defended the president against Lazarus Powell's attacks; on the next day in the House, Owen Lovejoy replied to Representative Charles J. Biddle's charges of tyranny, by stating, "The President of the United States is the last man in the world that should be charged with arbitrary power. That gentleman must know it, as every man knows it, and as, thank God, the great masses of the people not only believe it, but know it." On January 27, Samuel Shellabarger of Ohio countered Vallandigham's assertion that Lincoln started the war by citing the statement of the Confederate Secretary of War, who had boasted that the South started it with the attack on Fort Sumter. On February 2, even Thaddeus Stevens, generally Lincoln's radical critic, spoke of "our excellent and kind hearted President," and on the 5th, the *Independent* declared, "He that rejects Mr. Lincoln chooses Jeff Davis." Noah Brooks, regretting Republican attacks on Lincoln, concluded, "No wonder if our honest, patriotic, and single hearted Chief Magistrate looks over the heads of mere politicians to find his best friends most distant in the mass of the people, who love and reverence Abraham Lincoln for his noble and manly qualities of heart and mind. . . ."[5]

The defenders of the president persisted in their rebuttals, though only a few can be cited here. In Congress, on February 5, John Sherman, conceding that some might think the president was not the ablest man that had ever lived, called him "the instrument in the hands of Almighty God," praised his honesty, and expressed his belief that in all his measures, he had in view the safety, welfare, and honor of the country. Some two weeks later, Amasa Walker of Massachusetts disputed charges that Lincoln was a tyrant: "Abraham Lincoln a tyrant!" he exclaimed, "Never was there a greater misnomer. There is nothing of the tyrant about him. His idiosyncracies are not in that direction."

On February 28, the radical Ohioan Albert G. Riddle, said that, while the president might not be a genius, "He is an unimpassioned, cool, shrewd, sagacious, far-seeing man, with a capacity to form his own judgments, and a will to execute them; he possesses an integrity pure and simple as the white rays of light that play about the throne. It is this that has so tied the hearts and love of the people to him that will not unclose in the breath of all the demagogues in the land." William P. Sheffield of Rhode Island, though often critical, declared that, as Lincoln was at the helm of affairs, he must be sustained. The Ohioan Harrison G. Blake not only denounced the opposition for maligning the president because he would not follow Buchanan's policy, but also once more defended the Emancipation Proclamation. "I honor Abraham Lincoln for issuing that proclamation," Blake said. The Governor of Michigan assured the president of his approval, and the 112th Pennsylvania Volunteers resolved that they saw nothing in the administration that was either tyranny or usurpation.[6]

On March 3, 1863, an Enrollment Act was passed—the first federal draft. Not even this measure, unpopular as it was, undermined Lincoln's popularity. "President Lincoln has now been in office two years and what tremendous responsibility has rested upon him and is likely to rest upon him for the remainder of his term," wrote Aurelius Lyman Voorhis of the 46th Indiana Regiment. "Without doubt he is the right man in the right place and every loyal man should support him with their hands and voice." The Arkansas Methodist Episcopal Church resolved that it had "undiminished confidence in the patriotism of the Chief Executive of the nation" and pledged to him its hearty support, a sentiment that its New Jersey counterpart shared. Andrew Johnson thought the president was merely doing his duty in calling out troops, and when the executive issued a proclamation calling on all those absent without leave to return before April in order to be treated with clemency, the

Philadelphia Inquirer was certain that no man could find fault with it. The New York *Commercial Advertiser* only regretted that the proclamation had not been issued earlier, an assessment with which the *New York Spectator* agreed. At the same time, the *Atlantic Monthly,* equating Lincoln with Pericles, averred that "each stands illustrious as the last reach upward of the towering civilizations that respectively pushed them to eminence."[7]

On April 8, 1863, Lincoln went to inspect the Army of the Potomac, where he was welcomed by enthusiastic shouts wherever he went. The *Independent,* considering the visit well timed and well conceived, felt that the soldiers could see that he did not forget them. Sergeant Edwin Welles of the 107th New York Regiment wrote to his sweetheart that the president reviewed the troops and "managed to increase their admiration." And Pennsylvania Captain Francis Adams Donaldson reported, "It did us good to see 'Uncle Abe' taking the kindly interest he does in our welfare." Nevertheless, any number of soldiers disagreed. "Old Abe was here, and he looks as if he would soon go to kingdom come, and there is [sic] few in this army who would be sorry if he was there," the Massachusetts color sergeant Peter Welsh wrote to his wife, while Sergeant Thomas W. Smith of the 6th Pennsylvania Cavalry Regiment referred to "Father Linckum, the nigger Father," in reporting on the visit.[8]

Again, military and naval setbacks, which the Democrats again complained that the president kept joking about, did not diminish the regard in which Lincoln was held. When on April 7, 1863, Admiral Samuel Du Pont's attack on Charleston and Fort Sumter failed, the New York *Commercial Advertiser* expressed no surprise at the abuse of "rebel sympathizers," but concluded that it was pleasant to know that the president was very indifferent to it, that the administration had done its duty in the matter of this attack, although it was not in mortal hands to command success, and neither the president nor the secretary of the navy had left undone anything within their power to achieve a fortunate outcome for the operation.[9]

In April, the radical Joint Committee on the Conduct of the War, which was set up in 1861 to monitor the administration's military policy, issued its report. Excoriating McClellan but also anything but friendly to the administration, it caused Republican and independent newspapers to muse that Jefferson Davis could rejoice about the document. Several depreciated the attacks on the president, as did the Washington *Evening Star,* while *Harper's Weekly* called it an emphatic testimony to the sagacity of the president and on May 2 published a full page sketch of the executive, General Hooker, and their staff reviewing the Army of the Potomac. Others, totally devoted to Lincoln, thought the correspondence with McClellan showed that, of all the men in and about Washington, he was the best fitted to take command of the army in and about that city.[10]

On May 3 General Hooker suffered a serious and unexpected defeat at Chancellorsville, which constituted a low point for the administration. While General Sherman, often critical, expressed his pity for the president, Hamilton Fish, former New York governor and senator, in line with his moderate Republicanism, thought no army could succeed with Lee opposed to it in front and Lincoln, Stanton, and Wade hampering it in the rear. But as Lincoln's New Jersey admirer, James M. Scovel, after attending a meeting in Columbia, Pennsylvania, reported to the executive, "Our reverses do not seem to have even chilled the old spirit of the loyal people in that region. Every allusion to yourself was met by heartfelt applause, and the meeting broke up with three cheers for the President."[11] On May 11, in praise of Lincoln, the *New York Tribune* affirmed that "in all this land, no other man has evinced so much and such constant overruling anxiety that the Rebellion should be suppressed in such manner as to permit the speedy and complete restoration of fraternal feeling between North and South as he." And the *Inde-*

pendent reported that after Chancellorsville, Lincoln was shocked at first but—undaunted by the reverse—was ready to press the war forward again. At the same time, the *Belletristisches Journal* commented that Lincoln, carried to office by a party, was now "the darling of all parties that care about the people and freedom," and rightly enjoying an enviable popularity. Joining in the tribute, Ferdinand Benventano de Bosco in Rome wrote to the president on May 20 that his manner of administering the government had inspired the most lively admiration.[12]

Lincoln's physical appearance, however, created pessimistic comment. As early as January 20, naval Lieutenant Roswell H. Lamson wrote to a woman in Washington that the president looked "completely worn out—almost haggard, and seemed much depressed." In April, the Massachusetts businessman Stephen Minot Weld found him so thin and pale that many predicted Hamlin would be president soon, and John T. MacMahon of the 136th New York believed that when his time was up the chief executive would look ten years older than when he took office.[13] Though the general's friends said Lincoln had already improved, General Meade found that the president appeared careworn and exhausted, an opinion shared by the Vermont soldier Wilbur Fisk. In May, Jane Stuart Woolsey wrote to a friend in Europe that the president was older, grayer, and more harassed looking; but when Sidney George Fisher saw him in June in Philadelphia, he was much pleased by the executive's countenance, voice and manner. Finding that he was not awkward and uncouth as had been represented, the Philadelphian was impressed by the president's honest, intelligent, amiable countenance, calculated to inspire respect, confidence and regard.[14] Yet, considering the problems Lincoln was facing, his worn appearance was not surprising.

On April 13, General Burnside, in charge of the Department of Ohio, issued his Order No. 38, threatening all who defamed the government with arrest. When Vallandigham did so, he was incarcerated, tried and sentenced by a military commission to imprisonment for the duration of the war. This wartime severity became highly controversial and was not stilled when, on May 19, Lincoln banished the culprit to the Confederacy. While Republicans, eager to uphold the administration, thought the president's action a good idea, and felt that Vallandigham could not complain when sent where his affection lay, Democrats like Governor Horatio Seymour, equally anxious to damage it, considered the order an outrage and a violation of freedom of speech. Opposition newspapers condemned it, and in Albany, a protest meeting chaired by the railroad magnate and former mayor of the city, Erastus Corning, sent resolutions of remonstrance to the president, protests that were repeated elsewhere.[15]

When Lincoln replied on June 12, he rejected the remonstrance by relying on the need to suspend certain safeguards for personal liberty in cases of armed rebellion: "Must I shoot a simple soldier-boy who deserts while I must not touch a hair of a wily agitator who induces him to desert?" he wrote. The Washington *Daily Morning Chronicle* could not praise his document enough. "He has spoken at last," it wrote, "and with a plain and direct truth and sincerity that will go to all loyal hearts, and establish the fact that for a great principle no cause can ever be ultimately defeated, however it may be retarded or delayed." Others, both radical and moderate, called the answer "creditable to the President in every way," with *Harper's Weekly* labeling it a "very admirable reply" to the Democratic meeting. According to the *Independent,* it was "the most satisfactory state paper of the present administration." Unhappy though some were about the Vallandigham case, they nevertheless praised the letter's sincerity and purity of purpose, and welcomed the warm appreciation from all quarters for its admirable temper. Still other papers also praised it, and individuals were equally moved. Horace Maynard thought it annihilated Vallandigham;

John W. Forney considered it "the right word . . . spoken by the right man, at the right time, and William O. Stoddard called it "a grand document."[16]

In the meantime, the praise of the president and his actions continued. Benjamin B. French wrote that the more he saw of Lincoln, the more he was convinced of his superlative goodness, truth, kindness, and patriotism, and even his call for 100,000 more men did not meet with general criticism. An article in the *Daily Morning Chronicle* commented: "The wisdom of this measure will be apparent to every intelligent man, and the proclamation will demonstrate to the country that the Chief Magistrate and Commander-in-Chief is alive to every emergency. . . ."[17]

Democrats disagreed. "The great, autocratic '*I am*' of President Lincoln, in his recent letter to the Albany Committee, surpasses in impudence any document which has ever been submitted to the American people," commented the *New York Weekly News*. Like the *Brooklyn Eagle*, the paper also denied the comparison with Andrew Jackson asserted by Lincoln in the document, And the Columbus *Crisis* insisted that Lincoln and the King of Prussia used the same language in excuses for arbitrary arrests, a comparison likewise made by the *New-Yorker Staats-Zeitung*.[18]

At the same time, Burnside caused more trouble. When, at the beginning of June, he suspended the Chicago *Times*, Lincoln overruled him, an action that, as the *Chicago Tribune* pointed out, gave the lie to Copperhead papers. These papers, however, as exemplified by the New York *World*, merely stated that if the revocation stood by itself alone, it would be fine, but in connection with the Vallandigham case they only showed Lincoln's inconsistency.[19]

Although by late June 1863 Lincoln was subjected to much criticism—the *Chicago Tribune* was very unhappy about General Hooker's recall on June 27, and Alexander McClure thought people were "paralyzed for want of leadership"—these opinions soon changed, with Lincoln's appointment of the Pennsylvanian of George C. Meade to head the Army of the Potomac, the new commander's great victory at Gettysburg on July 1–3, and with Grant's capture of Vicksburg on July 4. "To the Administration at Washington, also, praise is due for the celerity and energy with which it has prepared for this ultimate defeat of Lee," commented the New York *Evening Post,* while others referred to "the grandeur of the President's position." Congratulations came from New York friends, who wrote, "You have the blessing of God. You will have the support of the people." The Maine Unitarian Societies adopted resolutions to be sent "to him who is at once Chief Magistrate of the Nation, and Father of the People, in token of our recognition of his Christian faithfulness to the cause of Human Right and Divine Justice. . . ." The Washington *Daily Morning Chronicle* wrote, "The Administration Vindicated," rhetorically asking, "Will not the impartial historians award due credit to our public servants who have been compelled to labor on in the midst of calumny and misrepresentation, and who now, when their plans and predictions are being realized in some of the most brilliant victories of our time, deserve the gratitude of their own countrymen and the admiration of the civilized world?"[20] From Vienna, the historian John Lothrop Motley, the American minister to Austria, not only sent his hearty congratulations, but added that never since Washington had any president taken office in such dark an hour and that the wise and good in every land had followed his steady march along the path of duty. When Lincoln issued a Thanksgiving Proclamation on July 15, it was called "one of the most beautiful compositions that ever emanate from the pen of one in authority," and characterized as "eloquent and beautiful."[21]

The Democrats however, refused to fall in line. "No Credit to the Administration," headlined the Chicago *Times,* maintaining that if Lincoln's policies had been carried out, Vicksburg would not have fallen. And they blamed him for the draft riots in New York that followed the victories.[22]

The riots, resulting in the lynching of blacks and attacks on Republicans, caused Governor Seymour to ask Lincoln to suspend the draft in New York. In a widely published letter, Lincoln refused, a decision that was extensively praised. His reply was labeled "kind, respectful, unruffled in temper, and as courteous as it is direct and manly in terms." The Springfield *Republican* believed that the president would be sustained in his decision; others referred to its "admirable tone," and the *Cincinnati Commercial* was also laudatory.[23]

Nor did the admiration for the president diminish. Benjamin Balch in Newburyport, Massachusetts, called him "our distinguished and beloved Chief Magistrate"; William Bebb at the Patent Office assured him that now that the war was waning, "we need you"; John Hay, his secretary and the later U. S. secretary of state, considering the problem of reconstruction, felt that "the old man is working with the strength of a giant and the purity of an angel to do this great work"; and Giuseppe Garibaldi sent him a message of admiration. "Heir of the thought of Christ and of Brown," he wrote, "you will pass down to posterity under the name of the Emancipator.[24]

Shortly afterward, on August 26, Lincoln wrote an answer to his old neighbor, James C. Conkling, who had invited him to attend a mass meeting of Union men in Springfield. Regretting his inability to leave Washington for so long a trip, Lincoln made clear his policies and his inflexible decision not to sign any compromise that did not restore the Union.[25]

This letter, too, met with widespread approval. "I delight in the President's plain letter to the plain people," the politically active merchant John Murray Forbes confessed to Charles Sumner. From Boston, the president heard that it was even better than expected; from Illinois he received "grateful thanks for it"; and Henry Wilson wrote, "May Almighty God bless you for your noble, patriotic, and Christian letter [which] will be on the lips and in the hearts of hundreds of thousands this day." The English visitor Henry Yates Thompson predicted that Lincoln would leave behind him a great reputation, and Charles Sumner thought he stated the case very well.[26] The *Chicago Tribune* identified it as "one of those remarkably clear and forcible documents that come only from Mr. Lincoln's pen." According to the New York *Commercial Advertiser,* the whole letter was breathing the spirit of the loftiest statesmanship and the most unselfish patriotism, and the Washington *Evening Star* thought it would meet with "the hearty approbation of all loyal and patriotic citizens everywhere." William O. Stoddard, stating that the people were rallying around the president and were ready to give him all the aid and support he might require, considered the letter worth as much as a victory. The *New York Times,* with a headline, "The Right Man in the Right Place," declared, "Abraham Lincoln is today the most popular man in the Republic," a characterization reprinted elsewhere. The nonagenarian Massachusetts politician and educator Josiah Quincy also expressed his gratitude for the "happy, conclusive, and effective letter." The Democrats' criticism was only to be expected.[27]

In the meantime, comparisons of Lincoln to Washington became more frequent. As early as March 21, 1862, the *New York Herald* had asserted that for the first time since the days of George Washington the administration of the national government had been lifted to Washington's platform of nationality. On February 2, 1863, John C. Hamilton wrote to the executive that there was "a remarkable analogy in the inner view of Washington's official civil career with that of President Lincoln"; John Lothrop Motley's letter of July 25, 1863 has already been mentioned. On September 14, 1863, General Peter Osterhaus supposedly told a Mississippi rebel near Vicksburg that all loved and venerated Washington, but that Lincoln was far superior and the greatest man the world had ever produced. Three days later, the Washington *Daily Morning Chronicle* found that "in general cast of mind and heart," Lincoln "probably more nearly resembles Washington than any of his predecessors." In Great Britain, the reformer Lord Brougham had allegedly remarked that the human fancy could not have created a combination of qualities more perfectly fitted for the scenes in which it was Washington's lot to bear a part, and the same consummate fitness for the times might be recognized in the man at the head of affairs of the United States in this second great crisis of its existence. The London *Star* observed that the Conkling letter was the manifesto of a truly great statesman, worthy of a Cromwell or a Washington. From Constantinople, Charles W. Goddard wrote that the Emancipation Proclamation would rank with George Washington's Farewell Address, and in its Thanksgiving Day illustration, *Harper's Weekly* showed Lincoln and Washington praying together. The comparison was to be made many times later on.[28]

Lincoln's popularity was so great that even when he issued a proclamation on September 15 suspending the writ of habeas corpus throughout the United States wherever necessary, the action, though widely criticized, was defended as "no doubt necessary." The Philadelphian Sidney George Fisher thought it had been wise to issue it in accordance with the act of Congress, and the *Brooklyn Daily Union*, commenting on the good faith of the president, added that he had decided to use his constitutional power to foil the efforts of sympathizers with treason at the North. "The necessity of the measure has long been apparent, and the proclamation comes none too soon," wrote the Springfield *Republican;* the *National Anti-Slavery Standard* extolled the suspension as "a powerful well directed blow at the rebellion. Other papers, as well as individuals, praised the "bold and wise" proclamation.[29]

Religious organizations also expressed their confidence in the chief executive. On September 15, the Universalists renewed their confidence in "our Chief Magistrate, whose honesty of purpose stand unimpaired" on the 24th, the Methodists, in their annual conference in Indiana expressed their appreciation in his humble and strong faith in an overruling providence and their sympathy with his measures and policy; and on October 3, the Baptists in Chenango—and some days later those in Wisconsin—followed suit, as did the United Brethren in Christ at their annual conference at Sandusky, Ohio on October 10, the Unitarians in Massachusetts on the 19th, and the New York State Baptist Missionary Convention on the 23rd—and all this in spite of the president's lack of membership in any church.[30]

On September 30, a radical delegation from Missouri asked the president to remove General John M. Schofield and to intervene in favor of the radicals in the state. Assuring the delegates that he considered them friends, he told them he preferred gradual to immediate emancipation and could not displace the general without cause. "The President never appeared to better advantage in the world," wrote his secretary John Hay, who had just spent two hours with him. "Though he knows how immense is the danger to himself from the unreasoning anger of that committee, he never cringed to them for an instant. He stood where he thought he was right and crushed them with his candid logic." The secretary also praised Lincoln's "superb" letter to Charles D. Drake, the leader of the delegation, with a more specific reply. The Washington *Daily Morning Chronicle* was certain that the country would endorse the judgment of the president; the New York *Spectator* found his reply "eminently proper"; the New York *Commercial Advertiser* commented that the president certainly had enough on his mind without being solicited to take up the burden of adjusting a political difficulty in Missouri; and the *Cincinnati Commercial* considered the letter "new evidence of his skill in dealing with the difficult questions presented by the times." The Democrats naturally approved of Lincoln's taking the side of the more conservative faction. Some radicals, however, expressed their disappointment.[31]

The praise of the president did not diminish. "It would be gratifying to the bottom of your heart, if you could hear and see the intense enthusiasm which greets every mention of your name at our public meetings," James M. Scovel informed him. J. Young Scammon in Chicago, most gratified to find how fast the people were learning to appreciate him, predicted, "You will be the next President of the United States to be freed and united under you." General Sickles thought Lincoln was justly sustained by the great mass of the nation, by the potential force of the press, and by the armies and fleets of the Union, and that it was no longer doubtful that history would assign him a conspicuous rank among the great rulers of the world. "Mr. Lincoln is consistent and persistent," the *Brooklyn Daily Union* wrote. "His main characteristic is a quiet, but stubborn pertinacity, which through every contingency, in the employment of every means, in all temptations, trials, and complications, holds steadily to one object. . . ." French Masons let him know that they felt he had shown himself by his moderation, prudence, and firmness worthy of the magistracy with which he had been entrusted. Even his call for 300,000 more troops met with approval, and General James C. Rice, maintaining that the soldiers would trust no one but Abraham Lincoln, predicted that, like Washington, he would ever live in the hearts of his countrymen.[32] The radical black leader Frederick Douglass concluded that the president would go down to posterity "as Abraham the Great, or Abraham the Wise, or Abraham the Eloquent," that he was all three, and that he would be remembered, if the country was saved, as Honest Abraham. In Pennsylvania, Josephine Forney Roedel, confessing that she had never seen or imagined such homage as the people bestowed upon Lincoln, was sure that the popular tide would increase so that he would surely be president for a second term.[33]

The 1863 elections, which ended favorably for the Republicans, were interpreted as indications that the people had supreme confidence in the government and that the masses approved of the administration's efforts to reestablish the national authority by force of arms. Indeed, Lincoln's name had helped greatly with the voters. Even Horatio Seymour, the Democratic governor of New York, admitted that he was not discouraged by the elections. "In the end the interests of the country may be advanced by giving to the Administration undisputed sway," he wrote to a supporter.[34]

On November 19, the president, whose writing and public speaking ability had often been questioned, delivered the famous Gettysburg Address at the dedication of the national cemetery to commemorate the battle. As is well known, Edward Everett, who delivered the principal speech at the event, wrote to Lincoln, "Permit me to also express my great admiration of the thoughts expressed by you, with such eloquent simplicity & appropriateness, at the consecration of the cemetery. I should be glad if I could flatter myself that I came as near to the central idea of the occasion, in two hours, as you did in two minutes." But he was not the only one to recognize the greatness of the address. Sidney George Fisher commented, "Mr. Seward made a good speech, Mr. Lincoln a very short one, but to the point and marked by his pithy sense, quaintness, and good feeling." James M. Scovel sent Lincoln a copy of an editorial in the Philadelphia *Evening Bulletin* concerning his "excellent speech at Gettysburg; Benjamin B. French spoke of the president's "brief, but most appropriate words, and David Wills of the Gettysburg Cemetery Commission, who had welcomed the visitor at the railroad station, asked for a copy of the manuscript.[35]

Many newspapers were enthusiastic. As the Springfield *Republican* put it, "Surprisingly fine as Mr. Everett's oration was in the Gettysburg consecration, the rhetorical honors [of] the occasion were won by Lincoln. His little speech is a perfect gem;

deep in feeling, compact in thought and expression, and tasteful and eloquent in every word and comma. Then it had the merit of unexpectedness in its verbal perfection and beauty."[35] The Washington *Daily Morning Chronicle* predicted that the address, though short, but glittering with gems evincing the speaker's gentleness and goodness of heart, would receive the attention and command the admiration of all the tens of thousands who would read it. The *Brooklyn Daily Union* referred to it as "a beautiful dedicatory address, and the *Chicago Tribune* called it "a gem." The *New York Spectator* correctly pointed out that "the real lesson of the occasion was briefly and pointedly expressed by the President, who, in ascribing all the glory and honor to the brave men living and dead who struggled in that bloody field, sought to draw fresh inspiration to duty and patriotism from their sacrifices and sufferings." *Harper's Weekly* found that "the few words of the President were from the heart to the heart. They cannot be read, even, without kindling emotion." The Democratic New York *World* was naturally critical, but reluctantly admitted that the speech was calculated to arouse deep feeling, while the equally Democratic Chicago *Times*, spoke of the "exceedingly bad taste" of the president's remarks. Even the always hostile London *Times* conceded that the address was in a somewhat different style from his former speeches. That Southerners disagreed was to be expected.[36]

After his return from Gettysburg, Lincoln came down with the varioloid, a mild form of smallpox. Rumors of his death frightened people. According to the *Brooklyn Daily Union*, men "almost refused to look at the contingency which would deprive the councils of the nation of that calm, wise judgment, that firm and deliberate will, that close sympathy with the people, that manly and enlightened sense of justice, and that unwearying assiduity which for nearly three years has guided and guarded them." Even the Democratic New York *World* expressed its unease as it was more afraid of Vice President Hamlin, whom it called an abolitionist, than of Lincoln.[37]

But he recovered quickly enough to deliver his important message and amnesty proclamation to Congress in December. These documents, too, met with favor, particularly the so-called Ten Percent Plan, an offer of amnesty and reconstruction to insurgents in seceding states provided 10 percent of the voters of 1860 were willing to pledge allegiance to the Constitution and acceptance of the Emancipation Proclamation. "The public mind, after due reflection . . . will accept it as another signal illustration of the practical wisdom of the President," wrote the *New York Times*. James A. Hamilton was so impressed with the two documents that he wrote to Lincoln, "The policy they indicate . . . do honor to your heart as well as to your head," and he predicted that his actions would immortalize him and establish his fame among "the greatest and best of this or any other country." Charles Sumner also spoke of the offer of amnesty and reconstruction with great satisfaction; the European author Count Agénor de Gasparin was much taken with Lincoln's excellent principles; Noah Brooks found the message "temperate, wise, statesmanlike, and broad in its treatment of the vexing questions of the time," and the Washington *Evening Star* was certain that every man's loyalty could be tested "by his adherence to or rejection of the common sense, practical and patriotic positions taken in the President's message." The Boston *Commonwealth* labeled the proclamation "one of the most memorable papers of this memorable era"; its fellow antislavery journal, the *National Anti-Slavery Standard,* delighted with Lincoln's refusal to retreat from the Emancipation Proclamation, referred to him as a "great magistrate, true to great interests committed to his charge," and the New York *Commercial Advertiser* expressed its admiration of the message and its accompaniment, which it called "wise and humane . . . an exemplification of the best qualities that compose the character of the President."

Other papers equally praised the message and the proclamation, and in England, the London *Spectator* praised the president's "impressive tone."[38]

Many radicals as well as their conservative opponents were pleased with it. As the *New York Herald* observed, "President Lincoln . . . has for some time been riding two political horses, and, with the skill of an old campaigner, he whips them—the radical horse 'a leetle ahead'—thus his message and his appended Proclamation of amnesty to the rebellion States." The radicals, Charles Sumner, Zachariah Chandler, Henry Wilson, George Boutwell, Owen Lovejoy, and Horace Greeley were delighted, as were the moderate Senator James Dixon of Connecticut, Maryland's Reverdy Johnson, and old Whigs like the later secretary of the navy Richard W. Thompson. As James Dixon, speaking for the moderates, wrote to Henry J. Raymond, the editor of the *New York Times,* "The President's Proclamation of amnesty cuts up by the roots Mr. Sumner's fatal heresy of State suicide. All who think as you and I do can cordially sustain it. If Mr. Sumner and his fellows can also do so, so much the better." Even in Kentucky, where Lincoln had been very unpopular in 1860, people liked the proclamation.[39]

A number of military men were most favorably affected by the documents. Wisconsin Captain Rufus R. Dawes wrote, "What a noble message from President Lincoln. I do not hesitate to say that I think him a great statesman, and what is better, an unselfish patriot. The high tone of this message, and the unflinching adherence to his great measure of Emancipation, must command the respect of the world. . . ." Jenkin Lloyd Jones from the same state called the document "true and honest, every word," and Major Thomas Wood Osborn not only liked the message but found it very timely.[40]

The Democrats, however, making the most of their opposition to emancipation, were outraged at Lincoln's demand that Southerners swear not only to support the Constitution but also to abide by the Emancipation Proclamation. The Columbus *Crisis* declared that the proclamation vindicated the paper's opposition to "Lincoln and the radical crazy advisers who hold him in their keeping," and that, if he succeeded in his plans, the Union was gone forever. The Albany *Atlas and Argus* thought it meant "simply the indefinite protraction of the war, the New York *World* called it absurd as a means to reconstruct the Union, and the *New-Yorker Staats-Zeitung* criticized the president's "hate-filled" conditions. As usual, the London *Times* was highly critical, while the *Moniteur* reported that opinions about the message were divided.[41]

While there was some doubt whether the Ten Percent Plan would work, the Washington *Daily Morning Chronicle* questioned why, if opponents doubted the plan, there were so many attacks on it. Nor, it continued two days later, was it a fraud as "our country never had a more upright and honest Administration than that which rules its destinies today and never did a purer man, not even the 'Father of his country' excepted, wield administrative or executive power." As the Iowa soldier Charles O. Musser wrote from Arkansas, the message and proclamation would be the means for redeeming the state from the hands of traitors, and the *Brooklyn Daily Union* called the establishment of a free state in Louisiana "the first fruits of the President's plan." Because 1864 was an election year, praise for the plan was soon combined with a call for Lincoln's renomination.[42]

5 Renomination and Reelection

According to Nathan I. Arnold's recollections, early in 1864 a newspaper editor asked Thaddeus Stevens to introduce him to some member of Congress friendly to Lincoln. Stevens took him to Arnold and said, "Here's a man who wants to find a Lincoln member of Congress. You are the only one I know." Even though Arnold disputed this assertion and responded that he knew many, the statement has been repeated through the years.[1] Yet it is far from the truth. Congressman after congressman defended Lincoln against attacks at the time, and the very fact that his renomination was correctly considered certain shows that he was very popular indeed, in and out of Congress.

In fact, predictions of Lincoln's nomination and election for a second term had been common for months. Reference has already been made to the endorsement of the Philadelphia Union League. On May 28, 1863, Noah Brooks wrote that no one was as likely to be nominated as Lincoln. "His honesty, faithfulness and patriotism are unquestioned," Brooks continued, "while his sagacity, ability and statesmanship has served to saved the country from ruin. . . . [W]e have been blessed by Providence in having such a man as Abraham Lincoln to hold in his hands greater powers than were ever before given to any President of the United States."[2] Considered the conservative candidate, he found favor for a renewed term with independent newspapers, seemed preferable to the radical Salmon P. Chase, a consistent rival, and was endorsed by religious organizations that hailed "with profound gratitude the reliance upon divine

providence so constantly exhibited in the official acts of our
most worthy President. . . ."[3]

By October, Elihu Washburne thought it was time to con-
sider the question of a second term, and the Republican victories in the 1863 fall elections in Ohio and Pennsylvania were
considered indications that both states were now declaring for
Lincoln in 1864. As one Michigan citizen wrote to her husband,
"You cannot think how we're rejoicing over the elections. A
death blow to copperheadism, surely, & those against the Gov
[ernment} & Union. . . . [We all trust that] Honest Old Abe will
be our next President . . ."[4]

The army was equally interested in Lincoln's renomination.
"It is the general opinion here that Lincoln will be reelected
President," James Horrocks of the 5th Battery, New Jersey Volunteers, informed his parents in England on November 11, 1863.
"Many of the papers express the same opinion." Thomas H.
Mann of the 18th Massachusetts also emphasized this trend.
"The army here are beginning to feel as tho' President Lincoln
would be elected by a vast majority for the next term and all I
have heard express their mind, asserting that he is the only one
they shall vote for." These opinions were bolstered by reports
that he was more clearheaded than most of his enemies were
willing to admit. As the radical *Independent* phrased it, "In time
of great peril Mr. Lincoln has shown himself to be superior to
his best generals, and simply because he has sound sense."[5]

The continuing demand for the president's renomination
furnished unmistakable proof of his popularity. W. P. Dole, the
superintendent of Indian affairs, heard from his correspondent
Uri Manly that the president had acted with great wisdom and
prudence and that there was no man living who had a deeper
hold on the hearts of loyal men than he. Lincoln himself was
told that he had touched the popular heart and secured his reelection beyond a peradventure should he desire it. On January
23, 1864, Horace Greeley heard that the president had already

been renominated by nine-tenths of the Republicans who did not aspire to be political leaders. Sigismund Kaufmann, a member of the 1860 New York electoral college that had voted for Lincoln, wrote to Washburne on December 12, 1863, "It is my firm opinion that we can find no better successor to 'honest Old Abe' than Abraham Lincoln. He ought to be the standard-bearer of all true and loyal men in 1864." According to the Lawrence *Kansas Tribune* during the same month, there was no better candidate for the presidency than Abraham Lincoln, and to bolster its prediction that Lincoln would be reelected in 1864, the Springfield *Republican* wrote, "Mr. Lincoln has proved himself a safe man, as well as honest, and his reputation for a sagacious and farsighted policy has grown continuously among the people."[6]

Thus, even before the campaign season of 1864 had begun, the president's popularity had assured him of widespread support for his renomination. His possible alternates, such as General Grant, Simon Cameron, and General Butler, could not really compete with him. Joseph Medill called the efforts for Grant and Chase "lost labor" since Old Abe had the "inside track," and Washburne was told that while Grant was great, it would be better to have the only good generals available on the battlefield and let Lincoln, who had really managed well, have the nomination. In January 1864, Schuyler Colfax stated that popular feeling seemed to be manifesting itself strongly in favor of the president's reelection. *Harper's Weekly*, speaking of the friends of the government, put it succinctly by stating, "[H]earty and unconditional as is their admiration for General Grant's military services, they have no less regard for the civil services of Mr. Lincoln. No man at this moment has so sure a hold of the national heart as the President."[7]

His supporters and other observers were full of praise for the executive. Effusive in its tribute and deprecating partisan wrangles, the Buffalo *Commercial Advertiser* stated, "The policy of Mr. Lincoln's administration has thus far been in this regard most salutary and wise. While, upon the one hand, he has ever been bold and unswerving in the straight line of his duty, having in view always the suppression of the rebellion and the vindication of the Federal integrity, he has, upon the other, strengthened his party by conciliating both wings of it. . . ."[8] The Washington *Daily Morning Chronicle,* in its endorsement, asserted, "The prevailing sentiment among the people is one of confidence in Abraham Lincoln and his Administration. No Chief Magistrate has been so severely tried, and yet no Chief Magistrate has administered our government with so much success and popularity. The American dwells with pride and satisfaction upon the Administrations of Washington and Jackson; and yet with all our veneration for these men . . . we can see in Abraham Lincoln the qualities that will make his name as dear. . . ." The Virginia Unionist John Minor Botts, though opposed to the Emancipation and Amnesty proclamations, nevertheless stated, "I think that Mr. Lincoln is by nature a vigorous, strong-minded and conscientious man; honest in his purposes, indefatigable in what he considers to be the duties of his office. In natural endowments I doubt if he is not quite equal, if not superior to any of those by whom he is surrounded."[9]

Endorsements for the renomination, which included unstinted praise, followed. In its endorsement of the president, the Kansas State Union Meeting at Topeka resolved "that to Abraham Lincoln more than to any other man, we owe our cheering prospects." The New Hampshire Union State Convention likewise resolved, in its call for renomination: "That Abraham Lincoln, by the exercise during the dangerous crisis in the nation's history of unequalled sagacity and statesmanship, of a moderation and prudence which experience has shown to be the highest wisdom, by his spotless integrity of personal character, above reproach and above suspicion, and by his slowly formed yet

unaltered determination that the triumph of the Constitution
and the Union over Secession and treason shall be the final triumph of liberty throughout the nation, has received and meri-
ted the abiding confidence of the people to an extent never
awarded to any other public man since Washington. . . ."[10]
Other state conventions followed suit, and the Union League of
Philadelphia's 24th Ward concluded, "The approaching down-
fall of the rebellion and the restoration of the Union demand in
our ruler the practical experience, the sagacity, the honesty of
purpose, and the single-heartedness which so pre-eminently
distinguish our present President. The exigencies of the time
require him, and the country cannot allow him to retire into
private life at the very crisis when his familiarity with all the
details of the situation renders his services more essential than
ever." The Camden Council of the Union League and its Trenton counterpart passed similar resolutions.[11]

Even some radicals, usually critical of the administration yet
eager for a Republican victory, favored Lincoln's renomination.
The ever dissatisfied Count Gurowski bemoaned this fact, which
was emphasized by Garrison's speech at the annual meeting of
the Massachusetts Anti-Slavery Society on January 28, 1864,
when he said:

There was a time when I had little confidence in Abraham
Lincoln, and very little respect for him. . . . But the time came
at last, when the President, unless he was determined to be
willfully and wickedly blind, was compelled to see that slavery
and the rebellion were indissolubly bound up together. . . .
Since that event (the issue of the Emancipation Proclamation), and in view of what has followed in the enrollment of
tens of thousands of colored soldiers, I have changed my
opinion of Abraham Lincoln. . . . Taking all these things into
consideration, especially in view of the fact that he has not
only decreed the liberation of every slave in Rebeldom for-

ever, but stands repeatedly committed, as no other man does, before heaven and earth, to maintain it as long as he is in office—in my judgment the re-election of Abraham Lincoln to the Presidency of the United States would be the safest, wisest course, in the present course of our national affairs. . . .[12]

Republican congressmen were never at a loss for words in their defense of their leader. In the House, the ever-faithful Nathan Arnold, in a long speech reviewing Lincoln's career, pointed out, "The masses of the people everywhere trust and love him. They know his hands are clean and his breast is pure. The people know that the devil has no bribe big enough, no temptation of gold or place, or power, which can seduce the honest heart of Abraham Lincoln." The Pennsylvanian Amos Myers asserted, "Politicians may think say and do as they please, but God and the people are for Abraham Lincoln." Iowa's Josiah B. Grinnell easily refuted Vorhees's charges that Lincoln was a usurper. The accusation was nonsense, he said; the president took his oath to the Constitution and all his acts had been in keeping with this oath. Pennsylvania's James K. Moorhead, stressing Lincoln's similarity to Jackson, declared, "They who denounce him as an usurper know little of his high conscientiousness, and regard but little that public interest which is, with him the pole star of duty;" Iowa's Sempronius H. Boyd defended him against accusations concerning a deal made with four Missouri congressmen to the detriment of General John M. Schofield, and Asabel W. Hubbard of Iowa angrily rejected accusations that the administration was responsible for sacrificed lives, when obviously the authors of the rebellion were responsible. In the Senate, Morton S. Wilkinson of Minnesota defended the President against Ben Wade's assertions that the executive had no right to issue an amnesty by emphasizing his powers as commander in chief of the armed forces; Wisconsin's

Oliver O. Howe pointed out that the president, faced with a revolt, nevertheless employed language less stringent than Jackson's, while Senator Jacob M. Howard of Michigan answered attacks by Kentucky's Lazarus W. Powell by pointing out that the state had refused to respond to the first call of a "patriotic President."[13]

By the end of February, the *New York Times* found that "The universality of popular sentiment, in favor of Mr. Lincoln's reelection, is one of the most remarkable developments of the time." That this statement was close to the truth was illustrated by the criticism of the Pomeroy Circular, a call for the nomination of Secretary Chase, signed by Kansas Senator Samuel Pomeroy and distributed among Republican congressmen. As David E. Long has pointed out, the circular effectively destroyed Chase's candidacy, one state organization after another endorsing the president. Ohio itself—Chase's home state—did the same, and Chase repudiated any connection with the document. Senator Wilkinson, showing that Lincoln had never taken one step backward since his inauguration, castigated it severely. The Washington *Daily Morning Chronicle* ridiculed its emphasis on the one-term principle; while Garrison's *Liberator,* acknowledging that Lincoln was open to criticism, criticized the memorandum on the grounds that it was necessary to have but one candidate, and as the Copperheads and the South desired a change, it asked, "Is it wise to gratify either of these parties?"[14] Chase himself heard from Richard C. Parsons that the effect of the circular in the Ohio legislature was to array men against each other, but that, in the end, party unity was necessary, and some Chase men had stayed in the caucus that voted to endorse the president. "I have seen the Lincoln movement growing & spreading of late," Parsons wrote, adding that Lincoln had "a vast personal popularity with the people." The president himself was told that the document would be rejected by a country "which sees the administration exposing corruption, extravagance, and rascality wherever found and pushing a victorious war all over the rebellious territory," and that the Emancipation Proclamation was an act that posterity would recognize as the "most imperishable monument of liberty and justice in the annals of time." As the *Chicago Tribune* wrote, "The people from Maine to Oregon are with Abraham Lincoln. They believe that he is their man to finish up this rebellion and lead the country to lasting peace."[15]

Early in March, Chase, embarrassed by his position as a member of the cabinet and challenger of his chief, withdrew as a candidate, an action widely hailed despite some doubts about its finality. "Senator Chase's withdrawal of this name from the list of aspirants for the Presidential nomination is hailed almost universally by the loyal press with great satisfaction," was the opinion of the *Brooklyn Daily Union*. The *Cincinnati Gazette* attributed the secretary's action to his desire for party harmony. And although the *Cincinnati Commercial* at first thought that the withdrawal did not make Lincoln's nomination certain, by March 14, it had changed its mind. "The people are clamorous for the re-election of the present incumbent of the Executive Chair," it wrote.[16]

Evidence of Lincoln's popularity multiplied. "The feeling for Lincoln is very strong here—His renomination seems now to be a foregone conclusion," the Maine Republican leader James G. Blaine informed Vice President Hamlin. "Never, before, in the history of the country, since Jackson elicited the homage and the confidence of the American People, did popular favor run higher and stronger for any man than it now does for Abraham Lincoln," commented the Harrisburg *Evening Telegraph* on March 4. As Nathan Arnold pointed out in Congress, among the reasons why the president should continue to enjoy the trust that had enabled him to accomplish so much was that he was "the most American of Americans." And an admirer in Albany, New York, wrote him, "Sir, I have ever been led to believe that you have been raised, as it were, by God to save this unhappy Nation from the jaws of treason. I firmly believe that it is by a Divine Providence, that through you and your noble honest purposes and your undoubted patriotism, that this nation has been saved." A Haverhill, New Hampshire, correspondent agreed, stating, "I believe you were just as much raised up by God for this crisis in our country's history as was Moses for his or Washington for his."[17]

As the time for the convention neared, these encomiums not only continued, but multiplied. From Tarrytown, New York, Lincoln heard that the Emancipation Proclamation had been translated in a Persian paper for Nestorians, so that even in distant Persia thousands were learning to revere his name. From Greenville, Illinois he learned from the writer William S. Waite that as he had done well, he had won the confidence of many who strongly opposed him in 1860. In an article for the St. Louis *Missouri Republican,* Waite had stated, "That Mr. Lincoln is a man of more than ordinary talents may be safely inferred. . . . He is universally esteemed as honest, no less than capable; amiable in deportment, kind hearted, harboring no malice against any man, but ever inclined to the god-like virtues of benevolence, forgiveness, and universal charity."[18] And George William Curtis wrote to John Murray Forbes on May 8, "In no conspicuous man do I see such a union of admirable qualities for the work at hand, as in Mr. Lincoln. He has a providential temperament for this emergency. Honesty, fidelity, sagacity, conviction, and an infinite patience. The last you will call weakness, reluctance, and all kinds of bad names. But it is his patience that makes him here and now, a truest kind of leader, and it will at last save us."[19]

Even in the border states, Lincoln's popularity tended to grow. As the Washington *Evening Star* pointed out, "The heartiness with which he was welcomed [at the Baltimore Fair], and the unbounded applause with which was greeted contrasted so broadly with the antagonism which he avoided on encountering on his first passage through the city after his election, that he must have been . . . keenly impressed by the change." According to the Unionist John A. Creswell's correspondents, the masses in Maryland were pro-Lincoln. In Kentucky, the editor Albert G. Hodges, to whom he had sent a letter explaining his stand on slavery, wrote to him, "It is with feelings of profound satisfaction I inform you, that every day since my arrival at home, I have been receiving information of your steady gain upon the gratitude and confidence of the people of Kentucky." Missouri, however, remained divided between radicals, generally hostile, and conservatives.[20]

The letter to Hodges on April 4, containing his statement, "If slavery is not wrong, nothing is wrong," received general approbation. The Springfield *Republican* called it "eminently characteristic, frank, direct and consistent with the frequently declared policy of the president on the subject to slavery, and the reasons for it," and praised its "honesty and straightforward logic." The *Philadelphia Inquirer,* considering it "admirable" labeled it "a manly, straightforward and ingenuous statement of the responsibilities which surrounded him in the discharge of his duties of this high office." And the *Brooklyn Daily Union* found it a most refreshing contrast to the circumlocutions of other politicians. In the army, Captain John M. MacKenzie was so delighted with it that he saw fit to congratulate the president. Even the cantankerous Count Gurowski, upon reading the Hodges letter, wrote, "Thank you! O, thank you! O, Mr. Lincoln!"[21]

A clear sign of Lincoln's undoubted popularity was the failure of the radical movement to substitute General Frémont as the presidential candidate. None of the prominent radicals, often critical of the executive, but eager to defeat the opposition, endorsed the general. The Cincinnati *Daily Commercial* called the Cleveland convention that nominated Frémont a "Body of impracticables," from whom the administration might well be parted, while the Washington *Daily Morning Chronicle,* remarking that the Copperheads had become enamored of Frémont, stated, "The most encouraging aspect of the present period, after the steady progress of our arms, is the confidence of the great body of the loyal people in Mr. Lincoln." Other papers had long before warned against a separate candidacy for Frémont, insisting that his program was not very different from that of the president.[22]

The military, too, tended to favor the president's renomination. On March 4, Orderly Sergeant John F. L Hartwell, then at Brandy Station, wrote to his wife and boy, "the soldiers almost <u>all</u> are in favor (as myself) of Lincoln's re-election as it will dash the last hope of the rebels to the earth unless they can get some nation at war with us & they become Allies." Major James A. Connolly, of the Army of the Cumberland, informed his wife that if he were where he could vote in the fall, he would vote for Lincoln, "if he is the candidate, which he ought to be." Henry R. Gardner, stationed in Louisiana, wanted "Lincoln for President and Grant for Commander in Chief." From a camp Near Culpepper, Secretary of the Interior John P. Usher heard from Clay Rice that four-fifths of the army desired the president's renomination. And on May 24, Lincoln received a letter from a soldier in Morganza, Louisiana, who assured him that the sentiment of the army was all right except for some officers whose whole business seemed to be to prepare the soldiers to vote against the president, but that they were few and of little account. Of course, there were a number of others who also did not share the sentiments of the majority.[23]

In Great Britain, even the hostile London *Times* admitted that a renomination of the president was probable. But it thought that he was too skillful a politician to trust too much to his personal popularity and that he had issued the Amnesty Proclamation to gain votes, while the *Edinburgh Mercury* commented, "What a ruggedly honest and sternly uncompromising soul is that which directs and governs the President of the great American Republic." The London *Spectator* praised the letter to Hodges, and in Paris, the *Moniteur* dwelled on the rivalry between the president and the secretary of the treasury and characterized the Red River campaign as a reelection device. The West Indies, too, took an interest in the campaign. An admirer from Barbados wrote, "Your public career has been hitherto marked by such characteristics as I deem worthy of entitling your name to a niche in the Temple of Fame."[24]

That the Democrats continued their attacks was natural. Charging the administration with issuing the "diabolical" Amnesty Proclamation in order to secure reelection, they maintained that the executive had broken every one of his promises. "If Mr. Lincoln's military sagacity were equal to his political cunning, we should have had peace long ago," commented the New York *World,* charging that he would control the convention and renominate and reelect himself with rotten boroughs of his own creation. The *New York Leader* labeled him "a coarse joker, whose wit has cost the country dear," and the Columbus *Crisis,* which claimed that he prostituted Yankee women by sending them to teach Negroes in Port Royal, where they became prostitutes, called his renomination ridiculous since he could not win. "The cant about 'Honest Old Abe' was at first amusing, it then became ridiculous, but now it is absolutely criminal," it added.[25] Lazarus Powell of Kentucky arraigned him for interfering in elections; Delaware's Willard Saulsbury attacked him for allegedly following in the footsteps of Caesar and predicted that if he were reelected, he would became a dictator, while Democratic papers chided him for the antislavery sentiments of the Hodges letter. And John Law of Indiana charged that "Faction, favoritism, folly seemed to have ruled the Administration. . . ." The Albany *Atlas and Argus* argued that Lincoln did not deserve a second term because he had been so weak and vacillating that the army had not succeeded in ending the rebellion, and when he was renominated, the paper called the convention fraudulent because Southern delegates were present.[26]

The South echoed these charges. As the fire-eater and Virginia agriculture expert Edmund Ruffin put it, "There is every indication that Lincoln (because of his iniquities) will be the favorite candidate of the all-powerful abolition party," while General Josiah Gorgas believed that the North was attempting to attain possession of state capitals so that it could institute state governments to influence the next election in favor of the president. The Richmond *Daily Dispatch* characterized his "confiscation program" as a slight modification of a highwayman's demands—your money *and* your life—and Confederate Senator Benjamin Hill wrote to Alexander H. Stephens that Lincoln's defeat would crush abolitionism so that peace would follow. As Hill phrased it, "His accession to power was the declaration of war. His continuance in power has been the continuance of war." The *Richmond Examiner,* with the headline "REX," referred to him as "the first Prince President, or *Stadtholder,* or Emperor of the United States," and echoed charges that he would not scruple to use any device, invent any falsehood, and shed any quantity of blood to perpetuate his power.[27]

On June 7, at the Baltimore convention of the Union party—as the Republicans now called themselves—Lincoln was unanimously renominated, with Andrew Johnson as his running mate. This success was an obvious proof of his popularity. "From near and far the people watch and wait, ready to accept, with a cheer that shall ring throughout the land, the name that stands at the portals of millions of loyal lips—Abraham Lincoln," wrote the *Chicago Tribune* on the day of the nomination. Two days later, the paper proudly averred, "The nomination of Mr. Lincoln . . . is the expression of the substantially unanimous voice of the entire people of the United States, so far as they favor the preservation of the Union and the suppression of the rebellion." The Washington *Daily Morning* Chronicle, echoing this sentiment, called the nomination the work of the people, in whose confidence and kindly regard, it explained, he had been steadily growing.[28] The *Cincinnati Commercial* used the same characterization, explaining, "There is no disputing the fact that the plain people has confidence in the President. He is the manner of man they understand. They know he means well for the whole country and give him credit for good sense as well as good intentions." Other papers commented that the Baltimore convention was the first to be "firmly and imperatively instructed by *the people*," that nomination was "a high compliment to Mr. Lincoln and a mark of just confidence in him and approval of his administration," and that that "Since the days of Washington no such spontaneous testimony has been given to the integrity, honesty, and ability of a Chief Magistrate as this enthusiastic endorsement of Abraham Lincoln by the people of the United States." The *Philadelphia Inquirer*, considering the nomination "a direct and unmistakable concession to the popular voice of the Union party . . . ," declared, "Whatever may be the differences of opinion as to his policy or his administrative ability, it is clear that for some paramount reason he has a powerful hold on the popular heart; and that reason is the firm belief in his integrity and patriotism, and the absolute singleness of his purpose with which has striven for three long years to restore the Union."[29] *Harper's Weekly*, continuing its support and again publishing a full-page sketch of the president and his secretaries, reminded its readers of its past favorable views and stated, "That he united perfect patriotism and great sagacity to profound conviction and patient tenacity, and this his conduct of our affairs has been, upon the whole, most admirable, and wise, we are more than ever convinced; and that no public man in our history since Washington has inspired a deeper popular confidence we have no doubt whatever that the result of the election will establish." The New York *Evening Post*, often a radical critic, also conformed. "Whatever may be said about his character," it opined, "or of his of administration of the government, it is not to be denied that he enjoys the favor and confidence of the people"; and according to its editor, William Cullen Bryant, the nomination took place, "in obedience to the public voice . . . pushed on the politicians whether willing or unwilling."[30]

Privately, many individuals likewise expressed their satisfaction with the nomination. Noah Brooks considered Lincoln's renomination "a foregone conclusion, a great majority of the delegates having been instructed beforehand in his favor, and the popular feeling was so evidently for him that the few chagrined and disappointed politicians hereabouts who were disposed to oppose him were quite swallowed up in the great wave of popular will." Congratulating Lincoln on his renomination, J. Russell Johnson of Carbondale, Illinois, sent him a letter on June 20, praising "the expression of the nation's heart laboring to give utterance of its confidence and appreciation of your great and noble services, and with a unanimity unprecedented in the history of this nation since the days of Washington." Even the secretary of the treasury, disappointed as he was, thought that the renomination of his rival "was required by the general sentiment of the Union men."[31]

Although the radicals were not enthusiastic about the result of the Baltimore convention, they recognized its inevitability in view of the president's popularity. In a report predating the nomination by a day, the *Independent* admitted, "Two-thirds of the members of Congress are 'radicals,' yet Mr. Lincoln would doubtless be nominated in a congressional caucus today, if it had the power to put up a candidate for the Republicans of the country. The reason is obvious: they know that he is popular, and believe that they can trust him. . . ." While believing it unmerited, the *National Anti-Slavery* Standard nevertheless conceded, "As long as the case stands as it now stands . . . we shall make straight paths for our President and follow with heart and soul after the banner of Abraham Lincoln!" Garrison went further when he declared, "Again I say that in regard to all his prominent military appointments, the President has acted up to all that loyalty and that abolitionism asked at his hands. . . . I hesitate not to declare that on the whole, politically speaking, the people cannot do better in my judgment, than to elect him for four years longer."[32] The *Commonwealth* was unhappy with the substitution of Andrew Johnson for Hannibal Hamlin, the former vice president, but it praised the emancipation platform endorsed by Lincoln. The *New York Tribune,* long opposed to a second term, in refuting the vilifications of the Democratic and Confederate press, which called Lincoln an ape, a hyena, or a jackass, now asked, "If that is a true characterization of one who has withstood such tests, overcome such impediments, and achieved such successes as Abraham Lincoln, then a democracy based on popular suffrage is an impudent fraud. . . ." By June 30, it reminded its readers that for many years the Whigs of Illinois had regarded him their strongest and ablest man. Ben Wade thought it would not be necessary to campaign much for the candidate. "The people have elected him already," he said, "and saved us a great deal of trouble."[33]

During the following election campaign, it was natural that the candidate should receive the encomiums of his supporters. Formerly unwilling backers like Horace Greeley's *New York Tribune* fell into line, and congressmen extolled his virtues. Orlando Kellogg of New York said, "While our armies are fighting our battles the people have nominated our worthy President for another term, and intend to elect him by an overwhelming majority. They have confidence in his patriotism and ability, and laugh at the silly charges of our enemies that he will rob them of their liberties and despoil them of their rights. They will sustain him in whatever he may do at this time for the salvation of the Union." Senator Thomas H. Hicks of Maryland, who had long been opposed to the president, proudly stated that he would vote for him now and that it was a godsend that he was elected to the presidency. Nathan Arnold defended him as usual; Henry Wilson pointed out that Democratic speeches would strengthen Lincoln more than any speeches on the Republican side of the chamber. Senator Wilkinson faulted the Democrats for comparing Lincoln to George III, as did the rebel Judah P. Benjamin, and Iowa's James Harlan defended him against attacks by Senator Garrett Davis.[34]

At the end of June, Lincoln finally accepted the resignation of Secretary Chase, who had frequently tried to withdraw. There was some criticism, but the *New York Herald* commented that the president should have let him go long before. The Springfield *Republican* thought "The pluck of the President . . . was admirable in the affair," and it praised the appointment of Senator William Pitt Fessenden of Maine in Chase's place, as did many others, the *Boston Journal* expressing its satisfaction that the president had the wisdom of discarding geographical prejudices by appointing two members from New England.[35]

Lincoln's call in July for 500,000 additional troops was, as usual, well received. The *Cincinnati Commercial,* noting that he was following the law, believed that speedy and effective reinforcement of the armies would result. Noah Brooks was moved by the fact that he was issuing the summons in the face of a general election. "He is determined to do his duty, let personal and political consequences be what they may," he mused. According to the Washington *Daily Morning Chronicle,* which thought that a few hundred thousand men would be worth ten times that many within three months, the levy was the very thing needed to inspire the confidence of the world in the ability of the American government and people to maintain the Union. The *Boston Morning Journal* believed the recruitment to be effective, and the *Brooklyn Daily Union* commented, "The President, seeing his duty clear, promptly and fearlessly performed it in issuing this call."[36]

The same paper also welcomed the widely criticized letter, "To Whom it may concern," in which Lincoln answered peace moves begun by Horace Greeley by stating he was willing to end the war on condition that the Union be restored and slavery ended. Pointing out that the letter showed that its estimate of the president's firmness and good sense was not an extravagant one, and that the peace plot was a Confederate effort to defeat his re-election, the paper said, "President Lincoln met this nice little plan with the direct good sense and firm principle that has so often baffled the trickery of his enemies." The Washington *Daily Morning Chronicle* also thought the whole movement was a scheme to entrap the administration into a false position before the country and the world for the benefit of the Democrats, and that the president had made his position clear by his consistency.[37] Attorney General Edward Bates, though surprised that the president allowed himself to be entrapped in the scheme, nevertheless found his letters "prudent." *Frank Leslie's Illustrated Newspaper* expressed its satisfaction that Lincoln saw through the game and effectively blocked it, while the *Boston Journal* also pointed out that the whole peace process was a Southern plot seeking long negotiations in Washington to weaken the Union army's resolve. "All this Mr. Lincoln has wisely and skillfully saved us from, by his timely little dispatch, 'To all (sic) whom it may concern,'" it wrote. The *Brooklyn Daily Union* was greatly taken with the firmness and good sense with which the president met the Southern scheme to defeat his reelection. William Lloyd Garrison, naturally impressed with the letter to Greeley, believed it contained truths every president would have asserted, and commented, "It is my firm conviction that no man has occupied the chair of the Chief Magistracy in America, who has more assiduously or more honestly endeavored to discharge all its duties with a single eye to the welfare of the country, than Mr. Lincoln."[38]

When Congress adjourned on July 4, Lincoln refused to sign the Wade-Davis Bill outlining a reconstruction plan more stringent than the president's, thus pocket vetoing it. A few days later, he issued a proclamation explaining his course. This action, though criticized by the radicals, seemed justified to many others. "It is sound and sensible and adds another to the many evidences of practical statesmanship exhibited by the President, which the people comprehend and appreciate," commented the friendly Springfield *Republican.* The paper also pointed out that the pocket veto was warranted on the grounds that it showed Lincoln's unwillingness to abide by only a single method of reconstruction. The *New York Times* mistakenly thought it indicated that there was no rift between Congress and the president and, though the bill's method of reconstruction seemed excellent, there might be circumstances that would justify a deviation from it, so that it was fortunate that the president did not sign it.[39] Andrew Johnson was delighted with the veto, but the radicals angrily expressed their disappointment. "What an infamous proclamation," Thaddeus Stevens wrote to Edward McPherson:

> The Pres. is determined to have the electoral votes of the seceded States at least of Tenn. Ark. La. Flor. Perhaps also of S. Car. The idea of pocketing a bill and then issuing a proclamation as to how far he will conform to it, is matched only by signing a bill and then sending in a veto. How little of the rights of war and the law nations our Pres. knows! But what are we to do? Condemn privately and applaud publicly!

Senator Wade and Maryland Representative Henry Winter Davis went so far as to issue a manifesto accusing the president of holding the electoral votes of the rebel states at the dictation of his personal ambition and reminding him that their support was of a cause and not of a man.[40]

In view of Lincoln's popularity, and the necessity of supporting a Republican candidate, the manifesto was widely criticized. The *New York Times* accused its authors of wanting a Democratic victory; the *Tribune,* in whose pages it was published, refused to support it, and even the *National Anti-Slavery Standard* deplored it, as did Garret Smith. Ben Wade's hometown paper, the Ashtabula *Sentinel,* called it "ill-tempered and improper," and Henry Stanbery, later attorney general of the United States, in a letter to Charles Sumner condemned it for only benefiting the Democrats, while Justice Noah Swayne, whom Lincoln had appointed to the Supreme Court, thought it would hurt no one but the authors themselves. It did, however, coincide with a low point in Lincoln's campaign.[41]

When in August several radicals, thinking they could finally dispense with the executive they had long distrusted, sought to substitute another candidate for the president, their efforts proved to be unpopular. Avowing that abandonment of Mr. Lincoln would mean the abandonment of all its principles, the Washington *Daily Morning Chronicle* argued:

> He stands as the central figure in the greatest war, of, per-haps, any age, and is the type of the most striking traits of a remarkable people. His simplicity, frankness, and careless-ness of conventional manners, accompanied by a sincere ob-servance of the essentials of good breeding, in his intuitive knowledge of men, his keen sense of the humorous, his clear perception of the common sense relation of things, he is one of the finest specimen of Western man."

The *Chicago Tribune,* conceding that not everything the president had done was correct, pointed out that never had anyone been forced to deal with such problems. "But never were the people of a great nation more unanimous in favor of sustaining any public officer than are the Union masses of the North in favor of Mr. Lincoln," it wrote.[42] Even those who would have preferred another candidate expressed their willingness to vote for the president, whose popularity had gone up and down more than once before, because of the Republicans' commitment to a restoration of the Union. Although it was said that Lincoln was becoming almost daily more unpopular, he was told that the people were becoming ever more attached to him, and if the politicians could be held at bay three weeks longer, everything would be all right. "The great heart of the nation is with you & if you will follow your own honest impulses it will triumphantly sustain you," he heard from Boston. A Philadelphian assured him that he could never be deprived of the good opinion of patriotic men; the radical Ohio Congressman Rufus P. Spalding let him know that he was resolved to sustain him; and a Massachusetts citizen wrote him that, as victory could be achieved with him but not with any other, the country looked to him as its savior in the terrible trouble and that by and by his name would stand side by side "with that of our own beloved Washington." A Cincinnati correspondent warned him not to withdraw as it would ruin the party, and the Bloomington, Illinois Republican Kitt Fell, assuring the president that no considerable portion of the American public was dissatisfied, asserted, "You are emphatically the people's candidate."[43]

The radicals' schemes came to nothing when the Democrats nominated General McClellan on a peace platform, and Sherman took Atlanta. Observing that a tremendous change had occurred since the nomination of McClellan and the victory at Atlanta, Theodore Tilton, the editor of the *Independent*, believed that it had created unanimity, and he too was for Lincoln, whom he had not previously supported. Concerning the proposed substitution of candidates, the Springfield *Republican* commented, "It is too late for such a change, if it were desirable;

and no man is mentioned, or can be, who will as fully unite the Union forces as Mr. Lincoln." Five days later, it made it clear that the capture of Atlanta, Farragut's victory at Mobile Bay, and the "disgusting" Democratic platform had revolutionized the political situation within one week, so that McClellan, who might have been elected ten days earlier, was now facing a majority for the president.[44] On September 7, Governor James T. Lewis of Wisconsin likewise wrote to Greeley and others that Lincoln would certainly be reelected, and for the honor of the nation, the interest of the party, and the good of humankind, he should remain the candidate. The *New York Times* also informed its readers that the outlook had changed after the recent victories; that it was now Lincoln or McClellan, and no one could undo the action of the Baltimore convention. The *Brooklyn Daily Union* was more specific. "The nomination of Mr. Lincoln went straight to the popular ear, and found firm lodgment there . . . ," it wrote. "The qualities which won for our noble President his abiding place in their confidence are not such as fade or fail. His calm deliberateness of judgment, his firmness in conclusions reached, his unimpeachable personal honesty, his unswerving fidelity to duty, and above all, that simple and earnest love of our popular institutions which always controls him, continue still to win and hold the respect of the people." The Illinois Union League passed a resolution against any change, stating "That our confidence in the integrity, patriotism and ability of our honored President is undiminished, and that we are utterly opposed to any efforts . . . to induce him to withdraw . . . being convinced that such a course will be attended with nothing but disaster and defeat, and as a consequence the destruction of the Union." And the *New York Tribune,* conceding that it had been opposed to an early convention, now fully endorsed Lincoln's reelection.[45]

Individuals again wrote Lincoln of their appreciation. From Cincinnati, D. H. Mears, believing that he of all men should be elected to finish the great work which he had been called in the Providence of God, that of serving the country, and freeing the slaves, advised him to unite with the Frémont electors. From Maryland, the German Lutheran minister G. Henry Vosseler wrote him that he was the only man "by the Lord's will to become our chief magistrate." The poet Laura Redden, thanking him for endorsing her poems, in a personal letter assured him, "The sympathies of the hearts of the people are with you to a great extent. I think that they appreciate the purity and sincerity of your motives in accepting your renomination. They understand that it is to carry out what you have begun and not for party and private purposes." From Indiana, F.W. Delang wrote, "Your victory over your competitor is an absolute necessity, the sinew of life for the United States. Any other man could tear down what you succeeded by wisdom and experience to build up during three hard years. None but you can overcome the storm and you are the only pilot to lead the ship into the harbor." And Mrs. A. E. Gridley of Hillsdale, Michigan confessed, "I shall never forget you as long as I live, and I will tell you that Washington, Jackson, Lincoln are all of our Fathers that I particularly admire."[46]

Correspondents did not address only the president himself. Lincoln's secretary, John G. Nicolay, heard from John M. Butler in Philadelphia, "We all feel the importance of the reelection of our worthy President"; a Cincinnati correspondent wrote to Horace Greeley, "If war is to continue, I want Mr. Lincoln to continue it. If peace is be secured, I want Mr. Lincoln to achieve it." And in Washington, John De Vries, in a letter to John Covode expressed the opinion that Lincoln's defeat would spell the end of the Union. By September, it was generally conceded that the president's reelection was no longer doubtful.[47]

Like John De Vries, most Republicans were certain that Lincoln's defeat would result in national ruin and that his reelection was essential for the defeat of the insurgents. Edward

Everett thought a change in administration would paralyze the military apparatus; consequently, though friendly with McClellan, he would vote for Lincoln. Henry Stanbery had not voted for Lincoln in 1860; but, as he wrote from Newport, Kentucky, "all my wishes, all my hopes are centered in one thing, and that is the crushing out of this rebellion by force of arms. . . . Whatever else may be said of Mr. Lincoln, no one can doubt that he has the same purpose, and that from the first to last he has never faltered in the great work." Thus, he did not wish to change executives. John Sherman likewise informed his brother, the general, that he believed Lincoln's election necessary to prevent disunion, so that he fully supported him.[48]

In September, John C. Frémont withdrew, and Postmaster General Montgomery Blair, under attack by the radicals, resigned from the cabinet. His brother, the general, wrote to their father, "I believe that a failure to re-elect Mr. Lincoln would be the greatest disaster that could befall the country and the sacrifice made by the judge (Montgomery) to avert this is so incomparably small that I felt it would not cost him a penny to make." The changes were welcomed, and Lincoln received grateful communications. "Thanks, many thanks for the cheering hope given by the removal of the P. M. General," he heard from Albany, New York. A telegram from H. W. Mitchell in Indianapolis informed him that "Our friends are entirely satisfied with your actions," while the *Boston Journal* regretted that Frémont did not manifest a higher opinion of the president in his letter of withdrawal.[49]

These encomiums increased as election time drew nearer. In an article, "Why the People Want Mr. Lincoln," the *Chicago Tribune* explained that

1. He is emphatically a man of the people, the most DEMO-CRATIC President we have ever had. . . . 2. He is an honest man. . . . 3. He is an able man. . . . 4. He has administered

the Government more satisfactorily to the people during the past four years than any of his predecessors since Washington have. . . . 5. He has been true to his oath to maintain the Union. . . . 6. He has, under the providence of God, been reasonably, honorably and even gloriously successful in the aggregation of his efforts to maintain the Union. . . . 7. In his military appointments he has been so liberal that not the shadow of a charge of political favoritism has ever been rested against him. . . . 8. He has committed no infraction of the constitution.

Harper's Weekly joined in this praise. "The great service that the President has done for this country and for civilization has often been considered in these columns," it announced, characterizing him as "so manly and modest a character, so faithful to every duty, so forgiving and so generous, with a sagacity so eminent, and exercised with so much intelligence and such an absence of guile that his strongest enemies and those of our country have no so ardent wish as to see him replaced. . . ." The radical *Wilkes' Spirit of the Times* thought it honored the Democrats that they were opposed by a President whom the rebels deeply hated, whose honesty and patriotism there had been no one to dispute, and who represented "a 'platform' which insists upon the integrity of the whole national domain."[50]

Throughout the final months and weeks of the campaign, constant references to Lincoln's honesty, patriotism, and consistency filled the papers and letters of supporters, and confidence in his reelection mounted constantly. "If Washington, as an instrument of Divinity, made good in revolution and delivered the American people from tyranny, you Sir, equally an instrument of Providence, have sanctified that revolution and saved the American people from a worse despotism," the president heard from Judge Rufus K. Williams of the Kentucky Court of

Appeals. The *Boston Journal* highlighted Lincoln's accomplishments in answer to attacks by the Tennessee politician Emerson Etheridge; John Sherman, in a speech at Sandusky, Ohio, praised him as a "noble and kind hearted . . . child of the people," and the Chicago *Illinois Staats-Zeitung* characterized him as an eminently virtuous man. As the Springfield *Republican* asserted, the president's reelection was virtually certain.[51]

The military, too, became ever more impressed with the commander in chief. Ever since Lincoln's nomination, the army's preference had been clear. Comments from soldiers bear this out. From Huntsville, Alabama, Private Jenkin Lloyd Jones of the Sixth Wisconsin Battery stated, "Abraham Lincoln nominated for the presidency by the Baltimore convention and Andy Johnson for vice president which gives satisfaction the large majority of the army. Hurrah for Old Abe!" George F. Crane of the 10th Illinois likewise wrote his mother on June 15, "The news of Abe's renomination was received with intense joy by the army, but the addition of Frémont blasts him forever in the eyes of the soldiers," and "Uncle Abe is the soldiers' choice," was the opinion of Charles O. Musser of the 29th Iowa. When the president visited the army on June 22, he was received with great enthusiasm, and sailors, too, hoped to be able to vote for him.[52] On July 11, Lincoln himself came under fire at Fort Stevens during Early's raid on Washington, and the military was favorably affected. Elisha Hunt Rhodes of the Second Rhode Island Volunteer Infantry noted that "As the President and many ladies were looking at us every man tried to do his best," and Dr. Daniel M. Holt wrote to his wife, "Father Abraham wife and son followed us in a carriage to the walls of the fort and here I lost sight of the good man. We have learned to love him as well as he appears to love his boys in blue, and we all would be willing to sacrifice anything for such a man and such a government." In August, a straw vote at an army hospital at Annapolis resulted in 237 for Lincoln, 32 for McClellan, and 1 for Frémont.[53] Although at that time the Republicans' difficulties were reflected by several negative opinions in the army,[54] by September Chaplain Samuel F. George of the 50th New York Engineers was able to write to Lincoln that, since McClellan's nomination, soldiers were coming over en masse. "We are satisfied with you," he added. "We want no other man at the helm until this rebellion is crushed, for we have tried you. . . . We can trust you and depend upon you. . . ." General James H. Kidd of the 6th Michigan Cavalry remarked, "Politics we care little about but think Lincoln ought to be reelected because we know he is all right. Somebody else *may not be.*" The army also appreciated his September draft call, and Colonel Thomas Sellat Mather of the 2nd Illinois Artillery informed Robert Lincoln that from his observation, the people and the army were with his father. Every single private soldier he had canvassed was for sustaining the executive.[55]

As in the country at large, as election time approached, Lincoln continued to gain in popularity among members of the army. "Old Abe is gaining strength lately here," Charles O. Musser of the 29th Iowa Regiment wrote his father from Little Rock on September 18, and repeated this statement one month later. Alfred L. Hough at Atlanta similarly remarked that McClellan was rapidly losing what friends he had had in the army and he had no doubt that Lincoln would have a large majority of the soldiers' vote. The Indiana volunteer George W. Squier explained to his wife why he would vote for the president. "In the first place, he has the experience which no other man in this nation has. He is eminently devoted to the *true* interests of the Government. He is a man who thinks and acts for himself. And last but not least he is a Christian."[56] Private Alonzo Miller of the 12th Wisconsin Infantry thought the election would have some effect on the war since Old Abe was the soldiers' choice and the rebels believed McClellan would make peace while Abe would fight. In Chattanooga, six days prior to the election, the

Wisconsin soldier John F. Brobst was convinced, as he stated, "And now all want to close up the game with Abe for President, and then the game will be up, the Union saved, and all things will be well with us." On election day, Corporal Bliss Morse, reflected, "This day we poll our vote for Abraham Lincoln, the man who represents the principles of Liberty, of Justice, and of the Righteousness which exalteth a Nation, of Peace and good will to all men—that Right may be the more firmly established forever in the land, and that it be a home for all men do we vote for Lincoln." After the president's victory, brought about in part by army votes, Thomas Morris Chester, the black Civil War correspondent, reported from before Richmond, that the reelection was "quite cheering to the army," which, if anything, was an understatement. Benjamin T. Smith in Sherman's army wrote in his journal, "News has reached us that Mr. Lincoln (honest old Abe) has been re-elected president, and there is great rejoicing by all the troops," an observation repeated by many others.[57]

As the campaign developed, Democratic charges became ever more abusive. Democrats were incensed at the president's reaction to Greeley's peace moves, emphasizing particularly his letter, "To Whom it may concern." The war was now no longer a war for the Union, charged the Columbus *Crisis,* but "a war for the Negro, and nothing else." Citing the *New York Herald's* assertion that with the letter Lincoln signed his own death warrant, The Albany *Atlas and Argus* wanted him impeached. "Caesar had his Brutus, Charles I his Cromwell . . . and we the People recommend Abraham Lincoln to profit by their example," it wrote. The Democrats reveled in the Republicans' and Lincoln's troubles in August, continually called him a tyrant and a widowmaker, and expressed fear that he might become a dictator. Accusing Mary Lincoln of buying china, asking for more than it was worth, and pocketing the difference, they questioned the president's honesty, they called him guilty of treason, homicide, kidnapping, arson, robbery, and all sorts of other crimes. And when the election results were in, they charged fraud, especially in connection with the soldiers' vote.[58]

As usual, Southern papers and individuals echoed these charges. As the British journalist George Augustus Sala observed, the Southerner allegedly knew the character of Abraham Lincoln. "He neither overvalues nor undervalues him. He accounts him a vulgar, cunning man, avaricious of power, bent on domination, callous of the popular consensus, determined to hang on to his office by the skin of his teeth." Thomas J. Key of the Confederate army wrote in his diary that the letters between Horace Greeley and the Confederate commissioners were dignified and would have resulted in humane acts "had it not been for the dictatorial and low note issued by Abe Lincoln in rejecting the commissions. . . . The President is determined to prosecute this inhuman war and will allow no one to approach him with the olive branch except on such humiliating terms as no gentleman or nation will accept." He tended to concentrate on the failed peace negotiations. Some even thought Lincoln would be preferable for the South, either because he was a greater fool than McClellan, or because the general would be a more skilled leader who would weaken the South by constantly offering peace on the basis of the Constitution. After the election, they feared it would mean many more years of war, and the Richmond *Dispatch* opined that "twenty millions surrendered their liberty to a vulgar tyrant . . . whose personal qualities are those of a low buffoon, whose most noteworthy conversation is a medley of profane jests and obscured anecdotes. . . ."[59]

Foreign opinion followed previous judgments. "What a ruggedly honest and sternly uncompromising soul is that which animates, directs and governs the President of the great American Republic . . . ," commented the *Edinburgh Mercury* after the renomination. "The way in which President Lincoln has slowly, though surely, carried out his Emancipation policy does him infinite Credit." In England, on August 4, Samuel Goddard praised Lincoln's handling of the Niagara peace conference. The editor of the *English Leader* wrote him, "Everyone who cares for freedom in this country regards your name not only with admiration but affection. . . . No President of America since the days of Washington has won the esteem of the liberal portion of the English nation as you have." In September, the Union and Emancipation Society in Manchester published an appeal to the People of Great Britain highlighting Lincoln's great achievements, and by October, the *Moniteur* was convinced of the certainty of the president's reelection. On October 15, *Le Siècle* enthusiastically stated, "Brothers of America, millions of men in Europe vote in their hearts with you for Lincoln! . . . Let principles be victorious in the election of Lincoln, and everything will be strengthened and encouraged on this side of the Atlantic."[60] In a letter to Greeley, John Bright pointed out that America's friends in Europe, though not believing Lincoln to be wiser than others, thought they had observed in his career a grand simplicity of purpose and a patriotism which did not change and which did not falter, and the London *Spectator*, considering Lincoln's reelection most likely, wrote, "It is certain that no party so strong for the reelection of a President has ever existed since Jackson's second return to office as exists in the United States for Mr. Lincoln." Its editor, John Campbell, addressed Lincoln directly, telling him, "You have achieved a mighty work, under an accumulation of obstacles, such as for variety, complexity, & magnitude, has never before surrounded the Ruler of any nation." Finally, lest his German friend Theodore Petrasch in Germany form the wrong opinion, Carl Schurz wrote to him:

> Your opinion of the President is too deprecatory. He is indeed a man without higher education and his manners harmonize little with the European conception of a dignity of a

ruler. He is an overgrown nature child and does not understand artifices of speech and attitude. But he is a man of
profound feeling, just and firm principles, an incorruptible
integrity. . . . He is the people personified; that is the secret
of his popularity. His government is the most representative
that has ever existed in world history. I will make a prophecy
which may perhaps sound strange at this moment. In fifty
years, perhaps much sooner, Lincoln's name will stand written upon the honor roll of the American Republic next to
that of Washington, and there it will remain for all time.[61]

Hostile foreign papers and individuals kept up their negative
assessments throughout the campaign. After the renomination,
the London *Times* commented that formerly only private per-
sons called Lincoln a buffoon; now it was a public matter, and
if he had been wise, he would never have accepted the renomination. It was appalled at Lincoln's alleged danger during Early's
raid and expressed the opinion that "To be told that the President of the Republic was very nearly taking refuge in a gunboat,
and that he was expected in New York, is not likely to raise the
Federal spirits." Criticizing the executive for not negotiating
with the Confederates except on terms unacceptable to them, it
charged that he was more interested in his reelection than in
military affairs. The *Moniteur,* commenting on the Niagara conference, published Confederate characterizations of Lincoln's
terms as those of a conqueror, mentioned the alleged unpopularity of the renewed call for 500,000 men, and highlighted his
difficulties in August. It, too, stressed the connection between
the election and the success of the Union armies. *Punch* published hostile cartoons, and the French traveler Ernest Duvergier
de Hauranne severely criticized Lincoln's decision not to exchange prisoners of war. Even the usually friendly London *Spectator* was disturbed by the terms Lincoln offered to the
Confederates. As it declared, "It is certainly a mistake that the

conference desired by the Commissioners did not take place. It was virtually granted once by the President, and then revoked without alleged reason. It places him in the attitude of coquetting with rebel emissaries, and of withdrawing precisely when he could have learned something of their plans."[62]

In spite of these accusations, however, all in all, the renomination and reelection campaign was another substantial proof of the president's popularity.

6 Triumph and Assassination

After his reelection, Lincoln enjoyed an unprecedented period of increasing popularity. The war was coming to a victorious close, so that it became ever more difficult for his opponents to charge him with inability to overcome the rebellion. Of course it all ended with his assassination, which almost immediately made him a national hero.

The praise started immediately. In the crowd listening to the president's acknowledgement of a serenade on November 10, an old man was heard to exclaim. "God is good to us; He has again given us as a ruler a sublime specimen of his noblest work—an honest man." The Philadelphia *Inquirer,* praising Lincoln's generous reference to his defeated opponent at this occasion, called him "a man with a true human heart in his bosom," and identified this trait with his hold upon the confidence and affection of the people. The speech also charmed the radical abolitionist Lydia Maria Child.[1] On November 9, the *Boston Morning Journal* commented, "The patriotic masses tell Abraham Lincoln that he is right in enforcing a vigorous prosecution of the war for the suppression of the rebellion, and that he is expected to continue right on to the end. . . ." Former Secretary of the Treasury Salmon P. Chase thought McClellan should not have received one vote, because, as he wrote, "Considered as men Mr. Lincoln is immensely his superior: considered as Representatives of ideas & Principles & Measures this superiority becomes immeasurable." The Washington *Daily Morning Chronicle,* reporting how Edward Everett praised the president, referred to him as "one of the purest and best of men." A Baltimore citizen assured Lincoln that he looked upon him as "a man who will receive the blessings of generations unborn," an idea shared by William L. Dayton, the American minister in Paris, as well as by Isaac Arnold. The Union Democrat and Edwards Pierrepont, later the attorney general, let him know that history would record how during his administration he emancipated four million slaves, and, he thought, "there will have been nothing like it in the roll of time." James Lothrop Motley, the Boston Brahmin and minister to Austria, wrote to Lincoln that the American people had found in him "a most fitting and fortunate impersonation." And *Frank Leslie's Illustrated Newspaper* published a cartoon entitled, "Jeff Davis's Nightmare, with the Confederate leader in bed, seeing Lincoln and asking, "Is that you, still there, LONG ABE?" Lincoln replies, "Yes, and I am going to be there FOUR years longer."[2]

Comparisons of Lincoln to George Washington were now almost commonplace. In Ohio, the Bellefontaine *Republican* was certain that, "No man since George Washington ever received such a unanimous endorsement by the people . . . a tribute which his worth, his great services to the cause of his country and humanity, his eminent statesmanship as developed during his whole administration deserved." Alfred Lacey Hough, soldiering at Chattanooga, also thought that "future history will place Mr. Lincoln's name next to Washington's, the first the founder and the second the preserver of the country."[2] William J. Kellogg in Peoria, Illinois argued that "the people will have cause to and will bless you and your fame will be as extended and enduring as that of the Father of his country Washington"; and the former Illinois legislator Anson S. Miller likewise insisted, "Your election has been secured with a unanimity unknown since the reelection of Washington." From Switzerland, Count Agénor-Etienne de Gasparin wrote him that having been elected, like Washington, for a second term, he was destined to be a founder after having been a defender. (*"vous êtes chargé comme lui de fonder après avoir défendu.*") In the American consulate at Hamburg, Germany, J. H. Anderson assured him that "your name, like that of the father of his Country, will go down to posterity loved and honored by the people of every civilized land," and the radical abolitionist Oliver Johnson let him know that: "A redeemed, disenthralled and regenerated nation will forever speak of your name with gratitude and reverence, as worthy to stand side by side with that of the 'Father of his Country.'"[4]

The delight of the military with the election results has already been mentioned, and the soldiers also evinced increased respect for their commander in chief. "Now that Abraham Lincoln is elected there can be but one heart and one voice (however honestly a portion of the nation may have opposed his reelection) . . . for united support of his administration and of the war," was the opinion of General James H. Kidd, of the 6th Michigan Cavalry. John H. Westervelt of the 1st New York Engineer Corps commented on the great rejoicing in the army at the election result; Commodore Thomas T. Craven of the *Niagara* in Antwerp ordered a 21 gun salute in honor of the event, and the Wisconsin volunteer John F. Brobst expressed his great satisfaction with the president's call for 300,000 more men.[5]

Lincoln's appointment of Chase as chief justice of the United States naturally pleased the radicals. Felicitating him on his decision, the *New York Tribune* wrote, "Mr. Lincoln will receive the thanks of the country that his judgment is so perfectly in accord with the popular wish." The *Commonwealth* agreed, as did the *Independent,* rejoicing that "the noble deed is done." Its editor was so delighted with the appointment that he sent a personal note of congratulations to the president. Noah Brooks commented that next to the Emancipation Proclamation, nothing had given such general satisfaction, because the president, true as ever to what he considered the public good, nominated his unsuccessful rival for the candidacy of the Union party. Nor-

man B. Judd, the American envoy to Prussia, was impressed
with Lincoln's magnanimity in appointing a man who had given
him nothing but trouble, and the Springfield *Republican* praised
him for putting aside personal feeling to "give us the best man
for the highest judicial position in the nation." But if the New
York *Evening Post* thought Chase was "wisely chosen" by the
president to preside over the Supreme Court, the *New York Herald* warned even before the appointment that it would mean
Lincoln's yielding to the radicals and delaying the peace for a
year.[6]

On December 5, 1864, the president submitted his annual
message, in which, among other subjects, he called for the rapid
adoption of the emancipation amendment. This message also
received general praise. "As often as the public have had reason
to exclaim, 'God bless Abraham Lincoln,' they will utter the
benediction with a new zest on reading his late message. It is
the best, in our opinion, he has yet written," stated the New
York *Evening Post*. The *Chicago Tribune* agreed, calling it the
most unexceptionable which had ever come from his pen. The
Boston *Morning Journal*, especially pleased with his lack of vin-
dictiveness and refusal to exalt over his election victory, referred
to it as "a good and sensible document that every man can
understand, and that nine-tenths of all patriotic men will ap-
prove."[7] "The verdict of all men is that the message is immensely strengthening for the President," stated Noah Brooks,
"and while it has all of the dignity and polish of a first-rate state
paper, it has the strong common sense, the partial knowledge of
details which will commend the document to the minds of the
'simple people.'" At any rate, he believed the president was "the
man for the times . . . a far greater and better man than our
own people think," and that the time would come when people
generally would concede his true merit and worth. And Charles
Francis Adams also expressed in a letter to his father his admira-

tion for the message, especially its endorsement of the antislavery movement.[8]

Many radicals were delighted with the president's stance on the constitutional change. "God bless Abraham Lincoln," the *Independent* wrote. "We never said it more heartily than on reading the noble Message to which Congress and the country have just lent listening ears. . . . Never before seemed he so noble in our eyes." The *Commonwealth*, praising the "confident tone" of the message, also praised the president's furtherance of the amendment. The *Liberator*, approving of his antislavery sentiments, agreed. "All honor to him," it stated. *Wilkes Spirit of the Times* called it "undoubtedly the most important document ever issued by an American Executive. . . . It now but remains . . . for him to pass through his term as the most popular of Presidents, and take rank in history as the greatest benefactor his country," it wrote. And in Congress, the arch radical Thaddeus Stevens labeled it "the most important and best message that has been communicated to Congress in the last 60 years," while asserting that "there never was a day since Abraham Lincoln was elected President that he has stood so high in the estimation of the people as at this moment."[9]

The Democrats, however, trying to overcome their defeat, kept up their attacks. As noted previously, they considered the election results fraudulent; according to the Albany *Atlas and Argus*, a change of only a few votes would have made all the difference. The Columbus *Crisis* bemoaned the fact that the people had become hero worshippers. Attributing the appointment of Chase to corruption, it equally bemoaned what it called the new chief justice's sitting in judgment on his own schemes. Nor did it fail to denigrate the annual message. "Such a production as President Lincoln's last message can scarcely be reviewed with the gravity which belongs to the importance of the subject," it commented. "Its atrocious features are so numerous and so prominent that they confront the reader in every paragraph and almost confound any attempt at analyzation by the mere force of their absurdity." The Albany *Atlas and Argus,* arguing that it showed that the nation was now involved in an abolition war, was equally critical.[10]

Following Lincoln's November triumph, the Europeans also expressed their renewed respect for him. On November 24, in a letter to the editor of the London *Daily Post,* Samuel Goddard, giving voice to English friends of the administration, stressed Lincoln's vast superiority to McClellan in intellect, force of character and reliability; the *Edinburgh Weekly Herald and Mercury* rejoiced that "Honest Abe" had been reelected; the *Manchester Examiner* wrote, "We heartily join with all who have faith in popular institutions . . . in offering our warmest congratulations to the people of the Northern States on the peaceful issue of this great contest." And James A. Putnam, at the consulate in Le Havre, pointed out to the president that liberal Europe was delighted with his victory. As he put it, "Your name is so identified with human progress and the free institutions which make this the noblest period in history, that your defeat would have been accepted abroad as the triumph of despotism." The London *Times* met with severe crticism on the Continent when, labeling the election result the first episode of the foundation of tyranny in the United States, it asserted that the war would now continue and that Lincoln would create mourning in every home for four years more. According to the *Independence Belge,* which thought the election reaffirmed the strength of the Northern government, these exaggerations were ridiculous, and it sufficed simply to point them out so that the good sense of the public would quickly dispose of them.[11]

The 1864 annual message also met with favor abroad. "A dry, shrewd tenacity has always been the characteristic of Mr. Lincoln's Messages, and the one transmitted to Congress on the 6th December is dryer, shrewder, and more tenacious than ever," reported the London *Spectator.* The London *Penny Illustrated*

Newspaper stated that Lincoln's character was no longer in question and that his statement that, if asked to reenslave people someone else would have to do it, would doubtless be written some day on his tomb. "Happy the man who can look forward to such a testimony to his life," it concluded. In France, the *Siècle* felt that after the message one could hardly be a partisan of the South, at least without breaking entirely with the idea of Western culture. Naturally, there were also some hostile comments, the London *Times* leading off with the assertion that it only meant more war, an opinion shared by Southern sympathizers in France.[12]

The South, having already interpreted the election results as an indication of a certain lengthening of the conflict, adjudged the message in a like manner. "His adherence to a purpose of emancipation of the slaves, and his employment of them in his armies will suffice for an indefinite prolongation of war . . . ," wrote the Confederate war clerk John B. Jones, an interpretation shared by Josiah Gorgas, the head of the Southern Ordnance Bureau. The *Richmond Enquirer* was of the same opinion; the Richmond *Dispatch* considered the message a call for unconditional surrender; and the Richmond *Sentinel* called it "commonplace, superficial, and feeble." But the feeling of Confederate pessimism was evident.[13]

The encomiums for Lincoln naturally continued. "The President has been elected upon a full and fair vote, and upon issues which were boldly proclaimed," insisted the *Philadelphia Inquirer.* "The nation backs him in his course of policy, and it will continue to sustain him by every means which may be necessary to the final triumph of the cause." In full agreement, the *New York Times* reflected that the election of Republican senators showed that the loyal states desired to sustain the president; and Mrs. C. Greene Breyton, the wife of a Rhode Island judge, addressed Lincoln as a most wonderful man who had done more than any other president by keeping the ship of state in good sailing order.[14]

As the new year started, peace moves and questions of reconstruction became paramount. In spite of Democratic attacks and suspicion of Confederate motives, Lincoln's handling of the efforts to achieve some settlement was well received. Early in January, he gave permission to the old Jacksonian Francis Blair to go to Richmond to see whether he could arrange for some settlement, and Blair went twice to the Confederate capital, where he met Davis, who agreed to a conference "to secure peace to the two countries." Lincoln replied that he was willing to confer "with a view of securing peace of the people of our common country," not yielding on his insistence of the restitution of the Union. In dealing with the mission, the *Philadelphia Inquirer* commented that, while Jefferson Davis was stubborn, so was Abraham Lincoln, but he had a stubborn people behind him and would not yield. The *New York Herald* was glad that Lincoln had blocked the Southern game to weaken the Union. And the *New York Tribune* pointed out that upon Blair's second trip, Lincoln, though thinking that the enterprise would not do any good, nevertheless showed his entire acquiescence in Blair's efforts by placing a United States steamer at Blair's command.[15]

In pursuance of a possible peace, in February, Lincoln met at Hampton Roads with a Confederate delegation that included Vice President Alexander H. Stephens. Though again attacked by Democrats as well as radicals, who opposed negotiations with the South, the president's handling of this conference and the general situation elicited numerous laudatory comments. The *New York Times* wrote:

> After Mr. Blair's volunteer diplomacy had, to a certain extent, committed the Government to a conference, nothing could be wiser, more patriotic, or more satisfactory, than the course pursued by President Lincoln. He gives the strongest possible

justification of his desire for peace by meeting personally with the rebel commissioners, and by giving the fullest most liberal consideration to every proposition and suggestion they had to offer. Yet he did not permit them for a single moment to believe, or even suppose, that peace was *possible at the cost of separation.*

The *New York Weekly Tribune,* also praising his efforts, thanked him heartily for his bearing at the conference. Its daily counterpart thought that Lincoln's honesty and frankness had been vindicated by Jefferson Davis's message on the subject; the Springfield *Republican* was attracted by Lincoln's shrewdness and thought that, though he did not play his cards "according to Hoyle," he tended to win nonetheless; and the *Cincinnati Gazette* was favorably affected by the "remarkable prudence with which Mr. Lincoln has conducted himself throughout this business."[16] A headline in the *Chicago Tribune* on February 11 read: "Mr. Lincoln's Duty Done," and two days later, commenting on his message about the meeting, the paper explained that "his brief, pithy sentences" gave the clue to the rebels' selfish aims in the conference. As the Washington *Morning Chronicle,* approving of Lincoln's terms of Union and emancipation, explained, the president had to see the Confederates if he wanted to maintain his standing in American or world opinion. The *New York Herald* considered the conference proof that Lincoln was one of the shrewdest diplomats of the day; Charles Francis Adams asserted that he looked to the president for honesty and shrewdness, and that in this matter he was not wanting in these respects. General Meade thought Lincoln's course ought to meet the approval of every patriot, while Thaddeus Stevens—again appearing in his rare role as Lincoln's defender—berated the opposition for censuring the president for not agreeing to Confederate terms. And from Europe, he heard that his work was admirable, while the Old World lacked leadership.[17]

Some radicals regretted that the executive had even consented to confer with the insurgents. While the *National Anti-Slavery Standard* recognized that the president knew that peace by negotiation was impossible, but wanted to satisfy the domestic opposition, the paper felt that he should not treat with Confederate leaders at all. By February 18, however, it announced that there was no longer any anxiety about the peace movements. Asserting that it did not share these fears because of its confidence "in the honesty and patriotism of the president," it pointed out that even his worst enemies had never considered him a fool. The New York *Evening Post* was more censorious. Because it was apparent that no peace could be made without disgrace to the Union, it regretted that the president should have risked his reputation for soundness of judgment by acting on a different conclusion.[18]

It is not surprising that the Albany *Atlas and Argus* considered the conference a mere administration device to satisfy the sentiment of humanity in the North and to arouse its indignation in case of rejection. Accusing Lincoln of throwing away the idea of influencing the people of the South, the paper charged him with "seeking in its stead the disadvantage of addressing to the Congress a repulsive and irritating proposition calculated to excite and embitter them . . . ." The New York *World* also characterized the conference as merely a maneuver by the president "to hoodwink and deceive the country for his benefit," and in the House of Representatives, Noah Brooks, declaring that Lincoln should have consulted Congress, maintained that he was hounded by the radicals, although the Democratic representative Samuel S. Cox thanked him for negotiating at all. Confederates thought the president's terms so dishonorable that they had united the Southerners for a more energetic prosecution of the war. Edmund Ruffin commented that while Stonewall Jackson had qualities of a leader, Lincoln had not one, "except duplicity and low cunning . . . ," while the *Richmond*

Whig had long been declaring that Lincoln's peace efforts were merely an attempt to keep the South from holding out for another campaign, after which it thought its triumph was assured.[19]

The question of reconstruction was closely tied to the passage of the Thirteenth Amendment. In his message, as has already been shown, Lincoln had urged the speedy passage of the emancipation measure, and though his further more positive support of its adoption was not publicly known, his advocacy of emancipation was popular. As Pennsylvania Representative Glenni W. Scofield argued in the House, "The President, in obedience to the advice of the people and the dictates of his own kind heart and unimpassioned judgment, has recommended that we should submit this amendment to the action of the States. Why should it not be done?" William Lloyd Garrison reminded Lincoln of the support he had given to him in word and print and wished him success and the passage of the amendment. Congress's final acceptance of the amendment on January 31 so delighted Henry Ward Beecher that he wrote to Lincoln, "Every step which you have, one by one, taken toward emancipation and national liberty is now confirmed beyond all change. You have brought the most dangerous and extraordinary rebellion in history, not only to a successful end, but have done it without sacrificing republican government even in its form. . . . Your position is eminent and impregnable." And as the *Belletristisches Journal* declared, "Let us not part from this subject without thinking of the one man who has earned a higher merit than any other. With the passage of this amendment Abraham Lincoln sees the fulfillment of the greatest wish of his heart; he used all his influence to achieve it. . . ," while *Frank Leslie's Illustrated Newspaper* celebrated Lincoln's part in it with a cartoon showing "Uncle Abe's Valentine," sent to Columbia with an envelope full of broken chains. But the reconstruction problem could not be solved during this session; the radicals refused to admit representatives from the states reorganized under the Ten Percent Plan and the pending Reconstruction bill was tabled. Others, however, praised the president for it. Senator Doolittle, for example, pointed out that it had worked very well in Louisiana, where more than 10 percent had voted. The *New York Tribune* even considered tabling the Reconstruction bill a good omen because Congress would adjourn soon and the editor had faith in Lincoln's managing the matter well until the legislators met again.[20]

The president's second inaugural gave rise to further praise. Three days before the event, a Boston admirer wrote him that he had done a great job and that the second inaugural would be greater than the first. The *Cincinnati Commercial* stressed the same point, and commentator after commentator reflected on the success of Lincoln's past policies. The *Philadelphia Inquirer* pointed out that he had been called to the executive office at a difficult time but had met the responsibilities forced upon him with courage, wisdom, and manliness. The *New York Times* lauded the first presidential term as "superlatively successful" in crushing the rebellion in the speediest way possible, and asserted that but for the great wisdom of Mr. Lincoln, the result would have been different. The Washington *National Intelligencer* asserted:

> As the military head of the nation, the people have shown unexampled confidence in Mr. Lincoln . . . . His measures of policy have been endorsed, or acquiesced in. The people have carried him into a second term of the presidency over open opposition, and caucus chicane of politicians of his party.

The *National Anti-Slavery Standard*, while characterizing Lincoln as not the ideal of a great statesman, nevertheless thought the inauguration was a great day for "us all" and doubted "whether such a man could have answered exactly such an exigency of just such a people as this so well as Mr. Lincoln has done." The artillerist Jenkin L. Jones mused that after four years of tempestuous sailing he had carried the good old ship of state through all breakers and hoped that during his second "voyage" he might know more sunshine and be as successful as before. The ever-changing *New York Herald,* commenting on the inauguration, not only called him "a most remarkable man," but also "the keenest of politicians and more than a match for his wiliest antagonists in the arts of diplomacy." And Benjamin B. French, impressed with the ceremonies, wrote, "It was a grand ovation of the *People* to their President, whom they dearly love."[21]

The second inaugural address, with its religious overtones and call for malice toward none and charity for all, which Ronald C. White Jr. has called "Lincoln's greatest speech," is generally considered to be second only to the Gettysburg address. The Washington *Evening Star* thought that "in pithy brevity, sagacity and honesty of purpose" it was "Lincolnian all over." The Springfield *Republican,* greatly moved by its invocation of divine judgment, concluded by stating, "There are many things the president might have said fitly and impressively. But what he did say he said frankly and nobly, and this inaugural address will be set down as, in character and circumstance, as remarkable an address as ever made." According to the *Chicago Tribune,* the address was impressive in its simplicity, and its leading characteristic was "its devout recognition of the oral and religious elements involved in the contest, in words which the people of the United States, as a Christian nation, will welcome from their Chief Magistrate." The Washington *Daily Morning Chronicle* stressed the difference between the first and second inaugural; finding the first apologetic and an appeal to the reason of the insurgents, it pointed out that in the second, "its author naturally took the tone of a master of the situation."[22]

Private individuals were equally appreciative. "What do you

think of the inaugural?" wrote Charles Francis Adams to his father. "That rail-splitting lawyer is one of the wonders of the day. Once at Gettysburg and now again on a greater occasion he has shown a capacity for rising to the demands of the hour which we should not expect from orators or men of the schools. This inaugural strikes me in its grand simplicity and directness as being for all time the historical keynote of this war . . . ." Noah Brooks commented on its "noble words, which might be printed in letters of gold," and Benjamin Moran wrote in his journal that it was "brief and sensible, and justly acknowledges the hand of Providence in our great trial." David Lane of the 17th Michigan Infantry considered it "the most remarkable state paper of modern times," resembling more the "production of one of Israel's ancient rulers than the Inaugural Address of a modern politician."[23]

To be sure, some radicals still had misgivings. Charles Sumner did not like the fact that the president had not mentioned the necessity of applying the Declaration of Independence—with its stress on equality—in reconstructing the states, though within a few weeks he came to believe that Lincoln's mind was undergoing a change about reconstruction. The *New York Tribune* criticized the omission of a strong appeal to the rebels for a cessation of hostilities, and the *Commonwealth*, while admitting that the inaugural was the touchstone of the national heart, also regretted the omission of a demand for black suffrage. The frequently critical New York *Evening Post*, however, thought that none who had agitated against slavery had presented the case "in such condensed, energetic language, as Mr. Lincoln has done," and the *Liberator* also praised it, particularly for the president's firmness about emancipation. The *Independent* pointed out that "His brief and pithy words—characteristic of their author's homespun style—were freighted with noble meaning, precious beyond all earlier utterances of his pen or tongue. . . ." And the *National Anti-Slavery Standard* reported that, with its stress on antislavery and religion, the address delighted all his friends.[24]

In spite of Lincoln's invocation of malice toward none and charity for all, the Democratic opposition remained hostile. The New York *World* charged him with substituting religion for statesmanship, and the Albany *Atlas and Argus,* complaining about the absence of any indication of his future policy, called it a profane and incoherent homily that shocked everybody. Southerners were equally unaffected by any offers of good will. They believed the address showed Lincoln's "utter lack of polish, education, and brains" and that the invocation of religion would only make the war more sanguinary. But abroad, the London *Times* finally had a good word to say about the man it had constantly abused. "We cannot but see," it wrote, "that the President, placed into the most important position to which a statesman can aspire, invested with a power greater than that of most Monarchs, fulfills the duties which destiny has imposed on him with firmness and conscientiousness, but without any feeling of exhilaration at success or sanguine anticipation of any prosperity." The London *Spectator,* declaring that no statesman ever uttered words stamped at once with the zeal of so deep a wisdom and so true a simplicity, likened Lincoln's characteristics to those of George Washington.[25]

During the remaining weeks of Lincoln's life, as the war was drawing to a close, his popularity was greater than ever. When he appointed a one-armed soldier as postmaster in Piqua, Ohio, the inhabitants thanked him profusely and passed a resolution that the appointment was "another proof of those principles of justice which have ever characterized him in all his acts. . . ." On March 28, the New Jersey Conference of the Methodist Episcopal Church resolved, "We have great respect for, and confidence in the Chief Magistrate of the Nation, and congratulate him, and the whole country, on the indication of returning peace . . . ," and on March 31, the *New York Times* announced that the whole country would sympathize with the president's conciliatory spirit of reconstruction. Then, on April 8, Lydia Maria Child wrote to her fellow radical, Ohio Congressman George W. Julian, "I think we have reason to thank God for Abraham Lincoln, with all his deficiencies, it must be admitted that he has grown continually; and, considering how Slavery had weakened and perverted the moral sense of the whole country, it was great good luck to have the people elect a man who was wiling to grow."[26]

On April 2, Richmond fell, and Lincoln went to visit the fallen enemy capital. But as Brooks pointed out, those who thought that he would make a personal parade or triumph of it did not know him. Of course, the local blacks were delirious with joy. As one of them said, "I know that I am free, for I have seen Father Abraham and felt him." At City Point, where he had gone to confer with General Grant, an English visitor found him "remarkably polite." And on April 9, the very day of General Lee's surrender, the Vermont soldier Wilbur Fisk, in his report to the Montpelier *Green Mountain Freeman*, wrote from the 6th Corps Hospital at City Point, which the president had visited to shake hands, "It was an unexpected honor, coming from the man upon whom the world is looking with so much interest, and the boys were pleased beyond measure. . . . The men not only revere and admire Mr. Lincoln, but they love him. May God bless him, and spare his life to us for many years."[27]

The victory at Appomattox and the imminent end of the war raised the president's popularity to unprecedented heights. Now, the main problem was the reconstruction of the seceded states, and even the arch-Copperhead Clement L Vallandigham, hoping for a merciful policy, averred, "If the President takes the proper course, he can have the support of the masses of men who have hitherto opposed him." On April 11, Lincoln was to address the people at the White House, with Reconstruction as his main theme. The Washington *Evening Star*, predicting that the visit to the mansion would give rise to a grand ovation, used the occasion to extol him again: "The grand traits of Mr. Lincoln's character, his magnanimity, patience, firmness, sagacity, and humanity, developed so conspicuously through the trying ordeal of the times, have won for him an amount of personal regard in this country that is apt to develop itself upon any and every opportunity, and which will have an exceedingly appropriate one tonight."[28]

The speech the president delivered that evening, in which he advocated limited black suffrage, was destined to be his last. . . . As the Washington *National Intelligencer* put it, "This remarkable speech is *wise* in *sentiment*; it is pervaded by the logic of the heart, while the keenness and clearness of perception and grasp of thought which distinguish it . . . are certainly remarkable." The *New York Herald* praised the "excellent" address, and the Washington *Evening Star* not only approved of his reconstruction policy in Louisiana, but lauded "the vein of strong sense and true patriotism which has invariably marked all the measures of his previous policy toward the rebellion everywhere 'crops out' on this occasion." The Springfield *Republican* liked the fact that he was flexible in his views on Reconstruction, properly believing in taking the best available plan and getting the best possible results from it; the *Philadelphia Inquirer* agreed, as did Noah Brooks.[29] The Washington *Daily Morning Chronicle,* referring to Lincoln's magnanimous speech, asserted that he constituted an exception to the general rule not to depend on one man, because none was so well fitted to deal with Reconstruction; the *Cincinnati Gazette* felt that the speech was very carefully considered as it was intended to foreshadow his policy of bringing the incendiary states back into their proper relationship with the national government; and the New York *Commercial Advertiser,* referring to the controversial nature of the speech, pointed out that, with his political shrewdness, which nobody could question, the president was appealing from the leaders of the party to the people in language "homely yet as expressive as . . . his own countenance. . . ." Noah Brooks, considering that the radicals opposed the speech, nevertheless reflected that the mass of the people had "an implicit and trustful faith in Lincoln," who had so often proven himself wiser than his critics.[30]

Because the president advocated only limited suffrage for the freedmen, many radicals were dubious about the speech. The chief justice was glad that he had come out for the franchise for intelligent and veteran blacks, but he regretted that he was not yet ready for universal or equal suffrage. Charles Sumner was of two minds: "The more I have seen of the Presdt. the more his character in certain respects has risen, & we must admit that he has said some things better than anybody else could have said them," he wrote to Chase. "But I fear his policy now." The radical *New York Tribune* believed the speech fell dead without effect on the audience. [31]

On April 14, 1865—three days after the speech—the actor John Wilkes Booth, a radical sympathizer with the South, who had noted that Lincoln advocated limited black enfranchisement and was heard to say, "That is the last speech he'll ever make," murdered the president at Ford's Theater. The reaction to this crime furnishes the final proof of the president's popularity. The New York *Commercial Advertiser,* in mourning about the calamity, stated, "Never before, since the President came from Springfield to assume the high duties of his office had he gained so large a share of public confidence as yesterday. His bitterest enemies were ready to trust him to the fullest extent, and the people felt that to him could be safely committed the measures of reconstruction." The St. Louis *Missouri Democrat* grieved: "The nation has lost a chief, whom it had loved and trusted." The *Chicago Tribune* stated, "that in Abraham Lincoln we have lost one whose place can never be filled, either in the executive chair or in our affections." As the New York *Christian*

Advocate and Journal reminded its readers, "The common sense of the nation is that he was eminently and incomparatively great." Louis Bryan Adams , the correspondent of the Detroit *Advertiser and Tribune,* reported from Washington that everyone was dumb and paralyzed with the great woe which had so suddenly come upon the nation and could not yet realize that "the man to whom the nation has looked up to with such faith and trust, is gone. . . ."[32]

The response to the assassination again gave evidence of the widespread tendency to compare Lincoln to Washington. Lincoln "had become to be regarded, and justly, as the savior of the country, a second Washington," wrote the Springfield *Republican.* The *New York Herald,* reporting the "appalling tragedy," pointed out, "The simple, genial, generous hearted, Honest Old Abe had taken a closer hold on the affections of the people than any of their chosen favorites since the days of Washington," and the *Cincinnati Commercial* agreed that "The bullet that pierced the head of President Lincoln touched the heart of the nation. No event since the death of Washington has so filled the land with sorrow." Carl Schurz believed that after Washington, Lincoln was our greatest president, and *Frank Leslie's Illustrated Newspaper* went even further by comparing Lincoln to Jesus Christ. "Christ died to make men holy; he died to make men free," it wrote.[33]

The military forces were deeply affected by the assassination. General Robert McAllister grieved to his wife, "O, what a loss to the country and the world. What a crime before God and Heaven! The army was and is united for Lincoln and the administration. The soldiers loved him!" George W. Squier wrote to his wife, "Almost every soldier feels he has lost a near and dear friend"; he also compared the fallen leader to George Washington, as many did. Chaplain Hallock Armstrong wrote to his wife from Petersburg, "History will record the name of Lincoln side by side with that of Washington," a sentiment the Michigan volunteer David Lane fully shared. Enlisted soldier Joseph R. Ward Jr., commented, "Our noble President, the idol of the people and the savior of the Republic, was snatched from us as if in a horrible dream, from which one hopes soon to awake."[34] Jenkin L. Jones described the great gloom among his comrades, all of whom regarded the loss like one of a dear relative, as did Elisha Hunt Rhodes of the 2nd Rhode Island Regiment. Chaplain John J. Hight of the 58th Indiana Regiment not only was shocked thunderstruck by the news of the assassination "of the purest and best president we have ever had," but also recorded the deep impression it made on the soldiers, "who speak of him with profound reverence." Massachusetts artillerist William Hamblin, commenting that the South had lost its best friend, noted the bad feeling prevailing in the army, and Private Benjamin T. Smith of Kankakee, Illinois, detected the same sentiment in Chicago. From near Montgomery, Alabama, the Wisconsin soldier James K. Newton told his parents, "Nowhere is such sincere sorrow felt as here in the army. No man, not even Grant himself, possesses the entire love of the army as did President Lincoln. We mourn him not only as a President but as a man, for we had learned to love him as one possessed of every manly principle."[35]

In Europe, even the long hostile London *Times* admitted that "it would be unjust not to acknowledge that Mr. Lincoln was a man who could not under any circumstances have been replaced," and thought that Englishmen could be proud of such a man of their "race." *Punch* published a cartoon entitled, "Britannia Sympathizes with Columbia," and the London *Spectator* commented that the South had lost its best friend, as Lincoln desired unity and peace with conciliation. Forgiving and generous as he was, he would have tendered "everything that was honorable, to the rebels of the South." In France, the conservative *Pays* called the deceased "a good man, a man of faith, and by character a great citizen," while the liberal *Siècle,* referring to

Lincoln as a martyr to a great cause who would be mourned by friends of liberty in the entire world, characterized him as the "austere and sacred personification of a great epoch, the truest expression of democracy." And in Germany, the *Frankfurter Journal* labeled the death of Lincoln and the putative assassination of Seward "terrible blows for the further peaceful development of the transatlantic republic."[36]

This time, even the Democrats and other opponents had to concede some good traits to their long-time antagonist. "Perhaps no member of this society appreciates more fully than I do, the difficult task which President Lincoln had to perform, and I am sure none can deplore his death more sincerely than I do," wrote former president Millard Fillmore. "It is well known that I have not approved of all acts which have been done in his name during his administration, but I am happy to say that his recent course met my approbation. . . ." The Albany *Atlas and Argus,* one of his most bitter critics, now admitted, "A wanton, cruel, infamous crime has taken off the Chief Magistrate of the country at a moment when all his endeavors were concentrated on the restoration of peace and when his heart was full of purpose of mercy. It is a crime against the nation, against humanity, against liberty that has been perpetrated." Maria Lydig Daly, the New York Democratic Unionist, after recounting the alleged faults with which she had always charged the president, now thought, "All this will be forgotten in this shameful, cowardly act of his assassination, whilst his heart was full of forgiveness to his enemies, and whilst he was planning the good of all, having only just now begun to understand the work which the South thrust upon him." Of course, there were some who disagreed, like the Maryland journalist William Wilkins Glenn, who still called Lincoln a dictator, and the Indiana Copperhead John Rupright in Adams County, who said he was damned glad Lincoln was dead, and whose friend George Judd told several ladies present that Lincoln died at 7 o'clock and went to hell. But these critics were in a distinct minority.[37]

Southern opinion varied. Confederate Captain Joseph Julius Wescoat, a prisoner of war at Fort Delaware, wrote, "Lincoln was assassinated last night. What a pity. What a pity." He was afraid that, as he put it, "we poor devils will have to suffer for his death," a sentiment shared by the Southern refugee Judith W. McGuire, who nevertheless thought that by his abolition theories he had caused the shedding of oceans of Southern blood, and according to scripture, by man his blood had now been shed. The Confederate war clerk J. B. Stone was afraid that the deed might be a calamity for the defeated Confederacy as it might render Northern troops more uncontrollable to perpetuate deeds of horror on Southerners. Near Athens, Georgia, Minerva Leah Rowles McClatchey called the act a "piece of unnecessary barbarity" because, though Lincoln had done a great deal of evil, he might have thought that he was right. Even Confederate Captain John Dooley, who accused the president of all the usual crimes attributed to him in the South, admitted that assassination was a bad method of getting rid of "the monster," and John A. Campbell, ex-supreme court justice, appreciating Lincoln's genuine sympathy for Southern bereavement and destitution, wrote to Horace Greeley, "My intercourse with President Lincoln, both here and at Hampton Roads, impressed me favorably and kindly to him." But there were those who unreservedly cheered for John Wilkes Booth.[38]

In conclusion, then, it is obvious that Abraham Lincoln was not at all the unpopular chief executive pictured by so many. Like every other president, he had his admirers and detractors, but unlike his successors and predecessors, he was compared to George Washington almost from the beginning. There was a general appreciation of his honesty, patriotism, and loyalty to the Constitution, as well as of his perfect representation of the American dream. Even though his writing and public speaking ability were often criticized, eventually any number of observers realized that the Gettysburg and Second Inaugural Addresses were outstanding. That he became a national hero immediately after the assassination was to be expected; but even prior to the crime, his future renown was often predicted. And in many ways, Lincoln's later fame was built on his previous encomiums. Almost immediately, the comparison to Washington was taken up; his honesty and integrity became an indispensable part of his fame; his kindness, common sense, and lack of passion were widely praised; and his self-possession and rise from rail-splitter to president frequently eulogized. The national hero of later years, the universally admired emancipator, and the glorious savior of the Union became the common heritage of the nation; if there were occasional criticisms, if the blacks lost some of their previous enthusiasm, these were exceptions. By and large, Lincoln has remained what his admirers saw during his administration: A great president, probably the greatest of them all.

Notes

Abbreviations

Appendix—Ap.
Compare—cf.
Congress—Cong.
Compiler—cpl.
Library of Congress—LC
Lincoln Papers—LP

Introduction

1. Merrill D. Peterson, *Lincoln in American Memory* (New York: Oxford, 1994), 1–35, passim.

2. J. G. Randall, "The Unpopular Mr. Lincoln," *Abraham Lincoln Quarterly*, II (June 1943), 255–80, esp. 256.

3. See below, passim.

4. *Sangamo Journal*, July 16, 1836, in Herbert Mitgang, ed., *Lincoln As They Saw Him* (New York: Rinehardt, 1956), 10–11.

5. *Sangamo Journal*, July 12, 1836, in ibid., 11–12.

6. Springfield *Illinois State Register*, Nov. 23, 1839, in ibid., 14–17.

7. *Sangamo Journal*, Oct. 15, 1841, Feb. 5, 12, 1846, in ibid., 26–27, 46–47.

8. *New York Tribune*, June 22, 1848; Anson S. Miller to Anson S. Henry, June 8, 1849; Judge David Davis to Lincoln Feb. 21, 1849, Abraham Lincoln Papers (hereafter referred to as LP), Library of Congress, Washington, DC (hereafter referred to as LC); microfilm.

9. *Quincy Whig* in Springfield, Illinois *State Journal*, Sept. 15, 1854; in Mitgang, *Lincoln*, 70; Augustus Adams to Lincoln, Dec. 17, 1854, LP; Elihu Washburne to Lincoln, Dec. 26, 1854, LP.

10. Elihu Washburne to Lincoln, Jan. 12, 1855; *New York Tribune,* June 20, 1856; *Chicago Tribune,* June 19, 1856; also in Mitgang, *Lincoln,* 90–92.

11. Owen Lovejoy to Lincoln, June 30, 1858, LP; Edward Magdol, *Owen Lovejoy: Abolitionist in Congress* (New Brunswick, N. J.: Rutgers Univ. Press, 1967), 204; *New York Times,* July 16, 1858.

12. New York *Evening Post,* Aug. 16, 27, 1858; James Aiken to Lincoln, Aug. 16, 1858; *New York Tribune,* Aug. 26, 1858; Hiram W. Beckwith to Lincoln, Aug. 31, 1858, LP; New York *Evening Post,* Sept. 7, 1858; Samuel Galloway to Lincoln, Sept. 1, 1858, LP.

13. Chester P. Dewey to Lincoln, Oct. 30, 1858, David Davis to Lincoln, Sept. 25, 1858, LP.

14. H. P. H. Brownell to Lincoln, Nov. 5, 1858, LP; B. Lundy to Lincoln, Nov. 22, 1858, LP; Anson G. Henry to Lincoln, Feb. 15, 1859, LP; *New York Times,* Mar. 24, 1859; T. J. Pickett to Lincoln, Apr. 13, 1859; Ethelbert P. Oliphant to Lincoln, July 28, 1859, LP.

15. *Weekly Dayton Journal,* Sept. 20, 1859, in David J. Ryan, "Lincoln and Ohio," in *Ohio Archaeological and Historical Publications,* I, XXXII (1923), 64; Horace Rublee to Lincoln, September 25, 1859, LP; William T. Bascom to Lincoln, Sept. 30, 1859, LP; Simeon Frances to Lincoln, Oct. 29, 1859 LP; L. L. Jones et al. to Lincoln, Nov. 29, 1859, LP.

16. Springfield, Illinois *State Register,* Nov. 23, 1839, Mar. 10, 1848, in Mitgang, *Lincoln,* 14–15, 57.

17. Harold Holzer, ed., *The Lincoln-Douglas Debates* (New York: Harper Collins, 1993; reprinted New York: Fordham University Press, 2004), 115, 141–42, 147, 150, 151.

18. *Allentown Democrat,* Jan. 9, 1861, in Howard Cecil Perkins, *Northern Editorials on Secession* (2 vols., New York: Appleton, 1942), I, 250; Oliver Johnson to William Lloyd Garrison, Aug. 9, 1860, in Walter Merrill, ed., *The Letters of William Lloyd Garrison* (6 vols., Cambridge: Harvard Univ. Press, 1971–81), IV, 687; The *Liberator,* July 13, Nov. 9, 1860; Columbus *Ohio Statesman,* September 17, 1859, in Ryan, "Lincoln and Ohio," 61–62; *Cincinnati Enquirer,* ibid., 98–99. The difference between the radicals and the conservatives was their attitude toward slavery; the former opposed any compromises with the South; the latter were more conciliatory.

19. Albany *Atlas and Argus,* May 19, 1860.

Chapter 1: Nomination and Election, 1860–1861

1. Springfield *Illinois State Journal,* Jan. 14, 1860.
2. Joseph M. Lucas to Lincoln, Jan. 26, 1860, LP; Charles Billinghurst to Lincoln, Feb. 8, 1860, LP; Charles Nook to Lincoln, Feb. 9, 1860, LP; Horace Rublee to Lincoln, Feb. 13, 1860, LP; *New York Times,* Dec. 5, 1859; David Herbert Donald, *Lincoln* (New York: Simon & Schuster, 1995), 235, 237.
3. *New York Tribune,* Feb. 28, 1860; Harold Holzer, *Lincoln at Cooper Union* (New York: Simon & Schuster, 2004); also in Mitgang, *Lincoln,* 158–59; William Cullen Bryant II and Thomas G. Voss, eds., *The Letters of William Cullen Bryant* (6 vols., New York: Fordham Univ. Press, 1984), IV, 142; James A. Briggs to Lincoln, Feb. 29, 1860, in Davie C. Mearns, *The Lincoln Papers* (2 vols, Garden City, NY: Doubleday, 1948), I, 231; Samuel Galloway to John Covode, Mar. 10, 1860, John Covode Papers, LC; E. D. Hay to Lyman Trumbull, Mar. 11, 1860, Lyman Trumbull Papers, LC.
4. Trumbull to Lincoln, Mar. 26, 1860; E. D. Hay to Trumbull, Mar. 11, 1860, Trumbull Papers; James Wilson to Henry Lane, Mar. 11, 1860; Henry Lane Papers, Indiana Historical Society; F. Finck to Lincoln, Apr. 16, 1860, LP.
5. *Chicago Tribune,* May 15, 1860.
6. *New York Tribune,* May 19, 1860; New York *Evening Post,* May 19, 1860; *Congressional Globe,* 36th Cong., 2nd Sess., 277–80, Ap., 417–19.
7. Daniel Ullman's speech at Newark, June 12, 1860, W. H. Lampert to Ullman, July 16, 1860, Daniel Ullman Papers, New York Historical Society, hereafter referred to as NYHS; T. J. Moore to Horace Greeley, July 5, 1860, Horace Greeley Papers, New York Public Library, hereafter referred to as NYPL; Leonard Swett to Lincoln, July 16, 1860, Joshua R. Giddings to Lincoln, May 18, 1860, Trumbull to Lincoln, May 10, 1860, LP; *Independent,* May 24, 1860; Hans L. Trefousse, *Benjamin Franklin Wade* (New York: Twayne, 1963), 128–29.
8. Charles Richard Williams, ed., *Diary and Letters of Rutherford B. Hayes* (5 vols., Columbus: Ohio State Archaeological and Historical Society, 1924), I, 555; Dr. A. Nourse to Hamlin, May 20, 1860, Hannibal Hamlin Papers, University of Maine, Columbia University, microfilm; Charles Sumner to Duchess of Argyle, May 22, 1860, in Beverly Wilson Palmer, ed., *The Selected Letters of Charles Sumner* (Boston: Northeastern Univ. Press, 1990), II, 24.

9. Allan Nevins and Milton Helsey, eds., *The Diary of George Templeton Strong* (4 vols., New York: Octagon, 1974), III, 28; James Miller to Seward, May 19, 1860, William R. G. Mellen to Mrs. Seward, May 21, 1860, D. Van Kleck to Seward, May 18, 1860, Seward Papers, Rochester University (microfilm).

10. Albany *Atlas and Argus*, May 19, 1860.

11. *Philadelphia Evening Journal*, in *New York Tribune*, May 24, 1860, also in Mitgang, *Lincoln*, 180–81; *Congressional Globe*, 36th Cong., 2nd Sess., 334; J. G. to Tilden, May 21, 1860, Samuel Tilden Papers, NYPL.

12. *Louisville Daily Courier*, May 26, 1860, in Dwight Lowell Dumond, *Southern Editorials on Secession* (New York: Century, 1931), 114; Richmond *Enquirer*, May 22, 1860.

13. *Congressional Globe*, 36th Cong., 2nd Sess., 2237; *New Orleans Bee*, in Springfield, Illinois *Journal*, June 2, 13, 14, in Mitgang, *Lincoln*, 191–92.

14. Lord Richard B. Lyons to Earl Russell, May 22, July 23, 1860, in James J. and Patience P. Barnes, *Private and Confidential Letters from British Ministers in Washington to the Foreign Secretaries in London, 1844–67* (Selinsgrove: Susquehanna Univ. Press, 1963), 233, 34.

15. *Edinburgh Review*, CXII (Oct. 1860), 581; Sigmund Diamond, ed., *A Casual View of America: The Home Letters of Salomon de Rothschild 1859–1861* (Stanford: Stanford Univ. Press, 1961), 43, May 22, 1860.

16. William Cullen Bryant to Lincoln, June 16, 1860, LP.

17. *Congressional Globe*, 36th Cong., 2nd Sess., Ap. 417–19; *Rochester Evening Express*, June 1, 1860, in LP; Colfax to Lincoln, May 26, 1860, LP.

18. N. S. Morrill to Justin Morrill, July 2, 1860, Morrill Papers, LC ; Samuel Hoffman to Lincoln, June 29, 1860, Alexander Ramsey to Lincoln, June 7, 1860, William M. Reynolds to Lincoln, July 25, 1860, LP; T. J. Moore to Horace Greeley, July 4, 1860, Greeley Papers, NYPL; Springfield *Illinois State Journal*, May 19, 1860.

19. *Momus*, June 2, 1860, in Gary L. Bunker, *From Rail-Splitter to Icon: Lincoln's Image in Illustrated Periodicals, 1860–1865* (Kent: Kent State Univ. Press, 2001), 35; Edward L. Pierce to Lincoln, July 20, 1860, LP.

20. Owen Lovejoy to Lincoln, June 10, 1860, Sumner to Lincoln, June 8, 1860, LP; *Douglass' Monthly*, June 1860.

21. J. Medill to Lincoln, June 19, 1860, in Mearns, ed., *The Lincoln Papers* (2 vols., Garden City, NY: Doubleday, 1948), I, 261–62; *New York Commercial Advertiser,* June 20, 1860.

22. Ibid., May 19, 24, 1860; *New York Tribune,* May 19, 21, 1860; *New Hampshire Palladium,* May 19, 1860, in LP; *New York Times,* May 19, 1860; *Harper's Weekly,* May 26, 1860; *Congressional Globe,* 36th Cong., 2nd Sess., 277–80, Ap. 417–25; James Doolittle to Hamlin, Aug. 19, 1860, Hamlin Papers; Leonard Swett to Lincoln, July 16, 1860, A. K. McClure to Lincoln, Oct. 19, 1860, LP.

23. Stephens to J. Henly Smith, July 10, 1860, in Ulrich Bonnell Phillips, ed., *The Correspondence of Robert Toombs, Alexander H. Stephens, and Howell Cobb* (Annual Report of the American Historical Association, for the Year 1911, II, Washington: 1913), 487; Greensborough, N.C. *Times,* Oct. 6, 1860, Hillsborough, N.C. *Recorder,* Nov. 14, 1860, in Donald E. Reynolds, ed., *Editors Make War: Southern Newspapers in the Secession Crisis* (Nashville: Vanderbilt Univ. Press, 1970), 130, 146; *Wilmington Daily Herald,* Nov. 9, 1860, in Dumond, *Southern Editorials,* 227; *Richmond Semi-Weekly Enquirer,* Aug. 10, 1860.

24. *Providence Daily Post,* Aug. 24, 1860, LP; Albany *Atlas and Argus,* May 19, 1860.

25. *Louisville Daily Journal,* Aug. 21, 1860, in Dumond, *Southern Editorials on Secession,* (New York: 1931) 164–65.

26. *Richmond Semi-Weekly Enquirer,* July 10, Aug. 17, 1860.

27. Montgomery, Alabama *Weekly Mail,* Oct. 26, 1860, in Reynolds, *Editors Make War,* 124–26; *Charleston Mercury,* July 9, 1860, in Emerson David Fite, *The Press Campaign of 1860* (Port Washington: Kennikat Press, 1967), 210; Montgomery, Alabama *Weekly Mail,* Oct. 26, 1860, in Reynolds, *Editors Make War,* 124–26.

28. *Chicago Tribune,* Nov. 7, 1860; *New York Tribune,* Springfield *Illinois State Journal,* Nov. 7, 1860; James M. Grimes to Lyman Trumbull, Nov. 13, 1860, Trumbull Papers, LC; for examples of these opinions, see *New York Times,* Nov. 8, 9, 1860; *Belletristisches Journal,* Nov. 9, 1890; Preston King to Samuel Tilden, Nov. 8, 1860, Tilden Papers, NYPL.

29. George Frisbie Hoar, ed., *Charles Sumner: His Complete Works* (20 vols., Boston: Lee & Shepard, 1900), VII, 78; *Independent,* Nov. 8, 1860; A. Brewer to Wade, Nov. 10, 1860, Benjamin F. Wade Papers, LC; *Congressional Globe,* 36th Cong., 2nd Sess., 101.

30. William S. Thayer to Bancroft Davis, Dec. 23, 1860, in Martin Crawford, ed., "Politicians in Crisis: The Washington Letters of William S. Thayer, Dec. 1860–March 1861," *Civil War History* 27 (Sept. 1987), 231–47; Wendell Phillips, *Speeches, Lectures, and Letters, 2nd Series* (New York: Arno Press, 1969), 294: *Liberator,* Nov. 9, 1860.

31. Albany *Atlas and Argus,* Nov. 8, 1860; William Medill to John S. Tuthill, Dec. 11, 1860, Medill Papers, LC; *Congressional Globe,* 36th Cong., 2nd Sess., Ap., 31–35; ibid., 179.

32. *New Orleans Daily Crescent,* Nov. 12, 1860, in Dumond, *Southern Editorials,* 230–31; Howell Cobb, *Letter . . . to the People of Georgia, Dec. 1860,* Jon L. Wakelyn, *Southern Pamphlets on Secession Nov. 1860– Apr. 1861* (Chapel Hill: Univ. of North Carolina Press, 1996), 88–92.

33. *Congressional Globe,* 36th Cong., 2nd Sess., 3–5, 11, 74; Jefferson Davis to Franklin Pierce, Jan. 21, 1861, Franklin Pierce Papers, LC; Robert Toombs to E. B. Pullin et al., Dec. 13, 1860, in Phillips, *Correspondence of Robert Toombs, Alexander H. Stephens and Howell Cobb,* 520; W. Gilmore Simms considered him a creature wholly unknown. Mary C. Simms Oliphant et al., *The Letters of William Gilmore Simms* (Columbia: Univ. of South Carolina Press, 1955), 295.

34. Douglas to 99 New Orleans Citizens, November 13, 1860, in Robert Johannsen, ed., *The Letters of Stephen A. Douglas* (Urbana: Univ. of Illinois Press, 1961), 501–02; Speech Against Secession, Delivered Before the Legislature of Georgia, Nov. 14, 1860, in Henry Cleveland, *Alexander H. Stephens in Public and Private With Letters and Speeches Before, During, and Since the War* (Philadelphia: National Publishing, 1866), 697; John Campbell to Daniel Chandler, Nov. 23, 1850, in "Papers of Hon. John Campbell, in *Southern Historical Society Papers,* (V, Oct. 1917), 9.

35. John Sherman to William T. Sherman, Nov. 26, 1860, in Rachel Sherman Thorndike, ed., *The Sherman Letters, Correspondence Between General and Senator Sherman. From 1837 to 1891* (New York: Scribner's, 1894), 86–87; P. H. Silvester to Ullman, Nov. 26, 1860, Ullman Papers; Mrs. Louisa Livingston Siemon to Lincoln, Dec. 10, 1860, in Mearns, ed., *Lincoln Papers,* II, 333.

36. Washburne to Lincoln, December 11, 17, 1860, in Mearns, ed., *Lincoln Papers,* II, 335, 344–45; George Worthington Dow to Edmund, Dec. 17, 1860, George Dow Papers, NYHS; Carl Schurz to Mrs. Schurz,

Dec. 17, 1860; Frederick Bancroft, ed., *Speeches, Correspondence and Political Papers of Carl Schurz* (3 vols., New York: Putnam, 1913), I, 168; Palmer, *Sumner*, II, 39.

37. Springfield *Illinois State Journal*, Dec. 21, 1860; C. R. Harrison to Trumbull, Dec. 22, 1860, Samuel Swift to Trumbull, Dec. 27, 1860, E. Stafford to Trumbull, Dec. 20, 1860, Trumbull Papers.

38. Warren J. Bell to Johnson, Jan. 2, 1861, in Leroy P. Graf and Ralph W. Haskins, *The Papers of Andrew Johnson* (17 vols., Knoxville: Univ. of Tennessee Press, 1967), IV, 116; C. H. Ray to Washburne, Jan. 7, 1861, Washburne Papers, LC.

39. Salmon P. Chase to George Opdyke, Jan. 9, 1861, in John Niven, ed., *The Chase Papers* (5 vols., Kent, OH: Kent State Univ. Press, 1993–98), III, 44–45; W. Jayne to Lyman Trumbull, Jan. 28, 1861, Trumbull Papers; Schurz to Mrs. Schurz, Jan. 29, 1861, in Joseph Schafer, ed., *Intimate Letters of Carl Schurz 1841–1869* (New York: Da Capo Press, 1970), 240. New York *Commercial Advertiser*, February 5, 1861; *Congressional Globe*, 36th Cong., 2nd Sess., 186–87, Ap. 121. Oris S. Ferry of Connecticut cited other founding fathers, as well as agreeing with Lincoln that slavery would eventually disappear. *Congressional Globe*, 36th Cong., 2nd Sess., 550.

40. *Cincinnati Gazette*, Jan. 5, 1861; *Cincinnati Commercial*, Jan. 7, 1861; Lyman Trumbull to Hannibal Hamlin, Jan. 2, 1861, Hannibal Hamlin Papers; Leonard Swett to David Davis, Jan. 1, 1861, David Davis Papers, LC.

41. St. Louis *Daily Missouri Republican*, Jan. 14, 1861, in Dumond, *Southern Editorials*, 293–95; *Congressional Globe*, 36th Cong., 2nd Sess., 149, Ap., 99, 123, 76–80, 196–99.

42. Springfield *Illinois State Journal*, Feb. 12, 1861; Garfield to Mrs. Garfield, Feb. 17, 1861, in Theodore Clark Smith, *The Life and Letters of James Abram Garfield* (2 vols., New Haven: Yale Univ. Press, 1925), I, 155; *Cincinnati Gazette*, Feb. 13, 1861. Two days earlier, Francis Springer of Springfield had already written him that God would make him second to none but George Washington. Francis Springer to Lincoln, Feb. 11, 1861, in Mearns, ed., *Lincoln Papers*, II, 436; New York *Sun*, Feb. 14, 1861.

43. Gaile Thornborough et al., eds., *The Diary of Calvin Fletcher* (9 vols., Indianapolis: Indiana Historical Society, 1978), VII, 54–55; *Portland Transcript* Mar. 2, 1861; *Harper's Weekly*, Mar. 9, 1861; also in

Harold Holzer, *Lincoln Seen & Heard* (Lawrence: Univ. Press of Kansas, 2000), 117; *New York Times,* Feb. 15, 1861; *Chicago Tribune,* Feb. 25, 1861; *Congressional Globe,* 36th Cong., 2nd Sess., 1068. On Apr. 21, however, *Harper's Weekly* published a flattering photograph of the new president. *Harper's Weekly,* Apr. 21, 1861.

44. *Congressional Globe,* 36th Cong., 2nd Sess., Ap., 300; *Congressional Globe,* 36th Cong., 2nd Sess., Ap., 246–50, 257–61, New Orleans *Daily Crescent,* Feb. 21, 1861, in Dumond, *Southern Editorials,* 265–67.

45. *Charleston Mercury,* Feb. 26, 1861, in Mitgang, *Lincoln,* 234; *Congressional Globe,* 36th Cong., 2nd Sess., 1397, 1067, 1151, Ap., 259, 233.

Chapter 2: The First Year

1. *Philadelphia Inquirer,* Mar. 5, 1861; New York *Commercial Advertiser,* Mar. 5, 1861; Springfield *Republican,* Mar. 5, 1861; *Cincinnati Commercial,* Mar. 5, 1861.

2. Edwin D. Morgan to Lincoln, Mar. 5, 1861, LP; Justin Morrill to "Louise," Mar. 5, 1861, Morrill Papers, LC; Francis Low to Trumbull, Mar. 7, 1861, John R. Jewett to Trumbull, Mar. 6, 1861, Trumbull Papers; *Frank Leslie's Illustrated Newspaper,* Mar. 9, 1861.

3. Donald B. Cole and John J. McDonough, eds., Benjamin B. French, *Witness to the Young Republic* (Hanover, N.H.: Univ. Press of New England, 1989), 348–49; Nicholas B. Wainwright, ed., *A Philadelphia Perspective: The Diary of Sidney George Fisher Covering the Years 1834 to 1871* (Philadelphia: Historical Society of Pennsylvania, 1967), 380; Neal Dow to Lincoln, Mar. 13, 1861, LP 4. *New York Tribune,* Mar. 5, 1861.

5. L. B. Conisius to John Albion Andrew, Mar. 6, 1861, Andrew Papers, Massachusetts Historical Society; Boston; The *Liberator,* Mar. 8, 1861.

6. Sumner to Duchess of Argyle, Mar. 19, 1861, in Palmer, *Sumner Letters,* II 61.

7. *New York Herald,* Mar. 5, 1861; Albany *Atlas and Argus,* Mar. 5, 1861; *Congressional Globe,* 37th Cong., Special Sess., 1436–37.

8. Ibid., 1436–38.

9. *New-Yorker Staats-Zeitung* (weekly), Mar. 7, 1861; Columbus *Crisis,* Mar. 7, 14, 1861.

10. *Richmond Semi-Weekly Enquirer*, Mar. 5, 7, 1861; John F. Marszalek, ed., *The Diary of Miss Emma Holmes 1861–1866* (Baton Rouge: Louisiana State Univ. Press, 1979). 11.

11. *Congressional Globe*, 37th Cong., Special Sess., 1436, 1439–46.

12. James D. Davidson to James B. Donnan, Mar. 6, 1861, in James D. Davidson, "Unionists in Rockbridge County," in *Virginia Magazine of History and Biography*, 73 (1965), 89–92; Jonathan Worth to B. G. Worth, Mar. 16, 1861, in J.G. de Roulhac Hamilton, ed., *The Correspondence of Jonathan Worth* (2 vols., Raleigh: Edward & Broughton, 1909), 134.

13. Raleigh *North Carolina Standard*, Mar. 9, 1861, in Dumond, *Southern Editorials*, 476–79; *Knoxville Whig*, Mar. 9, 1861, in Reynolds, *Editors Make War*, 191.

14. Charles C. Jones to Rev. C. C. Jones, Mar. 5, 1861, in Robert Manson Myers, *The Children of Pride: The True Story of Georgia and the Civil War* (New Haven: Yale Univ. Press, 1972), 655; C. Vann Woodward, ed., *Mary Chesnut's Civil War* (New Haven: Yale Univ. Press, 1981), 23; New Orleans *Picayune*, Mar. 6, 8, 1861.

15. London *Morning Chronicle*, Mar. 18, 1861; *Le Moniteur*, Mar. 21, 1861.

16. *Frankfurter Journal*, Mar. 18, 1861; The Regent Captains of San Marino to Lincoln, May 29, 1861, in Belle Becker Sideman and Lillian Friedman, eds., *Europe Looks at the Civil War* (New York: Orion Press, 1960), 55–56; London *Times*, Mar. 16, 18, 19, 1861.

17. Henri Mercier to Foreign Office, Mar. 7, 17, 1861, Archive, Ministère des Affaires Étrangères, Paris.

18. Sideman and Friedman, eds., *Europe Looks at the Civil War*, 42; F. A. Golder, "A Russian View of the American Civil War," *American Historical Review*, 26 (1921), 157. (Oct. 1920–July 1921), 157, n. 9; Eduard de Stoeckl to Prince Alexander Mikhhailovich Gorchakov, Mar. 12, 25, 1861, in Albert A. Woldman, *Lincoln and the Russians* (Cleveland: World Publishing Co., 1952, 43, 47–48; Rudolph Schleiden, Mar. 4, 1861, Schleiden Papers, LC, microfilm; Lord Lyons to Lord John Russell, Mar. 26, 1861, in Lord Newton, *Lord Lyons: A Record of British Diplomacy* (2 vols., London: Edward & Arnold, 1913), I, 34.

19. Justin Morrill to Mrs. Morrill, Mar. 1, 1861, Morrill Papers, LC; L. B. Canisius to Governor Andrew, Mar. 6, 1861, Andrew Papers.

20. *Philadelphia Inquirer*, Mar. 2, 1861; Charles W. Dennison to Lincoln, Mar. 11, 1861, LP.

21. For example, see John P. Crawford to Lincoln, Aug. 10, 1861, LP; Boston *Transcript,* Aug. 18, 1861, in *New York Tribune,* Aug. 22, 1861. Also see below, 20.

22. *Cincinnati Gazette,* Mar. 11, 1861; *Philadelphia Inquirer,* Apr. 1, 1861; New York *Commercial Advertiser,* Apr. 4, 1861; South Bend *Register,* April 4, 1861, in LP, Second Series.

23. John Greenleaf Whittier to Charles Sumner, March 29, 1861, in John B. Pickard, *The Letters of John Greenleaf Whittier 1861–1892* (3 vols, Cambridge, Mass.: Harvard Univ. Press, 1975), III, 11; William T. Sherman to John Sherman, Apr. 2, 1861, in Brooks D. Simpson and Jean V. Berlin, eds., *Sherman's Selected Correspondence of the Civil War* (Chapel Hill: Univ. of North Carolina Press, 1999), 71; Schuyler Colfax to Lincoln, March 6, 1861, Rufus King to Lincoln, Mar. 18, 1861, LP; George W. Dow to Cousin George, March 15, 1861, Dow Papers, NYHS.

24. James Wien Forney to Lincoln, Mar. 25, 1861, James A. McDougall to Lincoln, Mar. 23, 1861, LP.

25. Eleanor F. Strong to Johnson, Mar. 26, 1861, in Graf and Haskins, *Papers of Andrew Johnson,* IV, 434; Adam Gurowski to Lincoln, Mar. 12, 1861, LP; Adam Gurowski, *Diary* (3 vols., New York: Burt Franklin, 1968 repr.), I, 31; Sumner to Duchess of Argyle, Mar. 15, 1861, in Palmer, *Sumner Letters,* II, 61–64.

26. *Congressional Globe,* 37th Cong., Special Session, 1478, 1485; 1501–02; 1510; *Charleston Mercury* (tri-weekly), Apr. 6, 1861; LP, Apr. 8, 1861.

27. Webb to Lincoln, Apr. 11, 1861, LP; Washington *Evening Star,* Apr. 12, 1861; *New York Tribune,* Apr. 13, 1861; *New York Herald,* Apr. 16, 1861.

28. *Chicago Tribune,* Apr. 22, 1861; Jupiter Hesser to Lincoln, Apr. 15, 1861, Henry P. Tappan to Lincoln, Apr. 19, 1861, LP; Browning to Lincoln, Apr. 18, 22, 1861; *Belletristisches Journal,* Apr. 19, 1861; Sumner to Fessenden, Apr. 16, 1861, in Palmer, *Sumner Letters,* II, 65 *Harper's Weekly,* Apr. 13, 27, 1861; Horace W. Raper, ed, *The Papers of William Woods Holden 1841–1868* (Raleigh: Division of Archives and History, 2000), 120 is an example of Southern opinion.

29. *New York Times,* May 9, 1861, Henry Wilson to Lincoln, May 16, 1861, LP; *Philadelphia Inquirer,* May 4, 1861; John Esterbrook to Trumbull, June 29, 1861, Trumbull Papers.

30. *Cicninnati Gazette,* June 3, 1861; Springfield *Republican,* June 6,

1861; Washington *National Intelligencer,* June 30, 1861; *Philadelphia Inquirer,* June 1, 1861.

31. *Congressional Globe,* 37th Cong., 1st Sess., 41 (Willard Saulsbury's speech); *Brooklyn Eagle,* Apr. 13, 1861; Albany *Atlas and Argus,* Apr. 12, 1861; G. K. Warren to Van Buren, Apr. 20, 1861, Martin Van Buren Papers, LC; Columbus *Crisis,* June 27, 1861.

32. *Manchester Guardian,* May 3, 1861; *Frankfurter Journal,* May 3, 1861; *Moniteur,* May 23, 1861; Joseph Aspinwall to Lincoln, May 10, 1861, LP.

33. *Cincinnati Gazette,* July 6, 1861; New York *Sun,* July 6, 1861; Washington *National Intelligencer,* July 6, 1861; New York *Commercial Advertiser,* July 6, 1861; *Harper's Weekly,* July 20, 1861; Lucius Eugene Chittenden, *Invisible Stage: the Journal of Lucius Eugene Chittenden Apr. 10, 1861 to July 14, 1861* (San Diego: American Exchange Press, 1969), 130; Richard Milford Blatchford to Seward, July 6, 1861, Seward Papers.

34. Nicholas B. Wainwright, ed., *A Philadelphia Prospective: The Diary of Sidney George Fisher Concerning the Years 1834–1871* (Philadelphia: Historical Society of Pennsylvania, 1967), 396; F. A. McNeill to Washburne, July 9, 1861, Washburne Papers; Hamlin to Mrs. Hamlin, July 9, 1861, Hamlin Papers, microfilm, Columbia University; *New York Tribune,* July 14, 1861; *Congressional Globe,* 37th Cong., 1st Sess, 42, Edward McPherson, *The Political History of the United States of America During the Great Rebellion* (New York: Da Capo Press, 1972), 115.

35. *Congressional Globe* 37th Cong., 1st Sess., 56–80, 118–19, 142–43, 188–189.

36. *New York Times,* Aug. 1, 1861; B. F. Stein to Covode, July 31, 1861, Covode Papers, LC; Granville Moody to Lincoln, Aug. 10, 1861, Browning to Lincoln, Aug. 19, 1861, LP; William Reddich to Trumbull, July 25, 1861, Trumbull Papers; Philadelphia *Press,* Aug. 16, 1861.

37. New York *Commercial Advertiser,* Sept. 16, 18, 1861; Washington *National Intelligencer,* Sept. 23, 1861, Springfield *Republican,* Sept. 17, 21, 1861.

38. Frederick A. Aiken to Seward, Oct. 4, 1861, Seward Papers. He also heard the opposite from others. See Joseph Warren to Seward, Sept. 23, 1861, Edgar Conkling to Seward, Oct. 1, 1861, Seward Papers, University of Rochester (microfilm); *Philadelphia Intelligencer,* Oct. 23, 1861; New York *Commercial Advertiser,* Nov. 4, 1861.

39. Sumner to Henry Wadsworth Longfellow, Apr. 7, 1861, in Palmer, *Sumner Letters*, II, 64; Gurowski, *Diary*, I, 24 ff., 54; Wade to Elisha Whittlesey, Apr. 30, 1861, Whittlesey Papers, Western Reserve Historical Society, Cleveland, OH; George Boutwell to Andrew, Apr. 24, 1861, Andrew Papers; *Liberator*, July 12, 1861; George Loring to Butler, Aug. 6, 1861, in Jessie Ames Marshall, cpl., *Private and Official Correspondence of General Benjamin F. Butler During the Period of the Civil War* (5 vols., Norwood, MA: Private printing, 1917), I, 191–92.

40. Joseph Medill to Chase, Sept. 15, 1861, in Niven, *Chase Papers*, 3, 97; Sumner to Francis Lieber, Sept. 19, 1861, in Palmer, *Sumner Letters*, II, 79; *Liberator*, Sept. 20, 1861; *Cincinnati Commercial*, Sept. 16, 1861.

41. George B. McClellan to Mrs. McClellan, Aug. 16, 1861, McClellan Papers, New Jersey Historical Society, Newark, NJ; Albany *Atlas and Argus*, Sept. 18, 19, 1861; *New-Yorker Staats-Zeitung*, Aug. 29, September 19, 1861; Columbus *Crisis*, Sept. 19, 1861.

42. For example, Jonathan Worth, "To the People of Randolph County, Raleigh, May 1861," in J. G. de Roulhac Hamilton, ed., *The Correspondence of Jonathan Worth* (2 vols., Raleigh: Edwards & Broughton, 1909), 136–37; *Richmond Enquirer*, Aug. 12, 1861; Charles E. Jones to Mary Jones, Sept. 18, 1861, in Myers, *The Children of Pride: The True Story of Georgia and the Civil War*, 748; *Charleston Courier*, May 30, 1861.

43. *Moniteur*, Oct. 6, 1861; London *Quarterly Review*, 110 (July and Oct. 1861), 275; London *Times*, Aug. 23, 1861; *Frankfurter Journal*, Sept. 19, 1861; Bulwer Lytton, Speech Before the Harts Agricultural Society, Sept. 25, 1861, in Sideman and Friedman, eds., *Europe Looks at the Civil War*, 93–94.

44. New York *Commercial Advertiser*, Nov. 4, 1861; Victor Post Ranney, ed., *The Papers of Fredrick Law Olmsted*, Vol. 15, *The California Frontier 1863–1865* (Baltimore: Johns Hopkins Univ. Press, 1990), 222, n. 1; Chase to Richard Smith, Nov. 11, 1861, in Niven, *Chase Papers*, III, 108; *Philadelphia Inquirer*, Oct. 23, 1861.

45. *New York Tribune*, Nov. 2, 1861; *Frank Leslie's Illustrated Newspaper*, Nov. 23, 1861; *Cincinnati Commercial*, Nov. 6, 8, 1861; B. F. Wade to C. D. Dana, Feb. 3, 1861, C. D. Dana Papers, LC; *Harper's Weekly*, Nov. 23, 1861.

46. Hayes to Mrs. Hayes, Oct. 19, 1861, in Williams, ed., *Diary and*

Letters of Rutherford B. Hayes, II, 120; A. Alvord to Seward, Oct. 26, 1861, Seward Papers; Bennett to Lincoln, October 22, 1861, LP; Thomas Batman to Lincoln, Nov. 18, 1861, LP; Benjamin B. French Diary, Nov. 24, 1864, in Donald B. Cole and John J. McDonough, eds., *Witness to the Young Republic, a Yankee's Journal 1828–1870* (Hanover, NH: Univ. Press of New England, 1989), 381; Michael Burlingame, ed., *Dispatches from Lincoln's White House: The Anonymous Civil War Journalism of Presidential Secretary William O. Stoddard* (Lincoln: Univ. of Nebraska Press, 2002), 38.

47. Thomas Ewing to Lincoln, Nov. 18, 1861, Prince de Joinville to Lincoln, Dec. 1, 1861, Millard Fillmore to Lincoln, Dec. 16, 1861, LP; Henry L. Abbot to Mother, Nov. 30, 1861, in Robert Garth Scott, ed., *Fallen Leaves: The Civil War Letters of Major Henry Livermore Abbott* (Kent, OH: Kent Univ. Press, 1991), 83. For Lincoln's maneuvering of Seward, see David Herbert Donald, *We Are Lincoln Men: Abraham Lincoln and His Friends* (New York: Simon & Schuster, 2003), 160–62.

48. Sumner to John Bright, Dec. 23, 1861, Sumner to Wendell Philips, Dec. 8, 1861, in Palmer, *Selected Papers of Charles Sumner,* II, 85–87; August Belmont to William Lewis Dayton, December 10, 1861, Dayton Papers, Princeton University; A. W. H. Clapp to Lincoln, Dec. 31, 1861, LP; *Münchner Neuste Nachrichten,* Jan. 11, 1862.

49. Benjamin B. French Diary, Nov. 24, 1864, in Donald B. Cole and John J. McDonough, eds., *Witness to the Young Republic,* 381; New York *Commercial Advertiser,* Dec. 4, 1861; *Philadelphia Inquirer,* Dec. 4, 5, 1861.

50. Washington *Evening Star,* Dec. 4, 1861, cf. Washington *National Intelligencer,* Dec. 4, 1861; *New York Tribune,* Dec. 4, 1861; Springfield *Republican,* Dec. 4, 1861; *New York Times,* Dec. 4, 1861.

51. New York *World,* Dec. 5, 1861; T. S. Bell to Lincoln, Dec. 6, 1861, Edward Everett to Lincoln, Dec. 12, 1861, James A. Hamilton to Lincoln, Dec. 17, 1861, LP; *Cincinnati Commercial,* Dec. 11, 1861; Albany *Atlas and Argus,* Dec. 4, 1861.

52. Brewster to Mother, Dec. 4, 1861; *Independent,* Dec. 1861; Gerrit Smith to Thaddeus Stevens, Dec. 6, 1861, LP; *Belletristisches Journal,* Dec. 6, 1861; Sumner to Phillips, Dec. 8, 1861, in Palmer, ed., *Letters of Charles Sumner,* II, 85; Richmond *Enquirer,* Dec. 9, 1861.

53. W. T. Sherman to Thomas Ewing, Dec. 24, 1861, in Brooks D. Simpson and Jean V. Berlin, eds., *Sherman's Selected Correspondence*

of the Civil War (Chapel Hill: Univ. of North Carolina Press, 1999), 171; Resolution of the Legislature (General Assembly) of Maryland, Dec. 31, 1861, LP.

54. Davis to Lincoln, Jan. 7, 1862, Ellen Sherman to Lincoln, Jan. 9, 1862, Fernando Wood to Lincoln, Jan. 15, 1861, LP; *Congressional Globe,* 37th Cong., 2nd Sess., 404–05, 569; Springfield *Illinois State Journal,* Jan, 9, 1862; *Cincinnati Commercial,* Feb. 10, 1862.

55. H. A. S. Dudley to Covode, Jan. 21, 1862, Covode Papers; Edwards Pierrepont to Lincoln, Jan. 19, 1861, LP, Series II; *Frank Leslie's Illustrated Newspaper,* Feb. 1, 1862; *Philadelphia Inquirer,* Jan. 14, 1862; New York *World,* Jan. 14, 1862; *New York Herald,* Jan. 16, 1862.

56. *Congressional Globe,* 37th Cong., 2nd Sess., 462, 594, 453, 400.

57. Robert G. Shaw to Effie, Apr. 30, 1861, in Russell Duncan, ed., *Blue Eyed Child of Fortune: The Civil War Letters of Robert Gould Shaw* (Athens: Univ. of Georgia Press, 1992), 88; Robert Hunt Rhodes, ed., Elisha Hunt Rhodes, *All for the Union: A History of the 2nd Rhode Island Volunteer Infantry in the War of the Rebellion* (Lincoln, RI., 1985), 20–21; W. N. Colin to Lincoln, Jan. 25, 1862, LP. For unfavorable army views, see Nevins, *Wainwright,* 9; Stephen W. Sears, George B. *McClellan, The Young Napoleon* (New York: Ticknor & Fields, 1988), 114, 131–33. For retention of popularity, see below.

58. Richard Yates to Trumbull, Feb. 14, 1862, Trumbull Papers; James Segar to Lincoln, Jan. 24, 1862, LP, 2nd Series; F. L. Olmsted to Bertha, Jan. 28, 1862, in Ranney, *Olmsted Papers,* IV, 258; Strong, *Diary* IV, 204.

59. Washington *Evening Star,* Feb. 18, 1862; *Congressional Globe,* 37th Cong., 2nd Sess., 909; McClellan to Lincoln, Feb. 22, 1862, Andrew Curtin to Lincoln, Mar. 3, 1862, LP 3, 1862, LP; New York *Evening Post,* Mar. 4, 1862.

Chapter 3: The Second Year: Sustaining Popularity

1. Karl Marx and Friedrich Engels, *The Civil War in the United States* (New York: International Publishers, 1937), 155.

2. James H. Stokes to Trumbull, Mar. 17, 1862, Trumbull Papers; Henry Raymond to Lincoln, Mar. 15, 1862, Thomas H. Hicks to Lincoln, Mar. 18, 1862, LP; Stephen Minot Weld, *War Diary and Letters of*

Stephen Minot Weld 1861–1865 (Cambridge, MA.: Riverside Press, 1912), 72.

3. *Cincinnati Daily Gazette,* Mar. 7, 1862; *New York Tribune,* Mar. 8, 1862.

4. *Philadelphia Inquirer,* Mar. 7, 1862; Washington *National Intelligencer* Mar. 11, 1862; *Belletristisches Journal,* Mar. 14, 1862; Springfield *Republican,* Mar. 8, 27, 1862.

5. Edward Dicey, *Six Months in the Federal States* (2 vols., London: McMillan, 1863), I, 163; John W. Blassingame, ed., *The Frederick Douglass Papers* (5 vols., New Haven: Yale Univ. Press, 1979–1992), III 518; Gurowski, *Diary,* I, 167; *Liberator,* Mar. 14, 1862; Bud B. Chapman to Horace Greeley, Mar. 12, 1862, Greeley Papers.

6. *New York Tribune,* Mar. 17, 1862; *Congressional Globe,* 37th Cong., 2nd Sess., 62; New York *Sun,* Mar. 7, 1862.

7. Albany *Atlas and Argus,* Mar. 8, 1862; *New-Yorker Staats-Zeitung* (weekly) Mar. 12–15, 1862; *Richmond Enquirer,* Mar. 21, 1862.

8. *New York Tribune,* Apr. 6, 13, 1862; John Bright to George Bancroft, Mar. 29, 1862, Bancroft Papers; New York *Commercial Advertiser,* Apr. 8, 1862; London *Times,* Mar. 21, 1862; *Moniteur,* Mar. 25, 1862; Report of Procurateur Général Neveu-Lemoine, Nancy, Apr. 15, 1862, in Lynn M. Case, ed., *French Opinion on the United States and Mexico 1860–1867* (New York: Appleton, 1936), 259; *Münchner Neuste Nachrichten,* Mar. 21, 1862.

9. *Chicago Tribune,* Mar. 13, 1862; *Cincinnati Commercial,* Mar. 13, 1862; *New York Herald,* Mar. 13, 1862; *Cincinnati Gazette,* Apr. 10, 1862.

10. *Philadelphia Inquirer,* Mar. 10, 1862; Resolution of March 12, 1862, LP; *Harper's Weekly,* Mar. 20, 1862.

11. *New York Herald,* Apr. 1, 1862.

12. Washington *National Intelligencer,* Apr. 3, 1862; G. O. Pond to Trumbull, Apr. 4, 1862, Trumbull Papers; Abraham E. Smith to Washburne, Apr. 18, 1862, Washburne Papers.

13. *Boston Journal,* Apr. 19, 1862; *Congressional Globe,* 37th Cong., 2nd Sess., 1732–35; Columbus *Crisis,* Apr. 23, 1862.

14. A. Hart to Lincoln, Apr. 23, 1862, Stoddard to Lincoln, Apr. 23, 1862, LP; Mrs. Chapman Coleman, ed., *The Life of John J. Crittenden with Selections from His Correspondence and Speeches* (2 vols., Philadelphia: J. B. Lippincott, 1871), II, 346.

15. Ledru-Rolin et al. to Lincoln, Apr. 24, 1862, John B. Hepburn to

Lincoln, May 7, 1862, *New York Times,* May 23, 1862; James R. Robertson, ed., *The Civil War Letters of General Robert McAllister* (New Brunswick: Rutgers Univ. Press, 1965), 129; Emil and Ruth Rosenblatt, eds., *Hard Marching Every Day: The Civil War Letters of Wilbur Fisk 1861–1865* (Lawrence: Univ. Press of Kansas, 1992), 322–23.

16. *Cincinnati Commercial,* May 20, 1862.

17. New York *Commercial Advertiser,* May 20, 1862; *Philadelphia Inquirer,* May 20, 1862; Washington *National Intelligencer,* May 22, 1862; New York *Evening Post,* May 19, 1862; *New York Tribune,* May 20, 1862; McClellan to Mrs. McClellan, May 22, 1862, in Sears, *McClellan Papers,* 274.

18. Chase to Hunter, May 20, 1860, Medill to Chase, May 30, 1862, in Niven, *Chase Papers,* III, 202, 207; Garrison to Charles B. Sedgwick, May 20, 1862; J. W. Forney to John Russell Young, May 19, 1862, John Russell Young Papers, LC; Merrill, ed., *The Letters of William Lloyd Garrison,* V, 93.

19. New York *World,* May 28, 1862; Springfield *Republican,* May 31, 1862; *Chicago Tribune,* May 29, 1862; Curtis Goodsil to Washburne, May 31, 1862, Washburne Papers.

20. *Congressional Globe,* 37th Cong., 2nd Sess., Ap., 268–371, 210.

21. Sumner, *Works,* VI, 116–17; New York *Evening Post,* June 6, 1862; McClellan to Joel Barlow, Mar. 16, 1862, in Sears, ed., *McClellan Papers,* 213; *New York Times,* May 27, 28, 1862; W. T. Sherman to John Sherman, May 31, 1862, in Simpson and Berlin, *Sherman's Selected Correspondence During the Civil War,* 231.

22. *Philadelphia Inquirer,* July 18, 1862; *Cincinnati Daily Commercial,* July 19, 1862; Gurowski, *Diary I,* 241; *Congressional Globe,* 37th Cong., 2nd Sess., 3002, 3381, 2991.

23. New York *World,* June 21, 1861; Springfield *Republican,* July 8, 1862.

24. *Congressional Globe,* 37th Cong., 2nd Sess., 3150.

25. *Frank Leslie's Illustrated Newspaper,* July 19, 1862; Washington *Evening Star,* July 11, 1862.

26. Michael Burlingame, ed., *Dispatches from Lincoln's White House: The Anonymous Civil War Journal of Presidential Secretary William O. Stoddard* (Lincoln: Univ. of Nebraska Press, 2002), 88; *New York Herald,* Aug. 2, 1862; W. D. Kelley to Lincoln, July 23, 1863, LP.

27. *Cincinnati Gazette,* Aug. 20, 1862; New York *Spectator,* Aug. 18, 1862.

28. Roy P. Basler, ed., *The Collected Works of Abraham Lincoln* (9 vols., New Brunswick: Rutgers Univ. Press, 1953–1955), V, 388–389.

29. Albany *Atlas and Argus*, Aug. 26, 1862; *Cincinnati Commercial*, Aug. 25, 1862; *Philadelphia Inquirer*, Aug. 25, 1862; *Harper's Weekly*, Sept. 6, 1862; Orville H. Browning to Lincoln, Aug. 25, Sept. 17, 1862; George Ashmun to Lincoln, Aug. 25, 1862, William A. Stearns to Lincoln, Sept. 3, 1862, LP. For a radical critique, see *New York Tribune*, Aug. 20, 25, 1862.

30. McClellan to Mrs. McClellan, Sept. 2, 1862, in Sears, ed., *The Civil War Papers of George B. McClellan*, 428.

31. Strong, *Diary*, 259, also in Glenn M. Linden and Thomas J. Pressly, *Voices from the House Divided* (New York: McGraw Hill, 1995), 74.

32. Browning to Lincoln, Sept. 10, 1862. Timothy Tillman to Lincoln, Sept. 18, 1862, Wesleyan Methodist Church, Miami Conference to Lincoln, Sept. 6, 1862, William B. Totten to Lincoln, Sept. 12, 1862, LP; Stoddard, *Journal*, Sept. 14, 1862.

33. W.B. Lowry et al. to Lincoln, Sept. 23, 1862, G. F. Train to Lincoln, Sept. 25, 1862, B. Gratz Brown to Lincoln, Sept. 27, 1862, Hamlin to Lincoln, 1862, LP.

34. Gerald Schwartz, ed., *A Woman Doctor's Civil War: Esther Hill Hawks' Diary* (Columbia: Univ. of South Carolina Press, 1984), 25; Wade to Julian, Sept. 29, 1862, Julian-Giddings Papers, LC; Tilton to Lincoln, Sept. 24, 1862, LP; Charles Sumner in Boston's Faneuil Hall, Oct. 6, 1862, in Sumner, *Works*, IX, 199; the picture is reproduced in Holzer, *Lincoln Seen & Heard*, 25.

35. *Cincinnati Commercial*, Sept. 23, 1862; *Liberator*, Sept. 26, 1862; *New York Times*, Sept. 23, 1862; New York *Evening Post*, Sept. 23, 1862; Springfield *Republican*, Sept. 24, 1862; *Portland Transcript*, Oct. 4, 1862; *Chicago Tribune*, Sept. 23, 1862; *New York Tribune*, Dec. 23, 1862.

36. Mary Ann Anderson, ed., *The Civil War Diary of Allen Morgan Geer, 20th Regiment Illinois Volunteers* (New York: Cosmos Press, 1977), 55; Cecil D. Eby Jr., ed., David Hunter Strother, *A Virginia Yankee in the Civil War* (Chapel Hill: Univ. of North Carolina Press, 1961), 117; George Tillotson to wife, Sept. 24, 1862, Gilder-Lehrman Collection, 4558, Pierpont Morgan Library; George Whitman to Mother, Sept. 30, 1862, in Jerome M. Loving, ed., *Civil War Letters of George Washington Whitman* (Durham, NC: Duke Univ. Press, 1975, 71; Jo-

seph Jones to Wife, Oct. 3, 1862, Gilder-Lehrman Collection, Morgan Library, NY, 5981.

37. New York *World,* Sept. 24, 1862; Columbus *Crisis,* Sept. 24, 1862; Albany *Atlas and Argus,* Sept. 24, 1862; *Louisville Journal,* quoted in ibid., Sept. 29, 1862.

38. Thomas Ellis, *Leaves from the Diary of an Army Surgeon* (New York: John Bradbury, 1863), 10; Chicago *Times,* September 24, 1862, in Mitgang, *Lincoln as They Saw Him,* 303–05; *Brooklyn Daily Eagle,* Sept. 23, 1862; *New York Evening Express,* Sept. 23, 1862.

39. *Southern Illustrated News,* Nov. 2, 1862, also in *Punch;* William Kaufman Scarborough, ed., *The Diary of Edmund Ruffin* (3 vols., Baton Rouge: Louisiana Univ. Press, 1976), II, 453; *Richmond Dispatch,* Dec. 30, 1862; Charlotte Cleveland and Robert Daniel, "The Diary of a Confederate Quartermaster," *Tennessee Historical Quarterly,* XI (Mar. 1952), 78–91; Howard Swiggett, ed., *A Rebel War Clerk's Diary at the Confederate States Capital* (2 vols., New York: Old Hickory Bookshop, 1935), I, 157; John Q. Anderson, ed., *Brokenburn: The Journal of Kate Stone 1861–1868* (Baton Rouge: Louisiana Univ. Press, 1955), 145–46.

40. *Punch,* October 18, 1862; London *Times,* Oct. 6, 7, 14, 1862; Sarah Agnes Wallace and Frances Elma Gillespie, eds., *The Journal of Benjamin Moran* (2 vols., Chicago: Univ. of Chicago Press, 1949), II, 1077; *Edinburgh Review,* Oct. 1862; London *Spectator,* Oct. 11, 1862; *Moniteur,* Oct. 6, 10, 1862; *Frankfurter Journal,* Oct. 8, 1862; *Edouard de* Stoeckl's Report No. 69, Sept. 15, 1862, in Woldman, *Lincoln and the Russians,* 181–85.

41. Koerner to Trumbull, Oct. 14, 1862, Trumbull Papers; Samuel A. Goddard to Editor, *London American,* Oct. 12, 1862, in Samuel A. Goddard, *Letters on the American Rebellion 1860–1865* (London: Simkins, Marshall & Co., 1870), 252.

42. *New York Times,* Sept. 25, 26, 1862; *New York Tribune,* Sept. 25, 1862; *Philadelphia Inquirer,* Sept. 25, 1862; *Cincinnati Commercial,* Nov. 4, 1862; *Congressional Globe,* 37th Cong., 3rd Sess., 62–69, 70–71, 76–79; *Courier des Etats Unis,* Sept. 26, 1862.

43. *New York Herald,* Oct. 19, 1862; Francis Spring to Hawkins Taylor, Oct. 19, 1862, S. W. Oakey to Lincoln, Nov. 5, 1862, LP; Springfield *Republican,* Nov, 8, 1862; *New York Times,* Nov. 5, 7, 1862; *Cincinnati Gazette,* Oct. 17, 1862; *New York Tribune,* Nov. 4, 1862.

44. Schuyler Colfax to Lincoln, Oct. 18, 1862, LP, Series II; New York *Evening Post,* Oct 13, Nov. 5, 1862; Andrew Parker to Lincoln, Nov. 9, 1862, D. D. Field to Lincoln, Nov. 8, 1862, LP; George W. Penny to John Sherman, Nov. 7, 1862, J. D. Cooke to John Sherman, Nov. 8, 1862, John Sherman Papers.

45. Albany *Atlas and Argus,* October 29, 1862; S. L. M. Barlow to Horatio Seymour, Nov. 8, 1862, Seymour Papers, NYHS.

46. Daniel S. Dickinson to Lincoln, Nov. 9, 1862, Schuyler Colfax to Lincoln, Nov. 10, 1862, William Sprague to Lincoln, Nov. 11, 1862, James K. Morehead to Lincoln, Nov. 13, 1862, LP.

47. *Cincinnati Daily Commercial,* Nov. 10, 1862; *Philadelphia Inquirer,* Nov. 10, 1862; Caroline L. Frey to Ludlow Frey, Nov. 15, 1862, Frey Family Papers, NYHS; Cornelia Jay, *Diary of Cornelia Jay* (Rye, NY: Privately printed, 1924), 80; *New York Tribune,* November 10, 1862.

48. Alan T. Nolan, ed., *Rufus R. Dawes: A Full Blown Yankee in the Iron Brigade, Service with the Sixth Wisconsin Volunteers* (Lincoln: Nebraska Univ. Press, 1962), 105; Oliver Wilcox Norton to Sister, Dec. 6, 1862, in Oliver Wilcox Norton, *Army Letters 1861–1865* (Chicago: O. L. Downing, 1903), 128; Charles H. Moulton to Mother, Nov. 11, 1862, in Lee C. and Karen D. Drickhamer, eds., *Fort Lyon to Harper's Ferry: The Civil War Letters and Newspaper Dispatches of Charles H. Moulton* (34th Mass. Vol. Inf. (Shippenburg, PA: White Mane Publishing Co., 1987), 57.

49. Columbus *Crisis,* Nov. 5, 1862; *New York Evening Express,* Nov. 11, 1862; Albany *Atlas and Argus,* Nov. 22, 1862; Benjamin F. Butler to Henry Wilson, Feb. 22, 1863, Henry Wilson Papers.

50. *Philadelphia Inquirer,* Dec. 2, 1862; *New York Times,* Dec. 2, 1862; *Cincinnati Gazette,* Dec. 2, 1862; Washington *National Intelligencer,* Dec. 2, 1862; *New York Herald,* Dec 2, 1862; Oliver Wilcox Norton to Sister, Dec. 6, 1862, in Norton, *Army Letters,* 128; Calvin Fletcher, *Diary,* 583; James C. Mohr, ed., *The Conway Diaries: A Northern Family in the Civil War* (Pittsburgh: Univ. of Pittsburgh Press, 1920), 164.

51. Gerrit Smith to Burke Hinsdale, Dec. 12, 1862, in Smith, *Speeches and Letters,* I, 267; *Liberator,* Dec. 6, 1862, also quoted in *National Anti-Slavery Standard,* Dec. 13, 1862; Sumner to Wendell Phillips, Dec. 4, 1862, in Palmer, *Selected Letters of Charles Sumner,* II, 133; New York *Evening Post* Dec. 2, 1862; *New York Tribune,* Dec. 2, 1862.

52. Rev. C. C. Jones to Col. C. Jones, Dec, 8, 1862, in Myers, *The*

Children of Pride, 997; *Richmond Dispatch*, Dec. 6, 1862; Elizabeth Baer, ed., *Shadows on My Heart: The Civil War Diary of Lucy Rebecca Buck* (Athens: Univ. of Georgia Press, 1997), 164.

53. David Herbert Donald, *Lincoln* (New York: Simon & Schuster, 1995), 399–408.

54. Albany *Atlas and Argus*, Dec. 19, 1862; Wait Talcott to Trumbull, Dec. 19, 1862, Trumbull Papers; J. H. Trumbull to Lincoln, Dec. 31, 1861, certifying resolution of Dec. 21, LP; Hannah Ropes to Alice, Dec. 21, 1862, in John A. Bugardt, ed., *Civil War Nurse: The Diary and Letters of Hannah Ropes* (Knoxville: Univ. of Tennessee Press, 1980), 114; J. W. Forney to John Russell Young, Dec. 22, 1862, John Russell Young Papers, LC; Washington *Evening Star*, Dec. 22, 1862; *Harper's Weekly*, Jan. 3, 1863.

55. *Congressional Globe*, 37th Cong., 3rd Sess., 160, 92, 55.

56. Robert Gould Shaw to Effie, Dec. 23, 1862, in Shaw, *Blue Eyed Child of Fortune*, 271; Gurowski to John A. Andrew, Dec. 27, 1862, Andrew Papers; Sumner to Longfellow, Sept. 21, 1861, in Palmer, *Selected Letters of Charles Sumner*, II, 233; Samuel F. DuPont to Mrs. DuPont, Dec. 24, 1862, in John E. Hayes, ed., *Samuel Francis DuPont: A Selection from His Civil War Letters* (3 vols., Ithaca: Cornell Univ. Press, 1969), II, 318; Chandler to Mrs. Chandler, Dec. 10, 18, 1862, Chandler Papers; Chandler to Austin Blair, Dec. 22, 1862, Austin Blair Papers, Burton Collection, Detroit Public Library; *New York Tribune*, Dec. 23, 1862; James W. White to Wade, Dec. 22, 1862, B. F. Wade Papers.

57. Sumner to John Murray Forbes, Dec. 28, 1862, in Palmer, *Selected Letters of Charles Sumner*, II, 135–36; Georgianna M. W. Bacon, ed., *Letters of a Family During the War for the Union 1861–1865* (2 vols., privately printed, 1899), II, 493; C. Rush Plumly to Lincoln, Jan. 1, 1863, Julius Stahel to Lincoln, Jan. 1, 1863, John Bittmann to Lincoln, Jan. 1863, Barry Grey to Lincoln, Jan. 1863, with poem, Victor Gus Bloede and Katie to Lincoln, Jan. 4, 1863, LP; John Olney to Trumbull, Jan. 6, 1862, Trumbull Papers.

58. *New York Times*, Jan. 3, 1863; *Chicago Tribune*, Jan. 2, 1863; *Cincinnati Gazette*, Apr. 12, 1864; Springfield *Republican*, Jan. 1, 1863; New York *Commercial Advertiser*, Jan. 2, 1863.

59. *New York Tribune*, Jan. 2, 1863; Greeley to John Nicolay, Jan. 10, 1863, LP, II; *Independent*, Jan. 8, 1863; *Wilkes' Spirit of the Times*, Jan.

10, 1863; New York *Evening Post*, Jan. 2, 1863; *Liberator*, Jan. 2, Feb. 6, 1863; George Livermore to Sumner, Jan. 5, 1863. LP.

60. *Manchester Guardian*, Dec. 31, 1862, Sideman and Friedman, *Europe Looks at the Civil War*, 198–201; Henry Adams to C. F. Adams Jr, Jan. 23, 1863, in Worthington Chauncey Ford, ed., *A Cycle of Adams Letters 1861–1865* (2 vols., Boston: Houghton Mifflin, 1920), I, 243; C. F. Adams to Edward Everett, Jan. 23, 1863, Edward Everett Papers, MHS; Baptist Wriothesley Noel, *The Rebellion in America* (London: James Nisbet, 1863), 378; Edward Dicey, *Six Months in the Federal States* (2 vols., London: Macmillan, 1863), I, 190–92; Goddard to *London American*, January 31, 1863, in Goddard, *Letters on the American Rebellion 1860–1865*, 296; Edinburgh *Caledonian Mercury*, quoted in *New York Tribune*, Jan. 10, 1863; Alexander James to Douglass, Dec. 23, 1862, Fredrick Douglass Papers.

61. London *Times*, Jan. 20, 31, 1863; Wallace and Gillespie, *Moran Journal*, II, 1106; *Moniteur*, Jan. 25, 1863; De Bigorie de Lachamps, Jan. 24, 1863, in Case, *French Opinion*, 272; *Courrier du Havre*, Jan. 27, 1863, in George Blackburn, *French Newspaper Opinion on the American Civil War* (Westport, CT: Greenwood Press, 1997), 114.

62. Columbus *Crisis*, Jan. 7, 1863; Albany *Atlas and Argus*, Jan. 3, 1863; Allan Nevins, ed., *A Diary of Battle: The Personal Journals of Colonel Charles S. Wainwright* (New York: Harcourt, Brace & World, 1962), 156; *Congressional Globe*, 37th Cong., 3rd Sess., 373–77.

63. Springfield *Republican*, Feb. 2, 1863; Beth G. Crabtree and James W. Patton, *Journal of a Secesh Lady: The Diary of Ann Devereux Edmundston 1860–1866* (Raleigh, NC: Division of Archives and History, Department of Cultural Resources, 1979), 340–341; *Richmond Enquirer*, Jan. 3, 1963, quoted in *New York Tribune*, Jan. 7, 1863; *Southern Illustrated News*, Mar. 14, 1863.

64. *Congressional Globe*, 37th Cong., 3rd Sess., 245–246; *Philadelphia Intelligencer*, Jan. 9, 1863; H. R. Summers et al. to Lincoln, no date (prob. Jan. 1863), LP; Ralph Lute to Wade, Jan. 21, 1863, B. F. Wade Papers; J. W. Shaffer to Butler, Jan. 25, 1863, Marshall, *Butler Correspondence*, II, 589–90.

Chapter 4: Defeat and Victory

1. Robert A. M. Carroll to John G. Nicolay, Jan. 11, 1863 (telegram), LP; *Congressional Globe*, 37th Congressional 3rd Sess. 314–15, 535.

2. William Leighton to Hiram Barney, Jan. 13, 1863, LP; *Congressional Globe,* 37th Cong., 3rd Sess., 379; New York *Evening Post,* Jan. 20, 1863; Washington *Daily Morning Chronicle,* Jan. 20, 1863; *New York Tribune,* Jan. 21, 1863.

3. *New York Leader,* Jan. 24, 1863; *New York Evening Express,* Jan. 19, 1863; *New-Yorker Staats-Zeitung,* Jan. 21, 22; New York *World,* Jan. 19, 1863.

4. *New York Times,* Jan. 17, 1863; Gurowski, *Diary,* II, 96; *Chicago Tribune,* Jan. 19, 31, 1863.

5. *Congressional Globe,* 37th Cong., 3rd Sess., 379, 456, Ap., 67–68, 79–82; *Independent,* Feb. 5, 1863; Burlingame, *Lincoln Observed,* 22–24.

6. *Congressional Globe,* 37th Cong., 3rd Sess., 735, 1085, 1400, 1223, 1412; Austin Blair to Lincoln, Feb. 24, 1863; Washington *Daily Morning Chronicle,* Feb. 25, 1863.

7. Diary of Aurelius Lyman Voorhis, Mar. 4, 1863, in Steven E. Woodworth, *Cultures in Conflict: The American Civil War* (Westport, CT: Greenwood Press, 2000), 100; Isaac Warton et al. to Lincoln, Mar. 7, 1863, H. P. Beegle to Lincoln, Mar. 18, 1863, LP; Johnson's Speech at Washington Union Meeting, Mar. 11, 1863, in Graf and Haskins, *Papers of Andrew Johnson,* VI, 202; *Philadelphia Inquirer,* Mar. 12, 1863; New York *Commercial Advertiser,* Mar. 13, 1863; *Atlantic Monthly,* XI (Mar. 1863), 386. For the unpopularity of the Enrollment Act, see Columbus *Crisis,* Apr. 1, 1863, and *Congressional Globe,* 37th Cong., 3rd Sess., 1365, 1379, 1387.

8. Burlingame, *Brooks,* 44–45; *Independent,* Apr. 9, 1863; Edwin Welles to Netty Watkins, Apr. 8, 1863, in William Walton, ed., *The Letters of Edwin Welles from Antietam to Atlanta: A Civil War Courtship* (Garden City, NY: Doubleday, 1980), 36; Francis Adams Donaldson to Brother, Apr. 12, 1863, in J. Gregory Acken, ed., *Inside the Army of the Potomac: The Civil War Experiences of Captain Francis Adams Donaldson* (Mechanicsburg, PA: Stackpole, 1998), 219; Peter Welsh to Mrs. Welsh, Apr. 10, 1863, in Lawrence Fredrick Kohl and Margarit Cossé Richard, eds., *Irish Green and Union Blue: The Civil War Letters of Peter Welsh* (New York: Fordham Univ. Press, 1986), 84; Thomas Smith to Brother (Joseph W. Smith), April 10, 1863, in Eric J. Wittenberg, ed., *"We Have It Darn Hard Out Here," The Civil War Letters of Sergeant Thomas W. Smith, 6th Pennsylvania Cavalry* (Kent, OH: Kent Univ. Press, 1999), 79.

9. Albany *Atlas and Argus*, Apr. 21, 1863; New York *Commercial Advertiser*, Apr. 15, 1863.

10. *New York Herald*, Apr. 10, 1863; Washington *National Intelligencer*, Apr. 8, 1863; Washington *Evening Star*, Apr. 8, 1863; *Harper's Weekly*, Apr. 25, May 2, 1863; *Chicago Tribune*, May 23, 1863.

11. W. T. Sherman to John Sherman, May 29, 1863, in Simpson and Berlin, *Sherman's Selected Correspondence*, May 29, 1863; Hamilton Fish to B. V. Wise, May 8, 1863, B. V. Wise Papers, NYH; James M. Scovel to Lincoln, May 9, 1863, LP.

12. *New York Tribune*, May 11, 1863; *Independent*, May 14, 1863; *Belletristisches Journal*, May 23, 1863; Ferdinand Benventano de Bosco to Lincoln, May 20, 1863, LP.

13. Roswell H. Lamson to Kate Buckingham, Jan. 25, 1863, in James and Patricia McPherson, eds., *Lamson of the Gettysburg, the Civil War Letters of Lieutenant Roswell H. Lamson, U. S. N.* (New York: Oxford Press, 1997), 76; Stephen Minot Weld, *War Diary and Letters of Stephen Minot Weld 1861–1865* (Cambridge, MA: Riverside Press, 1912), 170; John Michael Priest, ed., *John T. McMahon's Diary of the 136th New York 1861–1864* (Shippensburg, PA: White Mane Publishing Co., 1963), 76.

14. George Gordon Meade to Mrs. Meade, Apr. 9, 1863, in George Gordon Meade, ed., *The Life and Letters of George Gordon Meade* (2 vols., New York: Scribner's, 1913), I, 364; Wilbur Fisk to Green Mountain Freeman, Apr. 13, 1864, in Rosenblatt, eds., *Hard Marching Every Day*, 64; Jane Stuart Woolsey to Friend in Europe, May 23, 1863, in Bacon, *Letters of a Family During the War for the Union 1861–1865*, II, 512–15; Wainwright, ed., *A Philadelphia Perspective*, 415.

15. Springfield *Republican*, May 23, 1863; *Cincinnati Gazette*, May 22, 1863; Horatio Seymour to Peter Cagger et al., May 16, 1863, Seymour-Fairchild Papers, NYH; *Brooklyn Eagle*, May 26, 1863; Albany *Atlas and Argus*, May 18, 28, 1863 and following days; Columbus *Crisis*, June 3, 1863; *New York Herald*, May 19, 1863.

16. Lincoln to Erastus Corning and others, June 12, 1863, in Roy P. Basler, ed., *The Collected Works of Abraham Lincoln*, (9 vols., New Brunswick: Rutgers Univ. Press, 1953, VI, 269; Washington *Daily Morning Chronicle*, June 16, 1863; New York *Evening Post*, June 15, 1863; *Harper's Weekly*, June 27, 1863; *Independent*, June 18, 1863; New York *Commercial Advertiser*, June 15, 1863; Washington *National Intelli-*

gencer, June 16, *New York Tribune*, June 16, 1863; Horace Maynard to Lincoln, June 18, 1863; John W. Forney to Lincoln, June 14, 1863, LP; Burlingame, *Stoddard*, 160; 1863; Washington *Evening Star*, June 16, 1863; examples are: New York *Spectator*, June 18, 1863, *New York Tribune*, June 16, 1863.

17. Cole and McDonough, eds., *Witness to the Young Republic*, 424; Washington *Daily Morning Chronicle*, June 16, 1863.

18. *New York Weekly News*, June 20, 1863; *Brooklyn Eagle*, June 20, 1863; Columbus *Crisis*, June 21, 1863; *New-Yorker Staats-Zeitung*, June 26, 1863.

19. *New York Tribune*, June 6, 1863; *Chicago Tribune*, June 6, 1863; New York *World*, June 6, 1863.

20. *Chicago Tribune*, June 30, 1863; A. K. McClure to Lincoln, June 30, 1863, E. Delafield Smith to Lincoln, July 8, 1863, L. F. Lovering to Lincoln, July 10, 1863, LP; New York *Evening Post*, July 6, 1863; *New York Herald*, July 9, 1863; Washington *Daily Morning Chronicle*, July 10, 1863.

21. John Lothrop Motley to Lincoln, July 25, 1863, LP; Washington *Daily Morning Chronicle*, Aug. 6, 1863; New York *Commercial Advertiser*, Aug. 5, 1863.

22. *Chicago Times, July 9, 1863*, quoted in Washington *Daily Morning Chronicle*, July 13, 1863; Albany *Atlas and Argus*, July 15, 18, 1863.

23. Washington *Daily Morning Chronicle*, Aug. 12, 1863; Springfield *Republican*, Aug. 12, 1863; *Philadelphia Inquirer*, Aug. 10, 1863; *Cincinnati Commercial*, Aug. 18, 1863.

24. Benjamin Balch to Lincoln, July 17, 1863, William Bebb to Lincoln, July 15, 1863, Giuseppe Garibaldi to Lincoln, August 6, 1863, LP; Tyler, "Lincoln in the Civil War," in *The Diary and Letters of John Hay* (New York: Dodd Mead, 1937), 73.

25. Basler, *Collected Works*, VI, 406–10.

26. John Murray Forbes to Charles Sumner, Sept. 8, 1863, in Hughes, ed., *Letters and Recollections of John Murray Forbes*, II, 59; John Goodrich to Lincoln, Sept. 3, 1863, N. Morris to Lincoln, Aug. 26, 1863, Henry Wilson to Lincoln., Sept. 2, 1863, Charles Sumner to Lincoln, Sept. 7, 1863, LP; Sir Christopher Chancellor, ed., *An Englishman in the American Civil War: The Diaries of Henry Yates Thompson 1863* (London: Sidgwick & Jackson, 1971), 62.

27. *Chicago Tribune*, Sept. 3, 1863; New York *Commercial Advertiser*,

Sept. 3, 1863; Washington *Evening Star,* Sept. 3, 1863; Burlingame, ed., Dispatches from Lincoln's White House, 109; *New York Times,* Sept. 7, 1863; Washington *Daily Morning Chronicle,* Sept. 17, 1863; *Cincinnati Gazette,* Oct. 10, 1863; *New York Weekly News,* Sept. 12, 1863; Albany *Atlas and Argus,* Sept. 4, 1863.

28. *New York Herald,* Mar. 21, 1863; John C. Hamilton to Lincoln, Feb. 2, 1863, LP; Gordon A. Cotton, ed., *From the Pen of a She-Rebel: The Civil War Diary of Emilie Riley McKinley* (Columbia: Univ. of South Carolina Press, 2001), 50; Joseph Wright to Lincoln, Sept. 18, 1863, quoting the London *Star* of Sept. 17; Charles Goddard to Lincoln, Oct. 19, 1863, LP; *Harper's Weekly,* Dec. 4, 1863; Washington *Daily Morning Chronicle,* Sept. 17, 1863 and *New York Times,* Sept. 7, 1863, constitute other examples of the comparison.

29. New York *Commercial Advertiser,* Sept. 16, 1863; Wainwright, ed., *Philadelphia Perspective,* 460–61; *Brooklyn Daily Union,* Sept. 16, 1863; Springfield *Republican,* Sept. 16, 1863; *National Anti-Slavery Standard,* Sept. 26, 1863; *Philadelphia Inquirer,* Sept. 17, 1863; Washington *Daily Morning Chronicle,* Sept. 17, 1863; New York *Spectator,* Nov. 17, 1863; *Cincinnati Gazette,* Sept. 17, 1863; E. D. Delafield to Lincoln, Sept. 17, 1863, LP. For Democratic criticism, see Albany *Atlas and Argus,* Sept. 21, 1863, and Loriphant to Manton Marble, Sept. 21, 1863, Marble Papers.

30. Richard Eddy to Lincoln, Sept. 15, 1863, John Laverty to Lincoln, Sept. 24, 1863, W. Y. Potter to Lincoln, Oct. 3, 1863, James Delaney to Lincoln, Oct. 15, 1863, Solomon Lindsay et al. to Lincoln, Oct. 10, 1863, George W. Rice to Lincoln, Oct. 19, 1863, C. L. Chandler to Lincoln, Oct. 22, 1863, LP.

31. Hans L. Trefousse, *The Radical Republicans: Lincoln's Vanguard for Racial Justice* (New York: Alfred A. Knopf, 1969); Dennett, Hay 97, 101; Washington *Daily Morning Chronicle,* Oct, 26, 1863; New York *Spectator,* Oct. 16, 1863; New York *Commercial Advertiser,* Oct. 3, 1863; Cincinnati *Daily Commercial,* Oct. 30, 1863, quoting the Boston *Advertiser; St. Louis Republican,* quoted in Washington *National Intelligencer,* Oct. 29, 1863.

32. James M. Scovel to Lincoln, Oct. 28, 1863; J. Young Scammon to Lincoln, Nov. 2, 1863, James C. Rice to Lincoln, Nov. 11, 1863, E. Benoit to Lincoln, Nov. 18, 1863, LP; *Brooklyn Daily Union,* Nov. 3, Oct. 7, 1863.

33. *Emancipation, Racism, and the Work Before Us,* Speech in Philadelphia, Dec. 4, 1863, in Philip S. Foner, *The Life and Writings of Frederick Douglass* (4 vols., New York: International Publishers, 1950–55), III, 608; "The Diary of Josephine Forney Roedel," Nov. 19, 1963, in *Tennessee Historical Quarterly,* 7, 390–411, 398.

34. Washington *Daily Morning Chronicle,* Nov. 5, 1863; New York *Commercial Advertiser,* Nov. 5, 1863; James Wien Forney to Lincoln, November 12, 1863, LP; Horatio Seymour to L. Lincklean, Nov. 14, 1863, Fairchild-Seymour Papers, NHS.

35. Edward Everett to Lincoln, Nov. 20, 1863, James M. Scovel to Lincoln, Nov. 23, 1863, David Wills to Lincoln, Nov. 23, 1863, LP; Wainwright, ed., *A Philadelphia Perspective,* 463; Cole and McDonough, eds., *Witness to the Young Republic,* 434–36. For examples of the criticism of Lincoln's writing and speeches, see *Liberator,* Dec. 5, 1862; Columbus *Crisis,* Nov. 18, 1863; *New York Evening Express,* Dec. 2, 1862; Springfield *Republican,* Feb. 18, 1861, Dec. 12, 1863.

36. Springfield *Republican,* Nov. 21, 1863; Washington *Daily Morning Chronicle,* Nov. 21, 1863; *Brooklyn Daily Union,* Nov. 20, 1863; *Chicago Tribune,* Nov. 25, 1863; New York *Spectator,* Nov. 23, 1863; *Harper's Weekly,* Dec. 5, 1863; New York *World,* Nov. 27, 1863; *Chicago Times,* quoted in *Brooklyn Daily Union,* Dec. 1, 1863; London *Times,* Dec. 4, 1863; Charleston *Mercury,* Nov. 27, 1863; War W. Briggs, *Soldier and Scholar: Basil Lannen Gildersleeve and the Civil War* (Charlottesville: Univ. of Virginia Press, 1998), 174.

37. *Brooklyn Daily Union,* Dec. 8, 1863; New York *World,* Dec. 5, 1863.

38. *New York Times,* Dec. 10, 1863; James A. Hamilton to Lincoln, Dec. 19, 1863, LP; Dennett, *Lincoln and the Civil War,* 134–35; Charles Sumner to John Bright, Dec. 15, 1863, in Palmer, *Selected Letters of Charles Sumner,* II, 214; Count Agénor de Gasparin to Lincoln, Jan. 7, 1864, LP; Burlingame, *Lincoln Observed,* 93–95; Washington *Evening Star,* Dec. 9, 1863; Boston *Commonwealth,* Dec. 11, 1863; *National Anti-Slavery Standard,* Dec. 19, 1863; New York *Commercial Advertiser; Cincinnati Commercial, Brooklyn Daily Union,* Washington *National Intelligencer,* Dec. 10, 1863 are examples of other papers favorably inclined toward the message; London *Spectator,* Dec. 26, 1863.

39. *New York Herald,* Dec. 11, 1863; Burlingame and Ettlinger, eds., *Inside Lincoln's White House,* 121–22; James Dixon to Henry J. Ray-

ins, ed., *A Diary of Battle: The Personal Journals of Colonel Charles S. Wainwright 1861–1868* (New York: Harcourt. Brace & World, 1962), 331; Francis Adam Donaldson to Jacob Donaldson, Mar. 3, 1864, in Acken, ed., *Inside the Army of the Potomac*) 433–36.

24. London *Times*, Feb. 4, 1864; *Edinburgh Mercury*, May 17, 1864, quoted in *New York Times*, June 12, 1864; London *Spectator*, May 14, 1864; *Moniteur*, Mar. 30, Apr. 21, 1864; James Ford Reed to Lincoln, Mar. 12, 1864, LP.

25. Columbus *Crisis*, Jan. 27, Feb. 10, Mar. 9, 1864; *New York Leader*, Jan. 2, 1864; *New-Yorker Staats-Zeitung*, Feb. 2, 1864; New York *World*, Feb. 6, 1864.

26. *Congressional Globe*, 38th Cong., 1st Sess., Ap., 55–71; 1276–83; Columbus *Crisis*, May 4, 1864; Albany *Atlas and Argus*, May 4, Mar. 4, June 9, 1864.

27. William K. Scarborough, ed., *Diary of Edmund Ruffin*, III, 381; Frank E. Vandiver, ed., *The Civil War Diary of General Josiah Gorgas* (Tuscaloosa: Univ. of Alabama Press, 1947), 84; Richmond *Dispatch*, Feb. 18, 1864; Benjamin Hill to Alexander H. Stephens, Mar. 14, 1864, in Ulrich B. Phillips, *Correspondence*, 635; Ward W. Briggs, *Soldier and Scholar: Basil Lannen Gildersleeve and the Civil War* (Charlottesville: Univ. of Virginia Press, 1998), 315–17.

28. *Chicago Tribune*, June 7, 9, 1864; Washington *Daily Morning Chronicle*, June 8, 1864.

29. *Cincinnati Commercial*, June 8, 1864; New York *Evening Post*, June 9, 1864; Springfield *Republican*, June 9, 1864; Washington *Evening Star*, June 9, 1864; *Philadelphia Inquirer*, June 9, 1864.

30. *Harper's Weekly*, June 11, 25, 1864; Bryant, *Letters*, IV, 363.

31. Brooks to George W. Herle, June 15, 1864, in Burlingame, ed., *Lincoln Observed*, 114; J. Russell Johnson to Lincoln, June 20, 1868, LP; Niven, ed., *Chase Papers*, IV, 396–97.

32. *Independent*, June 9, 1864: *National Anti-Slavery Standard*, June 9, 1864; *Liberator*, July 15, 1864.

33. *Commonwealth*, June 17, 1864; New York *Tribune*, June 24, 30, 1864; *Cincinnati Commercial*, July 8, 1864.

34. *New York Tribune*, June 24, 30, 1864; *Congressional Globe*, 38th Cong., 1st Sess., 2954–56, 2970, 3308, 3344–45, 3294.

35. Gurowski, *Diary*, IV, 267–68; *Cincinnati Daily Commercial*, July 1, 1864; *New York Herald*, July 1, 1864; Springfield *Republican*, July 2, 1864; *Boston Morning Journal*, July 2, 1864.

mond, Dec. 13, 1863, Henry J. Raymond Papers, NYPL; R. W. Thompson to Henry Lane, Dec. 27, 1863, Henry Lane Papers, Indiana Historical Society; John Daniel Smith and William Cooper, eds., *A Union Woman in Civil War Kentucky* (Lexington: Univ. Press of Kentucky, 2000), 176.

40. Rufus R. Dawes to M. B. G., Dec. 12, 1863, in Alan T. Nolan, ed., *A Full Blown Yankee of the Iron Brigade: Service with the Sixth Wisconsin Volunteers* (Lincoln: Univ. of Nebraska Press, 1962), 230–32; Jones, *An Artillery Man's Diary*, 153; Herb Crumb and Katherine D. Halle, eds., *No Middle Ground: Thomas Wood Osborn's Letters from the Field, 1862–1864* (Hamilton, NY: Edmondston Publishing Co., 1993), 183.

41. Columbus *Crisis*, Dec. 16, 1863; Albany *Atlas and Argus*, Dec. 10, 1863; New York *World*, Dec. 10, 1863 *New-Yorker Staats-Zeitung*, Dec. 17, 1863; London *Times*, Jan. 5, 1864; *Moniteur*, Dec. 28, 1863.

42. Washington *Daily Morning Chronicle*, Dec. 30, 1863, Jan. 1, 1864; Charles O. Musser to Father, Jan. 1, 1864, in Barry Popchuck, ed., *Soldier Boy: The Civil War Letters of Charles O. Musser, 29th Iowa* (Iowa City: Univ. of Iowa Press, 1995), 101–02; *Brooklyn Daily Union*, Jan. 21, 1864.

Chapter 5: Renomination and Reelection

1. Isaac Arnold, *The Life of Abraham Lincoln* (Chicago: Jansen, McClurg, 1885), 385–86, n. 2.

2. Supra, 82–3. Burlingame, ed., *Lincoln Observed*, 54; *New York Herald*, May 23, 26, 1863; New Orleans *Weekly True Delta*, June 14, 1863; Frederick Law Olmstead to Father, Oct. 30, 1863, in Ranney et al., eds., Vol. V of *The Papers of Frederick Law Olmstead*, 123; George H. Clapp to Lincoln, Sept. 24, 1863, LP.

3. *Chicago Tribune*, Nov. 3, 1863; *New York Daily Herald*, Oct. 9, Nov. 3, 5, 9, 1863; John Donnelly to Lincoln, Nov. 26, 1863, H. C. Townley to Lincoln, Sept. 29, 1863, LP.

4. Washburne to Lincoln, Oct. 12, 1863, Cameron to Lincoln, Oct. 10, 1863, James K. Morehead to Lincoln, Oct. 15, 1863, LP; Sophia Buchanan to Claude Buchanan, Nov. 5, 1863, in George M. Blackburn,

"Letters to the Front: A Distaff View of the Civil War," *Michigan History*, IXL (Mar. 1965), 56.

5. James Horrocks to Parents, Nov. 11, 1863, in A.S. Lewis, ed., *My Dear Parents An Englishman's Letters Home from the American Civil War* (London: Victor Gollancz, 1983), 46; Thomas H. Mann to Father, Nov. 18, 1863, in John H. Hennessy, ed., *Fighting With the Eighteenth Massachusetts: The Civil War Memoir of Thomas H. Mann* (Baton Rouge: Univ. of Louisiana Press, 2000), 195; *Independent*, Nov. 26, 1863.

6. Uri Manly to W. P. Dole, Dec. 9, 1863, Albert Smith to Lincoln, Dec. 12, 1863, LP; John A. Kasson to Greeley, Jan. 24, 1864, Greeley Papers; S. Kaufmann to Washburne, Dec. 12, 1863, Washburne Papers; Springfield *Republican*, Dec. 15, 1863; Lawrence *Kansas Tribune*, Dec. 23, 1863.

7. Joseph Medill to J. K. Forrest, Dec. 17, 1863, LP; M. Greitzner to Washburne, Jan. 26, 1864, Washburne Papers; New York *Daily Tribune*, Jan. 21, 1864; *Harper's Weekly*, Jan. 2, 1864.

8. Buffalo *Commercial Advertiser*, Jan. 11, 1864, LP.

9. Washington *Daily Morning Chronicle*, Jan. 14, 1864; John Minor Botts to John B. Frye, Jan. 22 1864, LP.

10. F. P. Baker to Lincoln, Jan. 7, 1864, LP; Washington *Evening Star*, Jan. 8, 1864.

11. John A. Hardenbrook to Lincoln, Jan. 23, 1864 (New York), George Bagner to Lincoln, Jan. 14, 1864 (Pennsylvania), Union League, 24th Ward, Philadelphia to Lincoln, Jan. 19, 1864, James Warrington to Lincoln, Jan. 20, 1864 (Camden) Bernard Stryker Jr. to Lincoln, Jan. 20, 1864 (Trenton), LP.

12. Gurowski, *Diary*, III, 59, 60; *Liberator*, Feb. 5, 1864.

13. *Congressional Globe*, 38th Cong., 1st Sess., 113–17, 473, 653, 1293–95, 952, 986, 1216, Ap. 85–98, 115. (In order of speakers mentioned.)

14. *New York Times*, Feb. 29, 1864; David E. Long, *The Jewel of Liberty: Abraham Lincoln's Re-election and the End of Slavery* (Mechanicsburg, PA: Stackpole Books, 1994), 36–37; *Congressional Globe*, 38th Cong., 1st Sess., 1027; I. B. Gara to Cameron, Feb. 26, 1865, James G. Blaine to Isaac Arnold, Mar. 3, 1864, James T. Lewis to Lincoln, Mar. 5, 1864 LP; Clark H. Chapman to Justin S. Morrill, May 16, 1864, Morrill Papers; *Cincinnati Commercial*, Feb. 29, 1864; Chase to Lincoln, Feb. 22, 1864, in Niven, *Chase Papers*, IV, 303–04; Washington *Daily Morning Chronicle*, Feb. 26, Mar. 15, 1864; *Liberator*, Mar. 18, 1864.

15. Richard C. Parsons to Chase, Mar. 2, 1864, in Niven, (pers, IV, 315–16; De Witt Chipman to Lincoln, Feb. 29, 1864, cago Tribune, Feb. 27, 1864.

16. *Brooklyn Daily Union*, Mar. 12, 1864; *Cincinnati Gazett* 11, 1864; *Cincinnati Commercial*, Mar. 10, 14, 1864.

17. James G. Blaine to Hannibal Hamlin, Mar. 8, 1864, H pers; Harrisburg *Evening Telegraph*, Mar. 4, 1864, LP; Mar *Congressional Globe*, 38th Cong., 1st Sess., 113–17, 1198–99 Place to Lincoln, Mar. 4, 1864, A. K. Merrill to Lincoln, Mar LP.

18. Henry L. Cobb to Lincoln, Apr. 6, 1864, William S. Lincoln, Apr. 9, 1864, LP.

19. George William Curtis to John Murray Forbes, Ma George William Curtis Papers, Staten Island Institute of the Sciences, Staten Island, NY.

20. Washington *Evening Star*, Apr. 20, 1864; John Frazier J A. J. Creswell, Mar. 24, 1864, J. A. K. Creswell Papers, LC; Hodges to Lincoln., May 27, 1864, Samuel T. Glover to Mo Bates, May 27, 1864, LP; William Frank Zornow, *Lincoln and Divided* (Norman: Univ. of Oklahoma Press, 1954), 64; Willia rish. *Turbulent Partnership: Missouri and the Union 1861–1865* bia: Univ. of Missouri Press, 1963), 183–85.

21. Springfield *Republican*, Apr. 29, 30, 1864; *Philadelphia* Apr. 29, 1864; *Brooklyn Daily Union*, Apr. 28, 1864; John M. M to Lincoln, Apr. 28, 1864, LP; Gurowski, *Diary*, III, 208.

22. *Cincinnati Commercial*, June 1, 1864; Washington *Daily* Chronicle, May 30, 1864; *Brooklyn Daily Union*, Mar. 19, 1864 field *Republican*, May 11, 1864.

23. John F. L. Hartwell to Wife and Boy, Mar. 4, 1864, in A well Britton and Thomas J. Reed, eds., *To My Beloved Wife a Home: The Letters and Diaries of Orderly Sergeant John F. L.* (Madison, NJ: Fairleigh Dickinson Univ. Press, 1997), 206; Connolly to Wife, Mar. 20, 1864, in Paul M. Angle, ed., *Thre the Army of the Cumberland* (Bloomington: Indiana Univ. Pr Henry R. Gardner to Parents, Mar. 29, 1864, in Kenneth E. Sh and Andrew K. Prinz, "A Yankee in Louisiana: Selections 1 Diary and Correspondence of Henry R. Gardner, 1862–1866," siana History V (Summer 1864), 284; J. Clay Rice to John 1 Apr. 4, 1864, N. H. Chrysler to Lincoln, May 24, 1864, LP; Al

36. *Cincinnati Commercial*, July 19, 1864; Burlingame, ed., *Lincoln Observed*, 127; Washington *Daily Morning Chronicle*, July 19, Aug. 4, 1864; *Boston Morning Journal*, July 20, 1864; *Brooklyn Daily Union*, July 19, 1864.

37. *Brooklyn Daily Union*, July 22, 1864; Washington *Daily Morning Chronicle*, July 22, 23, 29, 1864.

38. Beale, ed., *Bates Diary*, 388–89; *Frank Leslie's Illustrated Newspaper*, August 6, 1864; *Boston Morning Journal*, July 27, 1864; *Brooklyn Daily Union*, July 22, 23, 1864; Merrill, ed, *Garrison Letters*, V, 221–26.

39. Springfield *Republican*, July 9, 11, 16, 1864; *New York Times*, July 11, 1864.

40. Andrew Johnson to Lincoln, July 13, 1864, in Graf and Haskins, eds., *Papers of Andrew Johnson*, V, 80; Stevens to Edward McPherson, July 10, 1864, Stevens Papers; New York *Tribune*, Aug. 5, 1864.

41. *New York Times*, Aug. 9, 12, 13. 1864; *New York Tribune*, Aug. 5, 17, 1864; *National Anti-Slavery Standard*, Aug. 20, 1864; Smith, *Speeches*, II, 19–24; Ashtabula *Sentinel*, Aug. 17, 1864; Stanbery to Sumner, Sumner Papers; Noah Swayne to Lincoln, Aug. 19, 1864, LP.

42. Washington *Daily Morning Chronicle*, Aug. 19, 1864; *Chicago Tribune*, Aug. 13, 1864.

43. John Chipman Gray to Codman Ropes, Aug. 21, 26, 1864, in John Chipman Grey, *War Letters of John Chipman Gray and Codman Ropes* (Boston: Riverside Press, 1927), 376; Thomas J. Turner to Lincoln, Aug. 29, 1864, Albert Smith to Lincoln. Aug. 30, 1864, David Brown to Lincoln, Aug. 15, 1864, Rufus P. Spalding to Lincoln, Aug. 19, 1864, Charles E. Wiggin to Lincoln, Aug. 30, 1864, S.F. Cary to Lincoln, Sept. 1, 1864, Kitt H. Fell to Lincoln, Sept. 3, 1864, LP.

44. Theodore Tilton to John G. Nicolay, Sept. 6, 1864, LP, Second Series; Springfield *Republican*, Sept. 5, 10, 1864.

45. James T. Lewis to Horace Greeley, Sept. 7, 1864, Illinois State Grand Council, Union League to Lincoln, Sept. 8, 1864, LP; *New York Times*, Sept. 7, 1864; *New York Tribune*, Sept. 6, 1864.

46. D. H. Mears, Sept. 9, 1864, Laura Redden to Lincoln, Sept. 12, 1864, G. Henry Vosseler to Lincoln, Sept. 3, 1864, F. W. Delang to Lincoln, Sept. 14, 1864, Mrs. A. E.Gridley to Lincoln, Sept. 30, 1864, LP.

47. John M. Butler to John G. Nicolay, Sept. 17, 1864, LP; Mary L. Bonham to Horace Greeley, Sept. 22, 1864. Greely Papers; John De

Vries to John Covode, Sept. 16, 1864, Covode Papers. For examples of this concession, see Friedrich Engels to Karl Marx, Sept. 4, 1864, in Marx and Engels, *The Civil War in the United States,* 271–72; Richard Yates to Tilton, Greeley, et al., Sept, 1864, John D. Andrew Papers, James A. Connolly to wife, Sept. 25, 1864, in Angle, ed., *Three Years in the Army of the Cumberland,* 364.

48. Edward Everett to A. Burwell, Sept. 19, 1864, Edward Everett Papers; *Cincinnati Daily Commercial,* Sept. 19, 1864; John Sherman to William T. Sherman, Sept. 4, 1864, in Thorndike, ed., *Sherman Letters,* 239.

49. Francis Blair Jr. to Frances Blair Sr, Sept. 30, 1864, Otis Allan to Lincoln, Sept. 24, 1864, H. W. Mitchell to Lincoln, Sept. 22, 1864, LP; *Boston Journal,* Sept. 22, 1864.

50. *Chicago Tribune,* Sept. 26, 1864; *Harper's Weekly,* Sept. 24, 1864; *Wilkes' Spirit of the Times,* Oct. 1, 1864, LP.

51. Rufus K. Williams to Lincoln, Oct. 3, 1864, LP; *Boston Journal,* Oct. 5, 1865; Springfield *Republican,* Oct. 8, 10, 1864; Bartow A. Ulrich to Lincoln, Oct. 28, 1864, enclosing the *Staats-Zeitung's* German text.

52. Jenkin Lloyd Jones, *An Artillery Man's Diary* (Madison: Wisconsin Historical Commission, 1914), 218; George F. Crane to Mother, June 15, 1864, in Jennifer Bornsted, ed., *Soldiering with Sherman: Civil War Letters of George F. Crane* (DeKalb: Northern Illinois Univ. Press, 2000), 105; Charles O. Musser to Father, in Popchuck, ed., *Soldier Boy,* 137; *Portland Transcript,* July 2, 1864; Robert Daly, ed., *The Letters of William Fredrick Keeler, U. S. N., to His Wife, Ann* (Annapolis: U. S. Naval Institute, 1968), 179.

53. Robert Hunt Rhodes, ed., *All For the Union, A History of the 2nd Rhode Island Infantry in the War of the Great Rebellion As Told by the Diary and Letters of Elisha Hunt Rhodes* (Lincoln, RI: Andrew Mowbry, 1985), 170; James Greiner et al., eds., *A Surgeon's Civil War* (Kent, OH: Kent Univ. Press, 1994), 330; James I. Robertson, Jr., ed., *Sarah Morgan Dawson,* 211–12.

54. John L. Hartwell to Wife, Aug. 14, 1864, in Ann Hartwell Britton and Thomas J. Reid, eds., *To My Beloved Wife and Boy at Home: The Letters and Diaries of Orderly Sergeant John F. L. Hartwell* (Madison, NJ: Fairleigh Dickinson Univ. Press, 1997), 270, Harvey Reid to Father, Aug. 26, 1864, in Frank L. Byrne, ed., *The View From Headquarters, The Civil War Letters of Harvey Reid* (Madison: State Historical Society of Wisconsin, 1965), 181; Wainwright, *Diary,* 460.

55. Samuel F. George to Lincoln, Sept. 7, 1864, Thomas S. Mather to Robert Lincoln, Sept. 20, 1864, LP; Robert McAllister to Ellen and Family, Sept. 17, 1864, in James F. Robertson Jr, ed., *The Civil War Letters of General Robert McAllister* (New Brunswick, NJ: Rutgers Univ. Press, 1965), 95; James H. Kidd to Parents, Sept. 9, 1864, in Wittenberg, ed., *One of Custer's Wolverines*, 104.

56. Charles O. Musser to Father, Sept. 18, Oct. 18, 1868, in Popchuck, ed., *Soldier Boy* 155, 157; Robert C. Athearn, ed., *A Soldier in the West* (Philadelphia: Univ. of Pennsylvania Press, 1957), 218; George W. Squier to Wife, Sept. 1864, in Julie A. Doyle et al., eds., *The Civil War Letters of George W. Squier, Hoosier Volunteer* (Knoxville: Univ. of Tennessee Press, 1998), 78.

57. Alonzo Miller, *Diaries and Letters Written by Pvt. Alonzo Miller, Co. A, 12th Wisconsin Infantry . . .* (Milwaukee: J. C. Stolt and J. P. Cullen, 1961), 35; John F. Brobst to Mary, Sept. 27, 1864, in Margaret Brobst Roth, ed., *Well, Mary: Civil War Letters of a Wisconsin Volunteer* (Madison: Univ. of Wisconsin Press, 1960), 95; Lauren J. Morse, ed., *Civil War Diaries of Bliss Morse* (Pittsburg, KS: Pitcraft, 1963), 68; R. G. M. Blackett, ed., *Thomas Morris Chester, Black Civil War Correspondent: His Dispatches From the Virginia Front* (Baton Rouge: Louisiana Univ. Press, 1989), 185; Walton, ed., *Private Smith's Journal*, 183; Rhodes, ed., *All for the Union*, 196; Charles H. Lynch, *The Civil War Diary of Charles H. Lynch, 18th Conn. Volunteers* (Hartford: Privately printed, 1915), 135.

58. Columbus *Crisis*, July 27, Sept. 19, October 26, 1864; Albany *Atlas and Argus*, Aug. 10, 13, 17, Nov. 16, 1864; *New-Yorker Staats-Zeitung*, August 11/13, 1864; Gil R. Stormont, cpl., *History of the Fifty-Eighth Regiment of Indiana Volunteer Infantry, From the Manuscript prepared by John J. Hight* (Princeton: Press of the Clarion, 1895), 356; Ernest Duvergier de Hauranne, *A Frenchman in Lincoln's America* (Chicago: R. R. Donnelly & Sons, 1974), 292; E. V. Haughwood to Editors of the New York *World*, Sept. 26, 1864, Manton Marble Papers; S. J. Anderson to Jefferson Davis, Aug. 30, 1864, in Dunbar Rowland, ed., *Jefferson Davis, Constitutionalist, His Letters, Papers, and Speeches* (10 vols., Jackson, MS: Mississippi Dept. of Archives and History, 1923), VI, 325.

59. George Augustus Sala, *My Diary in America in the Midst of War* (2 vols., London: Tinsley Bros., 1865), I, 210; Wirt Armistead Cate, ed.,

Two Soldiers, the Campaign Diaries of Thomas J. Key, C.S.A., Dec. 7, 1863–May 17, 1865 and *Robert J. Campbell, U.S.A. Jan. 1, 1864–July 11, 1865* (Chapel Hill: Univ. of North Carolina Press, 1938), 113; Ruffin, *Diary*, III, 577; Younger, ed., *Inside the Confederate Government*, 174; George P. Erwin to Sister, Nov. 5, 1864, in Steven E. Woodworth, *Cultures in Conflict, The American Civil War* (Westport, CT: Greenwood Press, 2000), 165; John F. Marszalek, ed., *The Diary of Emma Holmes*, 382; Vandiver, ed., *Civil War Diary of General Josiah Gorgas*, 150; Richmond *Dispatch*, Nov. 9 1861.

60. *Edinburgh Mercury*, May 17, 1864, quoted in *Liberator*, July 12, 1864; Goddard, *Letters*, 448–52; George Jacob Holyoake to Lincoln, Sept. 4, 1864, LP; *Liberator*, Sept. 30, 1864; *Moniteur*, Oct. 3, 1864; *Le Siècle*, Oct. 15, 1864, quoted in *Liberator*, Nov. 18, 1864.

61. Washington *Evening Star*, Oct. 18, 1864; London *Spectator*, Nov. 19, 1864; John Campbell to Lincoln, June 10, 1864, LP; Schurz to Theodore Petrasch, Oct. 12, 1864, in Schafer, ed., *Intimate Letters of Carl Schurz*, 308–09.

62. London *Times*, July 4, 30, Aug. 5, Sept. 24, 1864; *Moniteur*, Aug. 4, 5, Sept. 8, Oct. 9, 1864; *Punch*, Aug. 27, Sept. 24, Nov. 5, 1864; Duvergier de Hauranne, 496; London *Spectator*, July 25, 1864.

Chapter 6: Triumph and Assassination

1. Washington *Daily Morning Chronicle*, Nov. 11, 1864; *Philadelphia Inquirer*, Nov. 11, 1864; Lydia Maria Child to Elizabeth Scudder, n.d, 1864, in Child, *Letters of Lydia Maria Child* (Boston: Houghton Mifflin, 1882), 183–84.

2. Boston *Morning Journal*, Nov. 9, 1864; Chase to George S. Dennison, Nov. 11, 1864, in Niven, *Chase Papers*, IV, 436–38; Washington *Daily Morning Chronicle*, Nov. 18, 1864; Robert A. Gray to Lincoln, Nov. 1864, William L. Dayton, Nov. 21, 1864, Isaac Arnold to Lincoln, Dec. 1, 1864, Edwards Pierrepont to Lincoln, Nov. 24, 1864, James Lothrop Motley to Lincoln, Nov. 28, 1864, LP; *Frank Leslie's Illustrated Newspaper*, Dec. 3, 1864.

3. *Bellefontaine Republican*, Nov. 11, 1864, in LP; Alfred Lacey Hough to Mary, Nov. 20, 1864, in Robert G. Ahearn, ed., *Soldiers in*

the West, *The Civil War Letters of Alfred Lacey Hough* (Philadelphia: Univ. of Pennsylvania Press, 1957), 230.

4. William J. Kellogg to Lincoln, Dec. 10, 1864, Anson S. Miller to Lincoln, Nov. 14, 1864, Agénor-Etienne de Gasparin to Lincoln, Nov. 24, 1864, J. H. Anderson to Lincoln, Dec. 2, 1864, Oliver Johnson to Lincoln, Dec. 21, 1864, LP.

5. James H. Kidd to Father, Dec. 5, 1864, in Wittenberg, ed., *One of Custer's Wolverines*, 111; Anita Palladino, ed., *Diary of a Yankee Engineer: The Civil War Story of John H. Westervelt, Engineer, 1st New York Volunteer Engineer Corps* (New York: Fordham Univ. Press, 1997), 186; Washington *Evening Star*, Dec. 10, 1864; John F. Brobst to Mary Englesby, Dec. 28, 1864, in Roth, ed., *Well, Mary*, 110.

6. *New York Tribune*, Dec. 7, 1864; *Commonwealth*, Dec. 10, 1864; *Independent*, Dec. 15, 1864; Henry C. Bowen to Lincoln, Norman B. Judd to Lincoln, Dec. 28, 1864, LP; Dec. 7, 1864; Burlingame, ed., *Lincoln Observed*, 151–52; Springfield *Republican*, Dec. 7, 1864; New York *Evening Post*, Dec. 6, 1864; *New York Herald*, Dec. 4, 1864.

7. New York *Evening Post*, Dec. 7, 1864; *Chicago Tribune*, Dec. 7, 1864; *Boston Morning Journal*, Dec. 7, 1864.

8. Burlingame, ed., *Lincoln Observed*, 150–51; Brooks to George Witherle, Dec. 10 1864, in ibid., 154–55; Charles Francis Adams to Father, Dec. 11, 1864, in Ford, ed., *Adams Letters*, II, 231.

9. *Independent*, Dec. 8, 1864; *Commonwealth*, Sept. 10, 1864; *Liberator*, Dec. 9, 1864; *Wilkes Spirit of the Times*, Dec. 17, 1864; *Congressional Globe*, 38th Cong., 2nd Sess., 124.

10. Albany *Atlas and Argus*, Dec. 3, 10, 1864; Columbus *Crisis*, Nov. 16, Dec. 14, 18, 1864.

11. Samuel Goddard to Editor of the *Daily Post*, Nov. 24, 1864, in Samuel Goddard, *Letters on the American Rebellion, 1860–1865* (London: Simkins, Marshall & Co., 1870), 475–77; *Edinburgh Weekly Herald and Mercury*, Nov. 26, 1864, LP; *Manchester Examiner*, quoted in *Liberator*, Dec. 23, 1864; James O. Putnam to Lincoln, Nov. 30, 1864, LP; *Independence Belge*, Nov. 25, 1864, in Sideman and Friedman, eds., *Europe Looks at the Civil War*, 265.

12. London *Spectator*, Dec. 24, 1864; London *Penny Illustrated Newspaper*, Dec. 31, 1864; *Siècle*, Dec. 22, 1864, in W. Reed West, *Contemporary French Opinion on the American Civil War* (Baltimore: Johns Hopkins Press, 1924), 95; London *Times*, Dec. 19, 1864; Procure-

urs Généraux Gaulot (Lyon), Dec. 28, 1864, Sandbreuiel (Amiens), Jan. 7, 1865, in Lynn M. Case, ed., *French Opinion on the United States and Mexico 1860–1867* (New York: Appleton, 1936), 291, 294.

13. Howard Swiggett, ed., *A Rebel War Clerk's Diary at the Confederate States Capital* (2 vols., New York: Old Hickory Books, 1935), II, 352; Sarah Woolfolk Wiggins, ed., *Journals of Josiah Gorgas* (Tuscaloosa: Univ. of Alabama Press, 1995), 148; *Richmond Enquirer*, Dec. 10, 1864, *Richmond Sentinel*, Dec. 10, 1864, quoted in *Cincinnati Commercial*, Dec. 16, 1864; *Richmond Dispatch*, Dec. 13, 1864.

14. *Philadelphia Inquirer*, Jan. 7, 1865; *New York Times*, Jan. 8, 1865; Mrs. C. Greene Brayton to Lincoln, Feb. 1, 1865, LP.

15. McPherson, *Political History, of the Union*, 566; *Philadelphia Inquirer*, Jan. 3, 1865; *New York Herald*, Jan. 5, 1865; *New York Tribune*, Jan. 21, 1865.

16. *New York Times*, Feb. 7, 1865; *New York Weekly Tribune*, Feb. 7, 1865; *New York Tribune*, Feb. 11, 1865; Springfield *Republican*, Feb. 6, 1865; *Cincinnati Gazette*, Feb. 15, 1865.

17. *Chicago Tribune*, Feb. 11, 1865; Washington *Daily Morning Chronicle*, Feb. 6, 1865; *National Anti-Slavery Standard*, Feb. 11, 18, 1865; Charles Francis Adams to Father, Feb. 7, 1865, in Ford, ed., *Adams Letters*, II, 253; George Gordon Meade to Wife, Feb. 9, 1865, in Meade, *Life and Letters*, II, 262; *Congressional Globe, 38th Cong.*, 2nd Sess., 734; D. Hohnfeld to Lincoln, Feb. 10, 1865, LP.

18. *National Anti-Slavery Standard*, Feb. 11, 18, 1865; New York *Evening Post*, Feb. 7, 1865.

19. Albany *Atlas and Argus*, Feb. 6, 13. 1865; New York *World*, Feb. 11, 1865; *Congressional Globe*, 38th Cong., 2nd Sess., 730–32, 735; Scarborough, ed., *Ruffin Diary*, III, 781; *Richmond Whig*, Jan. 21, 1865, quoted in New York *Commercial Advertiser*, Jan. 24, 1865.

20. *Congressional Globe*, 38th Cong., 2nd Sess., 144, 576–78; Garrison to Lincoln, Jan. 1865, Henry Ward Beecher to Lincoln, Feb. 9, 1865, LP; *Belletristisches Journal*, Feb. 10, 1865; *Frank Leslie's Illustrated Newspaper*, Feb. 25, 1865; *New York Tribune*, Feb. 23, 1865.

21. J. Z. Goodrich to Lincoln, Mar. 1, 1865, LP; *Cincinnati Commercial*, Mar. 4, 1865; *Philadelphia Inquirer*, Mar. 4, 1865; *New York Times*, Mar. 4, 1865; Washington *National Intelligencer*, Mar. 4, 1865; *National Anti-Slavery Standard*, Mar. 11, 1865; Jenkin Lloyd Jones, *An Artillery Man's Diary*, (Madison: Wisconsin History Commission, Feb. 1914),

309; *New York Herald*, Mar. 4, 1865; Cole and McDonough, eds., *Witness to the Young Republic*, 466.

22. Ronald C. White, Jr., *Lincoln's Greatest Speech, the Second Inaugural* (New York: Simon and Schuster, 2002); Washington *Evening Star*, Mar. 4, 1865; Springfield *Republican*, Mar. 6, 1865; *Chicago Tribune*, Mar. 6, 1865; Washington *Daily Morning Chronicle*, Mar. 6, 1865.

23. Charles. F. Adams Jr. to Father, Mar. 7, 1865, in Ford, ed. *Adams Letters*, II, 257–58; Burlingame, ed., *Lincoln Observed*, 168; Gillespie, ed., *Journal of Benjamin Moran*, II, 1395; David Lane, *A Soldier's Story: The Story of a Volunteer, 1862–1865* (privately printed, 1905), 256.

24. Charles Sumner to John Bright, March 13, 1865, Sumner to Richard Cobden, Mar. 27, 1865, in Palmer, ed., *Letters of Charles Sumner*, II, 273–74, 279; *New York Tribune*, Mar. 6, 1865; *Commonwealth*, Mar. 18, 1865; New York *Evening Post*, Mar. 6, 1865; *Independent*, Mar. 9, 1865; *National Anti-Slavery Standard*, Mar. 11, 1865.

25. New York *World*, Mar. 6, 1865; Albany *Atlas and Argus*, Mar. 6, 7, 1865; Martian Buck, "A Louisiana Prisoner of War at Johnson's Island," *Louisiana History*, IV, (1963), 241; Swigett, ed., *Rebel War Clerk's Diary*, II, 443; *London Times*, Mar. 17, 1865; London *Spectator*, Mar. 25, 1865.

26. Granville Moody to Lincoln, Mar. 27, 1865, Resolution of New Jersey Conference of the Methodist Episcopal Church, Mar. 28, 1865, LP; *New York Times*, Mar. 31, 1865; Lydia Maria Child to George W. Julian, Apr. 8, 1865, in James H. Barnes, "Letters of a Massachusetts Woman Reformer to an Indiana Radical," *Indiana Magazine of History*, Vol. 26 (1930), 36.

27. Burlingame, ed., *Lincoln Observed*, 180–81; Blackett, ed., *Chester*, 294–95, 297; James L. Robertson, ed., "English Views of the Civil War, Apr. 2–8, 1865," *Virginia Magazine of History and Biography*, Vol. 77 (1969), 211–12; Rosenblatt, eds., *Hard Marching Every Day*, 233.

28. Clement L. Vallandigham to Horace Greeley, Apr. 11, 1865, Horace Greeley Papers; Washington *Evening Star*, Apr. 11, 1865.

29. Washington *National Intelligencer*, Apr. 13, 1865; *New York Herald*, Apr. 3, 1865; Washington *Evening Star*, Apr. 12, 1865; Springfield *Republican*, Apr. 12, 1865; *Philadelphia Inquirer*, Apr. 13 1865.

30. Washington *Daily Morning Chronicle*, Apr. 12, 1865; *Cincinnati Gazette*, Apr. 13, 1865; New York *Commercial Advertiser*, Apr. 13, 1865; Burlingame, ed., *Lincoln Observed*, 183–86.

31. Niven, ed., *Chase Papers*, I, 527; Sumner to Chase, Apr. 12, 1865, in Palmer, *Letters of Charles Sumner*, II, 283–84; *New York Tribune*, Apr. 12, 1865.

32. Donald, *Lincoln*, 588; New York *Commercial Advertiser*, Apr. 15, 1865; St. Louis *Missouri Democrat*, Apr. 28, 1865, quoted in Howard K. Beale, ed., *The Diary of Edward Bates, 1859–1866* (Washington: Government Printing Office, 1933), 579; *Chicago Tribune*, Apr. 17, 1865; New York *Christian Advocate and Journal*, Apr. 20, 1865; *Detroit Advertiser and Tribune*, Apr. 15, 1865.

33. *Springfield Republican*, Apr. 15, 1865; *New York Herald*, Apr. 16, 1865; *Cincinnati Commercial*, Apr. 17, 1865; Mrs. Schurz to Carl Schurz, Apr. 21, 1865, in Frederick Bancroft, ed., *Speeches, Correspondence, and Political Papers of Carl Schurz* (6 vols., New York: G. P. Putnam & Sons, 1913), I, 253–54; *Frank Leslie's Illustrated Newspaper*, Apr. 29, 1865.

34. Robert McAllister to Ellen, Apr. 15, 1865, in Robertson, ed., *The Civil War Letters of General Robert McAllister*, 608; George W. Squier to Ellen, Apr. 15, 1865, in Doyle et al., eds., *This Wilderness of War* 103, 106; Hallock Armstrong to Mary Armstrong, Apr. 16, 1865, Hallock F. Raup, ed., *Letters from a Pennsylvania Chaplain at the Siege of Petersburg 1865* (London: Eden Press, 1961), 28; David Lane, *A Soldier's Story: The Story of a Volunteer 2862–1865* (Jackson, MI, printed 1905) 261–62; D. Duane Cummings and Daryl Hohweiler, eds., *An Enlisted Soldier's View of the Civil War: The Wartime Papers of Joseph R. Ward, Jr.* (West Lafayette, IN: Bell Publications, 1981), 168.

35. J. L. Jones, *An Artillery Man's Diary*, 323; Rhodes, ed., *All for the Union*, 231; Hight, *History*, 522–2; Pvt. William Hamblin to Wife, Apr. 16, 1865, in Annette Tapert, ed., *The Brothers' War: Civil War Letters to Their Loved Ones From the Blue and Gray* (New York: Times Books, 1988), 235; Clyde C. Walton, ed., *Private Smith's Journal: Recollections of the Late War* (Chicago: R. R. Donnelly, 1963), 212–13; Stephen E. Ambrose, ed., *A Wisconsin Boy in Dixie: The Selected Letters of James K. Newton* (Madison: Univ. of Wisconsin Press, 1961), 152.

36. London *Times*, Apr. 27, 1865; *Punch*, May 6, 1865; London *Spectator*, Apr. 20, 1865; *Pays*, Apr. 28, 1865, in Blackburn, *French Newspaper Opinion*, 132; *Siècle*, Apr. 27, 18, 1865; *Frankfurter Journal*, Apr. 27, 1865.

37. Speech at Buffalo Historical Society, May 9, 1865, in Frank H.

Severance, *"Millard Fillmore Papers,"* 2 vols. (Buffalo Historical Society Publications, X, XI, 1907), II, 106–07; Albany *Atlas and Argus,* Apr. 17, 1865; Hammond, ed., *Diary of a Union Lady,* 355; Lewis Griffith to O. P. Morgan, Apr. 23, 1865, in Harvey Wish, "Civil War Letters and Dispatches," *Indiana Magazine of History,* 33 (1937), 67.

38. Anne King Gregory, ed., "Diary of Captain Joseph Julius Wescoat, 1863–1865," *South Carolina Historical Magazine,* 49 (1958), 94; Judith W. McGuire, *Diary of a Southern Refugee During the War* (New York: Arno Press, 1972), 355–56; Swiggett, ed., *A Rebel War Clerk's Diary,* 479; C. Conn Bryan, "A Georgia Woman's Civil War Diary: The Journal of Minerva Leah Rowles McClatchey, 1864–65," *Georgia Historical Quarterly,* 51 (1967), 214; John Dooley, *Confederate Soldier: His War Journal* (Washington, DC: Georgetown Univ. Press, 1945), 195; John A. Campbell to Horace Greeley, Apr. 26. 1865, "Papers of Hon. John Campbell, 1861–1865," *Southern Historical Society Papers, New Series, IV* (Oct. 1917), 61–65. For examples of cheers for Booth and other favorable Southern views about the assassination, see John Q. Anderson, ed., *The Journal of Kate Stone 1861–1868* (Baton Rouge: Louisiana Univ. Press, 1955), 333, 341, 353; Earl Schenck Miers, *When the World Ended: The Diary of Emma Le Conte* (New York: Oxford Univ. Pres, 1957), 91 Davis, *The Image of Lincoln in the South,* 98–101.

Other Works by Hans L. Trefousse

Andrew Johnson: A Biography. New York: W. W. Norton and Company, 1997.

Ben Butler: The South Called Him Beast! New York: Octagon Books, 1974.

Benjamin Franklin Wade, Radical Republican from Ohio. Woodbridge, CT: Twayne Publishers, 1963.

Carl Schurz: A Biography. New York: Fordham University Press, 1998.

Causes of the Civil War: Institutional Failure or Human Blunder. Melbourne, FL: Krieger Publishing Company, 1983.

Germany and American Neutrality, 1939–1941. New York: Octagon Books, 1969.

Historical Dictionary of Reconstruction. Westport, CT: Greenwood Press, 1991.

Impeachment of a President: Andrew Johnson, the Blacks, and Reconstruction. New York: Fordham University Press, 1999.

Lincoln's Decision for Emancipation. Philadelphia: Lippincott, 1975.

The Papacy Confronts the Modern World. (With Frank J. Coppa.) Melbourne, FL: Krieger Publishing Company, 2003.

Pearl Harbor: The Continuing Controversy. Melbourne, FL: Krieger Publishing Company, 1982.

The Radical Republicans: Lincoln's Vanguard for Racial Justice. Baton Rouge, LA: Louisiana State University Press, 1975.

Reconstruction: America's First Effort at Racial Democracy. Melbourne, FL: Krieger Publishing Company, 1999.

Rutherford B. Hayes: 1877–1881. New York: Times Books, 2002.

A Short History of the Native Americans in the United States. (With Howard Meredith.) Melbourne, FL: Krieger Publishing Company, 2001.

Thaddeus Stevens: Nineteenth-Century Egalitarian. Mechanicsburg, PA: Stackpole Books, 2001.

What Happened at Pearl Harbor? Albany, NY: New College and University Press, 1958.

Index

Abbott, Henry Livermore, 32
Abolitionism, 40
Abolitionists, 41
Adams, Charles Francis, Jr., 62,
    120–21, 130
Adams, Charles Francis, Sr., 120–
    21, 125, 130
Adams, Henry, 62
Adams, Louis Bryant, 135
Albany *Atlas and Argus*: on 1860
    election, 7, 9; on first inaugura-
    tion, 18; on Frémont order, 13;
    on messages, 34, 40, 84; on
    Emancipation Proclamation,
    51, 63; on elections, 53, 121; on
    cabinet crisis, 51; on renomina-
    tion, 96; demand for impeach-
    ment, 112; on Blair conference,
    106, on 2nd inauguration, 131;
    on assassination, 137
Anderson, J. H., 119
Anderson, Robert, 23
Andrew, John Albion, 29; and 1st
    inauguration, 17–18; on cabi-
    net, 20
Antietam, battle of, 49
Appomattox, 132
Argyll, Duchess of, 4
Armstrong, Hallock, 135
Army: Lincoln's popularity in,
    36–37, 39, 43; Lincoln's visits

to, 46–47, 68, 110; and Emanci-
    pation Proclamation, 50–51;
    and McClellan's demotion, 56;
    and renomination, 86, 95; and
    1864 election, 110, 111, 119; and
    assassination, 135–36
Arnold, Nathan I., 90, 92, 101, 118;
    and Lincoln's alleged unpopu-
    larity, 85
Ashmun, George, 48
Ashtabula *Sentinel*, and Wade-
    Davis Manifesto, 104
Atlanta, seizure of, 105, 106
Atlantic Monthly, 68

Balch, Benjamin, 75
Baltimore, 1864 Union Conven-
    tion at, 97, 98, 99, 106
Bancroft, George, 40
Barbados, 96
Barlow, S. L. M., on 1862 elec-
    tions, 55
Bates, Edward, 102
Barney, Hiram, 65
Bebb, William, 75
Beecher, Henry Ward, 13, 127
Bell, T. S., 34
Bellefontaine *Republican*, 118
Belletristisches Journal: on Ft.
    Sumter, 23; on Lincoln's mes-

ins, ed., *A Diary of Battle: The Personal Journals of Colonel Charles S. Wainwright 1861–1868* (New York: Harcourt. Brace & World, 1962), 331; Francis Adam Donaldson to Jacob Donaldson, Mar. 3, 1864, in Acken, ed., *Inside the Army of the Potomac*) 433–36.

24. London *Times*, Feb. 4, 1864; *Edinburgh Mercury*, May 17, 1864, quoted in *New York Times*, June 12, 1864; London *Spectator*, May 14, 1864; *Moniteur*, Mar. 30, Apr. 21, 1864; James Ford Reed to Lincoln, Mar. 12, 1864, LP.

25. Columbus *Crisis*, Jan. 27, Feb. 10, Mar. 9, 1864; *New York Leader*, Jan. 2, 1864; *New-Yorker Staats-Zeitung*, Feb. 2, 1864; New York *World*, Feb. 6, 1864.

26. *Congressional Globe*, 38th Cong., 1st Sess., Ap., 55–71; 1276–83; Columbus *Crisis*, May 4, 1864; Albany *Atlas and Argus*, May 4, Mar. 4, June 9, 1864.

27. William K. Scarborough, ed., *Diary of Edmund Ruffin*, III, 381; Frank E. Vandiver, ed., *The Civil War Diary of General Josiah Gorgas* (Tuscaloosa: Univ. of Alabama Press, 1947), 84; Richmond *Dispatch*, Feb. 18, 1864; Benjamin Hill to Alexander H. Stephens, Mar. 14, 1864, in Ulrich B. Phillips, *Correspondence*, 635; Ward W. Briggs, *Soldier and Scholar: Basil Lannen Gildersleeve and the Civil War* (Charlottesville: Univ. of Virginia Press, 1998), 315–17.

28. *Chicago Tribune*, June 7, 9, 1864; Washington *Daily Morning Chronicle*, June 8, 1864.

29. *Cincinnati Commercial*, June 8, 1864; New York *Evening Post*, June 9, 1864; Springfield *Republican*, June 9, 1864; Washington *Evening Star*, June 9, 1864; *Philadelphia Inquirer*, June 9, 1864.

30. *Harper's Weekly*, June 11, 25, 1864; Bryant, *Letters*, IV, 363.

31. Brooks to George W. Herle, June 15, 1864, in Burlingame, ed., *Lincoln Observed*, 114; J. Russell Johnson to Lincoln, June 20, 1868, LP; Niven, ed., *Chase Papers*, IV, 396–97.

32. *Independent*, June 9, 1864: *National Anti-Slavery Standard*, June 9, 1864; *Liberator*, July 15, 1864.

33. *Commonwealth*, June 17, 1864; New York *Tribune*, June 24, 30, 1864; *Cincinnati Commercial*, July 8, 1864.

34. *New York Tribune*, June 24, 30, 1864; *Congressional Globe*, 38th Cong., 1st Sess., 2954–56, 2970, 3308, 3344–45, 3294.

35. Gurowski, *Diary*, IV, 267–68; *Cincinnati Daily Commercial*, July 1, 1864; *New York Herald*, July 1, 1864; Springfield *Republican*, July 2, 1864; *Boston Morning Journal*, July 2, 1864.

15. Richard C. Parsons to Chase, Mar. 2, 1864, in Niven, *Chase Papers*, IV, 315–16; De Witt Chipman to Lincoln, Feb. 29, 1864, LP; *Chicago Tribune*, Feb. 27, 1864.

16. *Brooklyn Daily Union*, Mar. 12, 1864; *Cincinnati Gazette*, Mar. 9, 11, 1864; *Cincinnati Commercial*, Mar. 10, 14, 1864.

17. James G. Blaine to Hannibal Hamlin, Mar. 8, 1864, Hamlin Papers; Harrisburg *Evening Telegraph*, Mar. 4, 1864, LP; Mar. 7, 1864; *Congressional Globe*, 38th Cong., 1st Sess., 113–17, 1198–99; Charles Place to Lincoln, Mar. 4, 1864, A. K. Merrill to Lincoln, Mar. 19, 1864, LP.

18. Henry L. Cobb to Lincoln, Apr. 6, 1864, William S. Waite to Lincoln, Apr. 9, 1864, LP.

19. George William Curtis to John Murray Forbes, May 8, 1864, George William Curtis Papers, Staten Island Institute of the Arts and Sciences, Staten Island, NY.

20. Washington *Evening Star*, Apr. 20, 1864; John Frazier Jr. to John A. J. Creswell, Mar. 24, 1864, J. A. K. Creswell Papers, LC; Albert G. Hodges to Lincoln., May 27, 1864, Samuel T. Glover to Montgomery Bates, May 27, 1864, LP; William Frank Zornow, *Lincoln and the Party Divided* (Norman: Univ. of Oklahoma Press, 1954), 64; William E. Parrish. *Turbulent Partnership: Missouri and the Union 1861–1865* (Columbia: Univ. of Missouri Press, 1963), 183–85.

21. Springfield *Republican*, Apr. 29, 30, 1864; *Philadelphia Inquirer*, Apr. 29, 1864; *Brooklyn Daily Union*, Apr. 28, 1864; John M. MacKenzie to Lincoln, Apr. 28, 1864, LP; Gurowski, *Diary*, III, 208.

22. *Cincinnati Commercial*, June 1, 1864; Washington *Daily Morning Chronicle*, May 30, 1864; *Brooklyn Daily Union*, Mar. 19, 1864; Springfield *Republican*, May 11, 1864.

23. John F. L. Hartwell to Wife and Boy, Mar. 4, 1864, in Ann Hartwell Britton and Thomas J. Reed, eds., *To My Beloved Wife and Boy at Home: The Letters and Diaries of Orderly Sergeant John F. L. Hartwell* (Madison, NJ: Fairleigh Dickinson Univ. Press, 1997), 206; James A. Connolly to Wife, Mar. 20, 1864, in Paul M. Angle, ed., *Three Years in the Army of the Cumberland* (Bloomington: Indiana Univ. Press, 1959; Henry R. Gardner to Parents, Mar. 29, 1864, in Kenneth E. Shewmaker and Andrew K. Prinz, "A Yankee in Louisiana: Selections From the Diary and Correspondence of Henry R. Gardner, 1862–1866," in *Louisiana History* V (Summer 1864), 284; J. Clay Rice to John P. Usher, Apr. 4, 1864, N. H. Chrysler to Lincoln, May 24, 1864, LP; Allan Nev-

"Letters to the Front: A Distaff View of the Civil War," *Michigan History*, IXL (Mar. 1965), 56.

5. James Horrocks to Parents, Nov. 11, 1863, in A.S. Lewis, ed., *My Dear Parents An Englishman's Letters Home from the American Civil War* (London: Victor Gollancz, 1983), 46; Thomas H. Mann to Father, Nov. 18, 1863, in John H. Hennessy, ed., *Fighting With the Eighteenth Massachusetts: The Civil War Memoir of Thomas H. Mann* (Baton Rouge: Univ. of Louisiana Press, 2000), 195; *Independent,* Nov. 26, 1863.

6. Uri Manly to W. P. Dole, Dec. 9, 1863, Albert Smith to Lincoln, Dec. 12, 1863, LP; John A. Kasson to Greeley, Jan. 24, 1864, Greeley Papers; S. Kaufmann to Washburne, Dec. 12, 1863, Washburne Papers; Springfield *Republican,* Dec. 15, 1863; Lawrence *Kansas Tribune,* Dec. 23, 1863.

7. Joseph Medill to J. K. Forrest, Dec. 17, 1863, LP; M. Greitzner to Washburne, Jan. 26, 1864, Washburne Papers; New York *Daily Tribune,* Jan. 21, 1864; *Harper's Weekly,* Jan. 2, 1864.

8. Buffalo *Commercial Advertiser,* Jan. 11, 1864, LP.

9. Washington *Daily Morning Chronicle,* Jan. 14, 1864; John Minor Botts to John B. Frye, Jan. 22 1864, LP.

10. F. P. Baker to Lincoln, Jan. 7, 1864, LP; Washington *Evening Star,* Jan. 8, 1864.

11. John A. Hardenbrook to Lincoln, Jan. 23, 1864 (New York), George Bagner to Lincoln, Jan. 14, 1864 (Pennsylvania), Union League, 24th Ward, Philadelphia to Lincoln, Jan. 19, 1864, James Warrington to Lincoln, Jan. 20, 1864 (Camden) Bernard Stryker Jr. to Lincoln, Jan. 20, 1864 (Trenton), LP.

12. Gurowski, *Diary,* III, 59, 60; *Liberator,* Feb. 5, 1864.

13. *Congressional Globe,* 38th Cong., 1st Sess., 113–17, 473, 653, 1293–95, 952, 986, 1216, Ap. 85–98, 115. (In order of speakers mentioned.)

14. *New York Times,* Feb. 29, 1864; David E. Long, *The Jewel of Liberty: Abraham Lincoln's Re-election and the End of Slavery* (Mechanicsburg, PA: Stackpole Books, 1994), 36–37; *Congressional Globe,* 38th Cong., 1st Sess., 1027; I. B. Gara to Cameron, Feb. 26, 1865, James G. Blaine to Isaac Arnold, Mar. 3, 1864, James T. Lewis to Lincoln, Mar. 5, 1864 LP; Clark H. Chapman to Justin S. Morrill, May 16, 1864, Morrill Papers; *Cincinnati Commercial,* Feb. 29, 1864; Chase to Lincoln, Feb. 22, 1864, in Niven, *Chase Papers,* IV, 303–04; Washington *Daily Morning Chronicle,* Feb. 26, Mar. 15, 1864; *Liberator,* Mar. 18, 1864.

mond, Dec. 13, 1863, Henry J. Raymond Papers, NYPL; R. W. Thompson to Henry Lane, Dec. 27, 1863, Henry Lane Papers, Indiana Historical Society; John Daniel Smith and William Cooper, eds., *A Union Woman in Civil War Kentucky* (Lexington: Univ. Press of Kentucky, 2000), 176.

40. Rufus R. Dawes to M. B. G., Dec. 12, 1863, in Alan T. Nolan, ed., *A Full Blown Yankee of the Iron Brigade: Service with the Sixth Wisconsin Volunteers* (Lincoln: Univ. of Nebraska Press, 1962), 230–32; Jones, *An Artillery Man's Diary*, 153; Herb Crumb and Katherine D. Halle, eds., *No Middle Ground: Thomas Wood Osborn's Letters from the Field, 1862–1864* (Hamilton, NY: Edmondston Publishing Co., 1993), 183.

41. Columbus *Crisis,* Dec. 16, 1863; Albany *Atlas and Argus,* Dec. 10, 1863; New York *World,* Dec. 10, 1863 *New-Yorker Staats-Zeitung,* Dec. 17, 1863; London *Times,* Jan. 5, 1864; *Moniteur,* Dec. 28, 1863.

42. Washington *Daily Morning Chronicle,* Dec. 30, 1863, Jan. 1, 1864; Charles O. Musser to Father, Jan. 1, 1864, in Barry Popchuck, ed., *Soldier Boy: The Civil War Letters of Charles O. Musser, 29th Iowa* (Iowa City: Univ. of Iowa Press, 1995), 101–02; *Brooklyn Daily Union,* Jan. 21, 1864.

Chapter 5: Renomination and Reelection

1. Isaac Arnold, *The Life of Abraham Lincoln* (Chicago: Jansen, McClurg, 1885), 385–86, n. 2.

2. Supra, 82–3. Burlingame, ed., *Lincoln Observed,* 54; *New York Herald,* May 23, 26, 1863; New Orleans *Weekly True Delta,* June 14, 1863; Frederick Law Olmstead to Father, Oct. 30, 1863, in Ranney et al., eds., Vol. V of *The Papers of Frederick Law Olmstead,* 123; George H. Clapp to Lincoln, Sept. 24, 1863, LP.

3. *Chicago Tribune,* Nov. 3, 1863; *New York Daily Herald,* Oct. 9, Nov. 3, 5, 9, 1863; John Donnelly to Lincoln, Nov. 26, 1863, H. C. Townley to Lincoln, Sept. 29, 1863, LP.

4. Washburne to Lincoln, Oct. 12, 1863, Cameron to Lincoln, Oct. 10, 1863, James K. Morehead to Lincoln, Oct. 15, 1863, LP; Sophia Buchanan to Claude Buchanan, Nov. 5, 1863, in George M. Blackburn,